T0339240

Stealing My Religion

Stealing My Religion

NOT JUST ANY CULTURAL APPROPRIATION

Liz Bucar

Harvard University Press

Cambridge, Massachusetts

London, England   2022

First printing

Library of Congress Cataloging-in-Publication Data

Names: Bucar, Elizabeth M., author.

Title: Stealing my religion : not just any cultural appropriation / Liz Bucar.

Description: Cambridge, Massachusetts : Harvard University Press, 2022. |
    Includes bibliographical references and index.

Identifiers: LCCN 2021062973 | ISBN 9780674987036 (cloth)

Subjects: LCSH: Religion and culture. | Cultural appropriation—Moral and
    ethical aspects. | Religion and sociology.

Classification: LCC BL65.C8 B83 2022 | DDC 306.6—dc23/eng20220314

LC record available at https://lccn.loc.gov/2021062973

Contents

Preface

Sharmila Sen, my editor at Harvard University Press, convinced me to write this book. It was June 2017 and I had just returned from my fourth time walking the Camino de Santiago. We were having a working lunch at a hipster cantina. Over a plate of flan that I refused to eat because, after a month in Spain, I was sick of desserts that jiggle, we discussed my next project. I threw out a few ideas and then said what I had to do first was write an article about cultural appropriation because my students had started to use it to shut down complicated ethical conversations. "They don't know what the term even means," I complained. "And they never consider that forms of religious borrowing might be harmful in the same way. I'm so annoyed about it. I have to get that out of my system first."

Sharmila looked up from her smoky mezcal concoction. "Wait, that is the book I want," she said. "What? No, it's not a book, it's just a journal article," I said. "It could be a book," she insisted. And then, just for fun and fueled by cocktails and jetlag, we sketched out what case studies I could include. Since I had just returned from a Catholic pilgrimage with non-Catholic students, that case study was a given. And I knew I had things to say about what happens when religious clothing becomes a fashion trend, things I hadn't had the space to address in my previous book, *Pious Fashion*. I suggested circumcision because I knew it made my students uncomfortable. And the whole point of this kind of book was going to be to make people squirm in their seats.

"No, yoga," she said. "Wait, yoga?" I replied, and then I was taking her more seriously. Part of my job while researching and writing this book was going to be leaning in on yoga? I'd have an excuse to do all the icky things, like spend time in an ashram, attend yoga retreats, or join a fancy studio. And then use those experiences to parse out what was so icky in the first place, as well as why I still wanted to do them. Elizabeth Gilbert's *Eat, Pray, Love,* but without all the sex and self-satisfaction. I was in.

The topic of this book — religious appropriation — is personal to me. I am, you could say, a repeat offender. Despite spending most of my professional career studying religion, I am part of the 29 percent of Americans who identify as religiously unaffiliated.[1] Yet I practice yoga. I lead an annual study abroad program on the topic of pilgrimage. I write about Muslim fashion and have worn it during fieldwork. The question of when religious borrowing is morally harmful and when it is not touches my personal and professional life.

This book is an opportunity to reflect on the benefits I gain from the religion of others as well as my responsibility to those traditions and communities. And Sharmila was right: that deserved more than a journal article.

Stealing My Religion

Introduction

When I was eleven years old, Madonna became my style icon. I tied mesh headbands in my permed hair, turned hot pink V-necked Forenza chunky sweaters backward, layered black rubber bracelets up to my elbows, and wore white fingerless lace gloves. All accessorized with a gold cross necklace and cross earrings.

Like Madonna, I was baptized Catholic, although I was raised Protestant. By age eleven, I refused to attend Sunday school, and yet even as I was rebelling against my religious upbringing, my personal style became visually more religious. I did not wear a cross in the 1980s as a Christian. I wore it as a tween following a pop-culture trend.

The story of the cross's journey from religious symbol to popular fashion accessory is filled with twists and turns.[1] It begins when Coco Chanel designed her now iconic enameled cuffs in the 1930s. Based on a design adopted by the Order of St. John in 1567, Chanel's accessory featured eight-pointed Maltese crosses of large gems. Other designers incorporated cross motifs. By the 1960s, oversize and bedazzled crosses were mainstream fashion, decadent accessories that elevated the wearer's sartorial game as a sign of her worldliness.

In the 1970s, evangelicals began to reclaim cross pendants as a sign of deep Christian commitments, and the accessory meant something theological again. Once that happened, cross jewelry was no longer cool as a form of borrowed spirituality. If I had been a tween in that decade, I would not have worn a cross.

Madonna changed that. When she wore a large cross in the 1989 MTV video "Like a Prayer," she was not communicating religious fidelity or obedience, but rather blasphemy and rebellion. "I know the moral majority is up in arms against me, but I consider that an achievement," Madonna said at the time.[2] She was able to change the mainstream meaning of cross jewelry in America again. In the late 1980s and early 1990s, it was no longer primarily associated with devotional piety or institutionalized Christianity because Madonna had turned the religious symbol into a provocation.

My decision as an eleven-year-old child to wear a cross did nothing to keep me in the Protestant church or reclaim my Catholic roots. It was all about being cool. This was the first time I stole my religion. It would not be the last. And I am not alone.

This book focuses on a class of religious borrowings I call religious appropriation: when individuals adopt religious practices without committing to religious doctrines, ethical values, systems of authority, or institutions, in ways that exacerbate existing systems of structural injustice. My use of the term "appropriation" is strategic. For most of my readers, the word will immediately invoke the idea of outsiders taking something from insiders—a distinction I'll say more about later—that causes harm. I want you to be primed to think of religious borrowings as potentially ethically fraught. The harmful ones I'll call religious appropriation.

In the American context, suggesting that there are cases of religious appropriation is controversial. Even as moral outrage over racial or ethnic appropriation is increasingly common, religious borrowing is accepted and even encouraged. In fact, the same people who are quick to call out cases of cultural borrowing as exploiting marginalized communities refuse to recognize that religious communities or practitioners can also be exploited when others adopt their practices in the name of politics, education, or well-being. This is especially true of secular liberals—a group I consider myself part of—who are suspicious of "organized religion" and think personal curation of religious practice severed from religious institutions, hierarchies, and doctrines is the only way to be religiously engaged and still free. But individuals who are themselves religiously affiliated also presume they can borrow the religious practices of others without becoming entangled in that religious tradition or community.

The goal of *Stealing My Religion* is not to convince readers to avoid interacting with the religion of others. Strict avoidance is likely impossible in our contemporary pluralistic world. Such avoidance might even sacrifice valuable forms of religious exchange as well as disempower the religious actors who want to open their practices to outsiders. And yet, borrowing can depend on and contribute to the oppression and marginalization of religious communities and individuals. It is one thing to accept that religious borrowing is part of our contemporary landscape. It is another to ignore the ethical implications of these borrowings. My first goal is to convince you to stop seeing all religious borrowing as morally benign. Some forms, including some very popular forms, are harmful.

My second goal is to think through how we can borrow in more responsible ways, by describing how religious practices are grounded in traditions and communities, identifying the range of exploitations borrowings cause, and understanding the systems of inequity and violence they reinforce. And while I think "cultural appropriation" is an overused and polarizing term, I also think it can be recuperated for this ethical work. I use the term "appropriation" to signal when I am discussing harmful cases of religious adoption. I use the term "religious borrowing" as a more general umbrella term that includes the possibility of adopting practices in ways that do not cause explicit harm.

In this book, three case studies demonstrate what kind of moral risk religious appropriation can entail, including communicating contempt for the deeply held values of religious communities, becoming involved in intrareligious debates, erasing religious history, and instrumentalizing religion for political, educational, and therapeutic goals. We justify borrowing religious practices of others based on the assumption that we can do so without risk of becoming religious in some way. But my three case studies will show that insisting that we can easily remain outsiders is one mechanism by which well-intended borrowing becomes harmful appropriation. When we appropriate religious practices, we are getting involved in religion.

Cultural Appropriation and Its Limitations

The academic use of the term "cultural appropriation" began in the 1920s when Harlem Renaissance scholars raised concerns about representations of African Americans in popular works, such as J. C. Harris's Brer Rabbit stories. In literary and art criticism, cultural appropriation became a term for a range of problematic actions, including possession of cultural objects by noncultural members or institutions (for example, most of the British Museum's holdings), representations of cultural experiences by outsiders to those cultures (for example, the voice appropriation of Brer Rabbit), and use of an artistic style by a nonmember (for example, Elvis Presley's 1956 recording of "Hound Dog," based on Big Mama Thornton's recording four years earlier). Today, the concept of cultural appropriation is used in a range of disciplines, including law, communications, anthropology, critical race theory, philosophy, and literary criticism, and to a lesser extent within religious studies in the context of American Indigenous religion and such Eastern practices as yoga.[3]

Generally speaking, "appropriation" is applied to cases where individuals or entities of the dominant culture take from the culture of marginalized communities, resulting in some harm or offense. The professional or disciplinary context in which appropriation is discussed determines what counts as appropriation, how it is defined, and the harm it causes. Lawyers, for instance, think about cultural appropriation as the taking of intellectual property without permission.[4] Legal scholarship on appropriation raises fascinating questions about the manner in which cultural appropriation might be related to copyright or patent infringement, and what legal mechanisms might prevent harms associated with cultural theft, such as intellectual property law.[5] But since religious ideas and practices cannot be owned like material property, and "permission" is difficult to establish given the heterogeneity of religious communities, these legal discussions don't fully capture the ethical complexity of religious appropriations.

Discussions of art and appropriation have similar limitations. For example, the central concern for philosophers of art in determining the moral acceptability of appropriation is whether the results are aesthetically successful or not.[6] An ethical analysis of religious appropriation has to also consider the implications to communities of religious practice and belief, not just the aesthetic success or failure of the appropriated form.

The variations in the way appropriation is used by different academic disciplines do cause some confusion over how best to apply this term to religious forms. And yet the barrier to exploring religious appropriation that I have encountered most often is the way appropriation is used outside the academy in rather anemic ways, ways that are polarizing instead of constructive. Most people encounter the idea of appropriation today not as academic jargon, but rather as a weapon of mainstream outrage. Celebrities' actions are often called out as cases of cultural appropriation, such as Gwen Stefani's bindi, Kim Kardashian's braids, and Katy Perry's geisha-themed performance. But any of us might be offenders by how we dress our kids for Halloween, where we find inspiration for home decor, or how we adorn our body. Aladdin costumes, Zen decorations, and hoop earrings have all been described as instances of cultural appropriation.[7]

I agree with the core ethical impulse of calling out cultural appropriation. Acts of appropriation by those of privilege—whether that privilege is based on race, gender, or class—often bring some sort of harm to those being appropriated. The playing field is not level, and thus even innocent borrowing from a minority culture is an exercise of privilege, frequently contributing to the disenfranchisement of already vulnerable people.

Yet the popular use of cultural appropriation lacks precision. It can refer to many types of borrowings, ignoring the fact that these cases might raise different ethical issues. And merely calling something cultural appropriation does not convince everyone that it is morally objectionable.

Most important, we rarely have discussions about cultural appropriation. The term is an accusation, a condemnation, an expression of moral outrage. Once it is deployed, conversation halts, as each party digs its heels in. This polarization assumes that the ethical implications of cultural borrowings are cut and dried, which they rarely are. I see this in my classroom all the time. Once the word "appropriation" is introduced into a conversation, students either retreat or feel emboldened to express indignation. Critics consider it an overly sensitive term, one that exemplifies political correctness gone bad, and that relies on essentialist notions of culture. Proponents point out that those critics are often part of communities of racial or economic privilege. And as everyone is convinced only they have the moral high ground, things can get pretty heated.

Novelist Lionel Shriver's keynote address at the Brisbane Writers Festival in 2016 was an occasion in which this dynamic played out. Shriver is best known for her 2003 novel *We Need to Talk about Kevin*, written from the point of view of a school shooter's mother. At the festival, Shriver, a white woman, delivered a speech arguing that accusations of cultural appropriation curtail literary creativity and potentially challenge an author's right to create fiction entirely. And she did this while wearing a sombrero.

Shriver's headgear was a reference to a recent incident at Bowdoin College in Maine, where a tequila-themed party with miniature sombreros resulted in a campus scandal. A strongly worded statement from the student government accused the party hosts of creating an environment where "students of color, particularly Latino, and especially Mexican, feel unsafe."[8] Shriver found the whole incident laughable, but also symptomatic of a state of cultural ultrasensitivity, one that she believed was an attack on the fiction writer's craft. "Because who is the appropriator par excellence, really?" she asked the audience. "Who dares to get inside the very head of strangers, who has the chutzpah to project feelings into the minds of others? . . . Who is the premier pickpocket of the arts? The fiction writer, that's who." She ended with the following declaration: "We fiction writers have to preserve the right to wear many hats—including sombreros."[9]

Shriver was implicitly drawing on the idea that some forms of artistic appropriation are justified by the aesthetic success of the art they produce. She went further by suggesting that fiction writers are, by trade, appropriators. But what she ignored entirely was the possibility that some novelists' cultural borrowings are not morally neutral because of existing systems of inequity.

Consider the reaction to Shriver's speech by author and media commentator Yassmin Abdel-Magied, who attended Shriver's 2016 keynote, at least until she walked out. She wrote about the event for the

Guardian. Abdel-Magied experienced Shriver's talk as "mocking those who ask people to seek permission to use their stories" and celebrating "the unfettered exploitation of the experiences of others."[10] To add insult to injury, the other listeners seemed to agree with Shriver. As Abdel-Magied wrote, "As chuckles of the audience swelled around me, reinforcing and legitimizing the words coming from behind the lectern, I breathed in deeply, trying to make sense of what I was hearing. The stench of privilege hung heavy in the air, and I was reminded of my 'place' in the world."[11] It was not only the existence of appropriation, but the writers' agreement that they had a right to engage in it, that was offensive to Abdel-Magied. As a Black Muslim woman of Sudanese heritage, Abdel-Magied belongs to communities that are marginalized. On that day, surrounded by predominantly white colleagues who seemed to agree with Shriver, Abdel-Magied was reminded that she was an outsider to her own professional guild.

I will have more to say about the role of oppression in religious appropriation, but for now I want to point out that the exchange between Shriver and Abdel-Magied was really a case of two people talking past each other. If we read Shriver generously, her concern was with drawing strict cultural boundaries that would prevent any form of cultural exchange. Abdel-Magied's concern, in contrast, was with the contexts of inequality and marginalization that make some forms of cultural borrowing exploitative. Both were convinced they had framed the issue of cultural appropriation correctly. It seems clear Shriver ignored that the harm of appropriation comes from the way it interacts with oppression. And while I am sympathetic to how the event made Abdel-Magied feel like an outsider in her own community of fellow writers, her piece in the *Guardian* did not address the issue of boundary policing that Shriver was trying to raise. This exchange was not a conversation about cultural appropriation, but rather was a display of moral righteousness, a common but problematic dynamic on this topic.

From the point of view of ethical understanding, conversations are often the means by which discernment and change occur. But such conversations rarely happen on the topic of appropriation because the term is so polarizing in public discourse. In this book, I try to rehabilitate appropriation to reimagine what this conversation could be about.

Stealing My Religion

The idea that inspired this book is that the moral implications of some forms of religious borrowing can be best understood through the framework of cultural appropriation. This use of appropriation depends on several theoretical understandings about such things as the boundaries between cultures, the nature of power, and the type of harm appropriation can cause. In addition, since I think appropriating from religions raises distinct ethical issues, I need to clarify how I am distinguishing religion from other cultural forms. Let's explore these theoretical concerns by taking a closer look at the title of this book, *Stealing My Religion*.

"Stealing" implies that (1) there is an object or practice of value, (2) being taken from its owner, (3) which causes some sort of injury. But all three of these dimensions—value, owner, injury—become complicated when we try to apply them to religion.

In the cases of religious appropriation that I explore in this book, the "thing being stolen" is not an object, but rather a religious practice whose value may not be quantifiable or even tangible. For the religious community, the practice is valuable because it does something that is beneficial for an individual practitioner or the community. Those outside a religious community who borrow a religious practice also presume it has a value, but in this case the value is assumed to be independent of its religious context. The benefits that animate the case studies that follow include expression of solidarity, religious literacy, and personal health.

As "stealing" implies that the practice is taken from its owner, how we understand religious ownership will affect which cases of appropriation we think deserve our attention. No person, community, or institution can legally own an entire religion. And this is especially true of abstract religious ideas and lived practices that intellectual property law often frames as "open source."[12] And yet to say that no one morally owns religion would be to insist that we have no responsibility to communities and traditions that claim religious ideas and practices as not only real, but ultimate truth.

At issue in the case studies in this book is what form of ownership of a practice a religious community might reasonably claim, based on its members' shared experiences of that practice. One way to ground this claim to ownership is to recognize that shared practices are what create a religious community, because they promote a sense of common identity and group connection.[13] When one of these practices is taken by someone outside the group, the group members' right to privacy is violated and a powerful mechanism for creating group identity is undermined.[14]

If group intimacy is what establishes the right to ownership, only a group member could make a legitimate claim of appropriative harm. This introduces another challenge: who is an insider? Having a clear and fixed criterion about who counts as a group insider versus an outsider will reinforce stereotypes and generalizations about a group, obscure forms of oppression within a group itself, and leave out members who don't fit the dominant mold.[15] We need a way to determine insider status without slipping into cultural essentialism, which itself is harmful.

One way to sidestep the issue of having to adjudicate who counts as an insider is to rely on self-reports. In this book, for instance, I give weight to appropriative claims made by self-identified religious insiders. However, even this approach has limitations. Religious communities are highly heterogeneous. Individual members will have different interpretations of what counts as a core religious practice and will experience appropriation by outsiders in different ways based on their lived experiences. There won't necessarily be a group consensus about whether a form of borrowing causes harm. And those who agree there is harm might disagree on what that harm entails. In fact, even religious insiders might engage in practices that fellow group members experience as appropriation, given internal debates about the "right" way to practice.

Another problem I have noticed with mainstream conversations on religious appropriation is that if any group member gives permission to borrow, it is interpreted as absolving a potential appropriator of any moral responsibility. Who is deemed capable of giving permission for an entire religious community matters. Often, clergy or institutional leaders are allowed to act as spokespersons. And yet, this relies on hierarchies of power and erases internal diversity.

Take, for instance, the range of Catholic reactions to the 2018 Met Gala, the extravagant annual fund-raising event for the Metropolitan Museum of Art. The 2018 theme, "Heavenly Bodies: Fashion and the Catholic Imagination," meant the who's who of fashion, film, and music industries walked the red carpet in their stylists' wildest interpretations of Catholic fashion. Some celebrities came dressed as religious figures. Singer Katy Perry was a golden Versace angel, with six-foot feathered wings and above-the-knee shiny boots. Actor Jared Leto was a blinged-out Gucci Christlike prince. Actress Zendaya was a silvery Joan of Arc in a chain-link Versace design. Singer Lana Del Rey was so very Marian, dressed in a Gucci tribute to Our Lady of Sorrows: a long white gown with gold embellishment and seven daggers piercing her chest. The singer Rihanna, one of the hosts of the event, came dressed as the pope. She wore a jewel-encrusted white Maison Margiela cloak and minidress with a matching miter, the medieval papal headgear. Others incorporated Catholic aesthetics as design elements. Singer Ariana Grande got some attention for her Vera Wang garment that turned Michelangelo's "Last Judgment" from the Sistine Chapel into a flowing chiffon gown, an image of the resurrected Christ placed strategically on her chest. Actress Sarah Jessica Parker paired her Dolce & Gabbana gold brocade gown with a complete Neapolitan nativity scene on her head.

As soon as images for the Met Gala began to circulate, Catholic Twitter started buzzing with moral outrage using the tag #MyReligionIsNotYourCostume. But these complaints were drowned out by high-profile cultural critics and fashion reporters who defended the event, relying in part on the Vatican's support of it. The Vatican donated forty items to the exhibit. Cardinal Gianfranco Ravasi, the Vatican's president of the Pontifical Council for Culture, even attended the Met Gala. As Jessica Andrews of *Teen Vogue* put it, "cultural appropriation implies a lack of consent and participation."[16] For her, Vatican endorsement got everyone off the hook.

But given that religious communities have multiple members with varying life experiences, we should be suspicious when agents granting permission occupy positions of relative privilege, since they are less likely to feel the sting of appropriation as exploitation. To avoid reinforcing forms of inequality within religious communities, in this book I pay special attention to insiders who are marginalized as female, Black, brown, or have other identities that make them more susceptible to systems of inequity.

This is all to say that considering existing power dynamics, including those within a religious community, is important when determining whether borrowing causes appropriative harm. An act of cultural borrowing is not wrong just because it transgresses a cultural boundary; for example, because an outsider borrows a cultural practice of an insider. It is wrong because of the way it interacts with existing oppression of specific groups in ways that further contribute to their oppression.[17] Put differently, borrowing becomes stealing when a dominant or privileged group borrows from a marginalized one. Borrowing in the other direction is assimilation, not appropriation, and not the focus of this book.

I have found American political theorist Iris Young's concept of "structural injustice" helpful for understanding how the conditions of oppression make some instances of borrowing forms of appropriation. Young developed this term to refer to a systemic condition that "exists when social processes put large categories of persons under a systematic threat of domination or deprivation of the means to develop and exercise their capacities, at the same time as these processes enable others to dominate or have a wide range of opportunities."[18] In my discussion of religious appropriation, that means capitalism, sexism, racism, orientalism, and Christian hegemony are all relevant forms of structural injustice.

In the case of religious appropriation, a shallow understanding of power—one that does not account for structural injustice as overlapping forms of domination—can prevent the identification of exploitation. This is why some commentaries dismissed concerns raised by lay Catholics over the Met Gala. They assumed that Catholicism was not eligible to be stolen because of the power and influence of the Roman Catholic Church. Let's revisit Andrews's commentary for *Teen Vogue* in which she wrote, "cultural appropriation hurts the powerless, and the Catholic Church is one of the most powerful institutions in the world." Andrews had a point. Roman Catholicism has been an imperial force in the world for much of its history, and it operated as such in precolonial America. Pope Alexander VI gave Spain the exclusive right to acquire territory and to trade in the New World with his 1493 papal bull Inter Caetera. The Spanish Requerimiento of

1513 used Catholic theology to justify forced conversion, land sei-
zures, and violence against Indigenous peoples.

But none of this political and institutional history means lay Catholics can't be discriminated against. On the contrary, we have a robust history of anti-Catholicism in the United States. Many of the first
settlers were Protestant, and they did not have a generous view of
Catholics. In fact, after the continent's Indigenous peoples, Catholics
were among the very first to become disenfranchised on North American soil. In 1642, the Colony of Virginia passed a law prohibiting
Catholic settlers. In 1719, Rhode Island denied Catholics voting
rights. Even Maryland, a colony established in 1632 explicitly as a
haven for Catholics facing persecution in Europe, outlawed Catholicism and banned Roman Catholics from public office by 1689.

There was a resurgence in US anti-Catholic sentiment in the nineteenth and twentieth centuries in response to waves of Catholic immigrants from Ireland, Italy, Poland, Quebec, and Mexico, especially
within the Ku Klux Klan and other nativist organizations. And today,
Hollywood loves to take cheap shots at Catholics, as James Martin
has recently argued in an essay titled "The Last Acceptable Prejudice?" for *America Magazine*.[19]

I disagree with Andrews's assessment that Catholics can't experience exploitation when outsiders borrow their practices. In fact, one
entire case study in this book is devoted to an instance of religious
appropriation involving a Catholic pilgrimage. But I agree with her
impulse that what makes appropriation harmful is past and ongoing
systems of inequality and marginalization. And certainly, some groups,
such as religious minorities, are more likely to experience harm. But
the issue of power in cases of religious appropriation is not as simple as
categorizing some religions as immune from exploitation just because
they are associated with powerful institutions or leaders.

One reason religious appropriation is so common is that we assume
there are no victims, or at least no victims that have a legitimate claim.

Thus, identifying various forms of exploitation experienced by diverse religious actors will be an important aspect of this book. I prefer the term "exploitation" to "harm," because it reminds us that the injury depends on forms of structural injustice and is thus a form of moral harm.[20] But it is also important to note that exploitation in cases of religious appropriation is not the same as in other forms of cultural appropriation.

Economic exploitation is the most common way of describing the harm caused by cultural appropriation, particularly when the products of the labor of one group are monetized by another group in ways that reinforce asymmetrical power dynamics. The exploitation of religious appropriation can be economic—Madonna commodified Catholic aesthetics to promote her brand. But it can also be ideological. Religious practices are co-opted for political agendas, religious histories are erased, and stereotypes are reinforced. Sometimes, that exploitation is about the corrupting of the practices themselves, insofar as they are extracted from their original context or disconnected from larger religious ideas and beliefs. Other times, exploitation comes from leveraging the value of a religious practice for personal benefit. In still others, it is about reinforcing orientalist narratives that encourage the appropriation in the first place. Understanding these exploitations helps clarify how religious practices are specific types of cultural phenomena, and thus we might need to take extra care when we borrow them.

American philosopher Joel Feinberg has a concept I have found useful for thinking about the exploitation involved in stealing the religion of others: profound offense.[21] In the context of criminal law, he makes a distinction between minor and profound offenses. Examples of the latter include voyeurism, desecration of venerated symbols, and mistreatment of a corpse. Actions that are profoundly offensive do more than put us in an unpleasant state of mind. They are an affront to our core values and sense of self. Religious practices build group intimacy and religious identity, but they can also be the foundation for how an individual sees themselves, the world, and the very meaning of life. Religious appropriations that are profoundly offensive disrupt these worldviews. They are enacted heresy.

What "my" refers to in *Stealing My Religion* depends on your perspective. It could mean, "Someone is stealing religion from me," or "I am stealing religion from someone." The ambiguity is intended to make space for the diverse relationships my readers will have to this topic. For some of you, the sting of appropriation I discuss will be personal, such as when campaigns adopt your religious clothing for political agendas or when the wellness industry promotes sanitized versions of your own religion to you as therapy. But for many of my readers, you will be on the other side of the table, borrowing the religion of others in the pursuit of what you consider to be nonreligious goals.

If the term "stealing" signals my presumption that appropriation is exploitation, the "my" in the title suggests this book is also a confession: I myself have appropriated religion. My Madonna phase, my yoga practice, some of my pedagogical choices, even my politics—these have all involved appropriating the religious practice of others. I am not presenting myself as a role model. I am a cautionary tale. I have stolen my religion in problematic ways, in ways that I am embarrassed by. My experiences with religious borrowing show how challenging navigating the ethics of religious appropriation can be, even for an expert in ethics and religion such as myself. But when I acknowledge these mistakes, take moral responsibility, and reflect on what I could have done better, I hope they become teachable moments.

I also want you to see yourself in this topic. In the early stages of writing, *Stealing Your Religion* was this book's working title because I think most Americans are guilty of stealing their religion. Likely, there are things you do that place you in the world, give you pleasure, contribute to physical or mental health, and so on, which are rooted in religious traditions you do not identify with. I am not trying to catch you in a "gotcha moment," but I do want you to consider how these religious borrowings might impact others. There are lots of reasons that so many of us steal our religion, but I want to put a significant amount of blame on liberalism. This ideology's emphasis on individual freedom and self-management encourages the curation of a personal spirituality instead of submitting to the authority of a religious institution or community.[22]

As I define religious appropriation, anyone can engage in it. But certainly, it is easiest to identify this practice in the United States among two groups: "spiritual but not religious" (SBNR) and non–religiously affiliated who self-describe as "nones." I would argue that anyone who calls themselves SBNR is in danger of engaging in religious appropriation, since they insist they are religious outsiders but also intentionally engage in ad hoc religious borrowings. Nones' refusal to affiliate with organized religion does not mean this group is irreligious either. Author Tara Isabella Burton describes nones as "the religious mix and matchers, the theologically bi- and tri-curious who attend Shabbat services but also do yoga, who cleanse with sage but also sing 'Silent Night' at Christmastime."[23] Insisting that they have no religious affiliation while acting religiously "bi- and tri-curious" is a situation ripe for religious appropriation.[24]

More generally, the agents of appropriation discussed in this book can be described in a couple of ways. Much as I depend on self-reports for determining who is a religious insider, I have selected case studies in which borrowers concede that they are not part of the religious community in which the practice they adopt originated.[25] In fact, assuming they can remain an outsider is part of what enables them to appropriate the practice in the first place. A non-Muslim woman who wears a hijab for the day as a political symbol. A Camino pilgrim who describes himself as an atheist. A yoga practitioner who insists her practice is merely therapeutic. As we will see, these individuals work hard to remain religious outsiders by rejecting religious doctrines, norms, and metaphysics. They don't dispute religious boundaries. In fact, the distinction between insiders and outsiders is fundamental to their comfort with ad hoc borrowing.

There are versions of religious appropriation that most of us would agree are immoral, such as the Nazi Party's use of the *svastika*, the Hindu symbol of good fortune. But, in this book, I focus on cases of religious appropriation where the intent is meaningful engagement because these are the situations that tend to avoid ethical scrutiny. The agents of appropriation in my three case studies are all motivated by goals that would be considered "good" if judged by the tenets of liberalism: solidarity with a religious minority under attack, education through experiential learning, and the pursuit of health and well-being.

However, intentions do not determine whether an action is just, because they do not predict how that action will be experienced by others.[26] Instead, we need to consider whether the action results in oppression because it relies on or reinforces existing forms of structural injustice. Asymmetrical power relations, not intentions, are how we determine the exploitation of appropriation. In fact, since the borrowing agent likely occupies a position of relative privilege, they are not in a position to see, much less understand, appropriative harm. Good motivations don't get us off the hook.

An outcome might even be in direct opposition to the appropriator's intended effect. We will see, for instance, how forms of solidarity hijab, displayed and worn to combat gendered Islamophobia, were experienced as further marginalization and powerlessness by Muslim women. If the goal of my study abroad program on the Camino was to increase religious literacy, in practice, it reinforced a Christian-centric narrative of Spanish history. Respite yoga, which has the goal of cultivating personal health, risks abuse of the borrowing agent.

Most of the appropriators of religion discussed in this book are white because white supremacy means that those who are white are more likely to feel entitled to appropriate the religion of others. But religious appropriation is not something that only white people do.

Let me use an example that was circulating on my Twitter feed in November 2020, as I was writing the first draft of this introduction. To promote her upcoming shoe collection for Reebok, Grammy winner Cardi B was featured on the November *Footwear News* cover styled as Durga, the many-armed Hindu goddess.[27] Wearing a candy apple strapless gown, against a hot pink background, Cardi B held a shiny red shoe from her collection with two arms. Another eight arms fanned out and over her head, showing off her signature three-inch coffin nails and upper-arm tattoos. The text reads, "The Power of Cardi B," a clear reference to Durga's reputation as a fierce warrior goddess.

Several of my Twitter mutuals, knowing I was working on religious appropriation, DMed me the *Daily Mail* piece on the ad, which they referred to as "homage to the Hindu goddess Durga." Then, I noticed some of Desi Twitter expressing outrage. @My_DesiGirl tweeted "Cardi B appropriating Hinduism and y'all call it fashion . . . disrespectful."[28] "Cardi B using Durga Maa to sell trainers??" wrote @GeetaChelseaFC. "When are people gonna realize our gods and goddesses aren't there to be mimicked."[29]

But not everyone agreed. For many, the fact that Cardi B was a Black woman meant the power differential present when white people appropriate from Black people was missing. For the same reason that Rihanna's pope costume at the 2018 Met Gala got a pass, as did Beyoncé's appearance dressed as an Indian woman in Coldplay's 2016 video "Hymn for the Weekend," some argued that Cardi B, as a Black woman, couldn't be guilty of appropriation.

I agree that there is something particularly egregious when white people appropriate practices associated with nonwhite communities. But a racial Black-white binary is not the only way whiteness is involved in creating exploitative conditions for appropriation. Critical race theory encourages us to think beyond this binary to understand that "each disfavored group in this country had been racialized in its own individual way and according to the needs of the majority group at particular times in its history."[30] Assumptions about race are at the core of how many dominant groups assert their superiority over others. For instance, religious minorities are racialized, but not always in ways that follow a simply Black-white binary.

Returning to the example of Cardi B, this popular singer might be Black, but she is also a Western woman appropriating an Eastern image to promote her celebrity brand. She is vulnerable to anti-Black racism in the United States, but also the beneficiary of orientalism and capitalism—which are also expressions of white supremacy. Cardi B's race doesn't mean her Durga cosplay is morally neutral because, even as a Black woman, she lives within a context where the relationship between race and power goes beyond the Black-white binary.

Cardi B apologized for the ad campaign, making this case of religious appropriation unlike so many others, by posting the following in an Instagram story:

> When I did the shoot, the creatives told me I was going to represent a Goddess; that she represents strength, femininity, and liberation, and that's something I love and I'm all about. And though it was dope, if people think I'm offending their culture or their religion I want to say that was not my intent. I do not like offending anyone's religion; I wouldn't like it if someone did it to my religion.[31]

This was an imperfect apology that focused on explaining her intention, instead of acknowledging why it was exploitative to sell a sneaker with imagery representing a Hindu goddess. But her admission that offense was caused by her not understanding the religious tradition she was borrowing from is commendable. "Maybe I should've done my research. I'm sorry. I can't change the past but I'm gonna do more research for the future."[32]

Cardi B is an example of how religion complicates our understanding of who the perpetrators of appropriation can be. Usually in discussions of cultural appropriation, racial identity is how we determine who the insiders and outsiders are. But in the context of borrowing religion, it becomes clear that people of color are not immune from exploiting others. My point is not to cast blame on communities of color, but rather to show that anyone is a potential stealer of religion. Religious or not religious. White, brown, or Black. We are all potentially the subject of *Stealing My Religion.*

Finally, a preliminary description of what I mean by "religion," the final word in the book's title, may be helpful. Since the academic study of religion emerged within the Western academy, the discipline is itself a product of empire, white supremacy, and Christian hegemony.[33] This history means forms of structural injustice are embedded in dominant analytical and theoretical approaches in the field.[34] And today, religious studies scholars disagree on how to define religion. This doesn't mean that the category of religion is not useful for focusing our attention on particular sorts of human activity, but rather that any definition will always be partial, emphasizing some things and missing others.

A second challenge to defining religion is, ironically, how often it is used. We are all familiar with the concept of religion, and yet few of us understand traditions that are not our own. So, while most Americans would insist they know what religion is, religious literacy is actually quite low here. "I know it when I see it" is not a definition of religion precise enough to be valuable for careful analytical work.

These two challenges—problematic origins of religion as an academic discipline and a fuzzy public understanding of religion—mean that how we define religion will dictate what we end up paying attention to.

For this book I need to define religion in a way that has enough precision to explain what makes religious appropriation distinct from other forms of cultural appropriation, without neglecting that religion is a flexible and evolving category. My working definition of "religion" can be summarized as *everyday human practices that are connected to histories of interpretation, systems of ethics, and broader metaphysical and cosmological claims.* This definition is influenced by both theological and anthropological scholarly approaches to religion, so let's look at those more carefully.

American historian of religion Jonathan Z. Smith was a giant in the field of religious studies. He spent most of his career at the University of Chicago, where I earned my doctorate. Although by the time I attended graduate school he was teaching infrequently, his understanding of religion had an enormous effect on my training because it helped shape how the Divinity School organized its courses and faculty into different areas. In his widely read and cited essay "Religion, Religions, Religious," Smith observed that religious studies scholars tend to use either theological or anthropological definitions of religions. Much of my coursework fell into these two categories; and in my work, I combine both these approaches.

My courses at the University of Chicago on ethics, for example, took a theological approach to religion. The most common formulation I read in graduate school was that of the Protestant theologian and philosopher Paul Tillich, who understood religion to be defined by an "ultimate concern."[35] For Tillich, not all "ultimate concerns" were equal; he would even have considered some erroneous, and certainly he had in mind Christian theism when he spoke of religion. But if we remove this bias from his definition, what we are left with is that religion is a "worldview" that entails both beliefs and practices, but for which orientation to an ultimate concern leads the way.

In contrast, anthropological definitions of religion emphasize religion as a human activity by focusing our attention on how social, political, and economic contexts are constantly forming systems of symbols that give meaning to human life.[36] Much of my coursework on the history of religion at the Divinity School—such as courses focused on the role of gender or authority in religious communities—assumed this definition of religion. One advantage to thinking about religion as culture in this way is that it allows us to take seriously religious practices and not just religion as belief. Malory Nye, author of the popular introduction to religious studies *Religion: The Basics*, provides an anthropological understanding of religion organized around defining religion grammatically as a verb instead of a noun, something I have found helpful in my teaching:

> I would argue that culture is not a thing in itself; it is a process, a form of activity that is ongoing and fluid; it is something that is done by people. One way to describe this may be to say that culture is culturing (as an activity, not as a thing)—when we practice our culture we are culturing. . . . This is also a way in which we can describe the practice of religion, as a process of religioning (as doing religion, rather than thinking of religion as a thing in itself).[37]

My goal is to combine theological and anthropological definitions of religion to draw our attention to religious practices that exist in webs of power but that are also grounded in ultimate concerns. Put another way, religion entails culture, but a distinct type of culture—one that is associated with the supernatural, god/gods, or simply decentering human agency.[38] This means that when we look at cases of the appropriation of religion, we need to pay attention to the impact on the ultimate concerns—which we find expressed in histories of interpretation, systems of ethics, and broader metaphysical and cosmological claims—as well as the meanings of the practices themselves.

The reader will notice that throughout this book, I reject the idea that spirituality is somehow qualitatively different from religion. In doing so, I know I am going against conventional wisdom as well as a long history of use of the term "spirituality" in the American context. Today, most of my students, friends, and family would insist that spirituality is distinct from religion, but most of my colleagues in religious studies would not.

As early as the nineteenth century, American liberal thinkers within the transcendentalist movement identified spirituality as the most desirable aspect of religion. These thinkers urged each person to rely on their own experience to find, in Ralph Waldo Emerson's words, "an original relation to the universe."[39] This set the stage for contrasting spirituality, associated with the individual, against religion, associated with the institution of the church.[40] Spirituality without religion was further popularized by such groups as Alcoholics Anonymous (AA) in the 1930s and 1940s when its founder, Bill Wilson, developed a therapy model that drew heavily on the idea of spiritual experience as central to recovery but without ties to institutional religion. Six of AA's famous twelve steps refer to a deity—"God," "Him," or "a Power greater than us"—even as many of AA's foundational documents emphasize that the organization is open to anyone seeking sobriety. The organization began to use the label "spiritual but not religious" to describe its program.[41]

The idea of customizing our spiritual practice, in which all religious traditions are part of a self-service buffet bar for us to pick and choose from, made its way into mainstream US culture during the nation's spiritual revisionism of the 1960s. This was a time of increased access to the religion of others through globalization and immigration, but also one of increased suspicion of religious institutions and authority because of countercultural movements. As Americans began to feel free to borrow from a wide range of religions, curating our own collection of beliefs and practices to solve a whole host of problems such as anxiety, immorality, obesity, and alienation, "spiritual but not religious" as an identity began to gain popularity.[42] By 2000, the concept showed up on a Gallup poll in which 30 percent of US respondents identified as SBNR.[43]

But the juxtaposition of religious and spiritual does more moral and political than meaningful descriptive work. When I ask my students, for instance, what defines something as spiritual, they give such answers as "a connection to something bigger than us," "a search for meaning," or "deepened consciousness." All positive attributes. In contrast, they associate negative things with religion, such as the oppressive authority of religious institutions and leaders or strict moral codes. "Spirituality" is the term that gets assigned to "good religion."[44]

My specific concern with the insistence that spiritual and religious are distinct is that this idea eases the way for appropriating the religious practices of others. For one, it allows us to claim we are engaging in borrowed spiritual practices without necessarily "becoming religious." Since we are only adopting the bits that "work for us," without buying into doctrines, dogmas, or values, we assume we can safely remain outsiders. But for many religious traditions, correct practice does not necessarily come after belief. In fact, practice may be the way beliefs, as well as virtues and larger orientations in the world, are created. Following Malory Nye, if religion is a verb we do instead of a noun we possess, if we are doing the religious things, we are doing religion, independent of our declared affiliation or ideological commitments.[45]

Furthermore, the spiritual/religious distinction encourages us to think that practices only become "good" once unpinned from religious traditions and institutions. That is, when we insist a practice is spiritual, not religious, we are claiming access to an "authentic" version of the practice, one unsullied by the hierarchies, institutions, norms, and doctrines of religion. And yet, this distillation by an outsider is an exercise of both cultural imperialism and conquest.

Finally, I want to be explicit about how my understanding of religion is shaped by critical race theory. On one hand, the connection between race and religion is historical. Theologian and scholar of Black Church studies J. Kameron Carter argues in *Race: A Theological Account* that the genesis of race is in attempts by Christians to differentiate themselves from Jews by casting them as a racialized group. Carter calls this the racial imagination. It included not only a distinction, but also a hierarchy, because this racialization was a way to explain why Christians were superior to Jews. Taken together, Carter calls these two moves (racial imagination and racial hierarchy) the theological problem of whiteness.[46] When we see white supremacy play out in the case studies in this book, we are witnessing a theological legacy.

We are supposed to be a nation founded on the value of religious freedom, but in practice, we have historically protected only expressions of religion that look like white Protestantism.[47] Anything else is discarded, encouraged to assimilate, or as we will see, up for adoption by self-proclaimed religious outsiders. Put differently, in the United States, secularism is not a lack of religion, but institutionalized white Protestantism, and it creates a form of entitlement that justifies the instrumentalization of practices of religious minorities.

If Americans are more sensitive to racial appropriation than to religious appropriation because we assume that only the first is involved in white supremacy, then we are missing the extent to which the latter also depends on whiteness. The ideology of whiteness is manifested in various ways in forms of religious appropriation; for instance, when practices associated with brown bodies are adopted by white agents, when histories of racism are erased, and when forms of appropriation position white Americans as the proper interpreters of the "true" meaning of a practice. The case studies in this book illuminate the ways race is part of what makes religious appropriation possible and popular in the first place, and then perceived as morally neutral.

Three Case Studies

Religious borrowing and combining has always existed. It occurs when religious communities interact, when religious traditions spread into new areas, and when new technological possibilities encourage religious beliefs to shift. There is even a term used to refer to the process of adapting Christian teachings and liturgy for non-Christian cultures: inculturation. And certainly, borrowing and combining is how some religious traditions are formed in the first place, such the Cuban diaspora religion Santería.

Some religious communities have doctrinal reasons for actively trying to convert people to their beliefs, which might make them seem more welcoming to religious borrowing. Evangelical Christians, for instance, believe they have a duty to spread the "good news" to those outside their community, based on their interpretation of Matthew 28:19–20. Likewise, Islam welcomes newcomers into the community.[48] But the goal of a proselytizing religion is that a convert will eventually accept beliefs, not just try on practices. It is one thing for a religious community to share its practices and beliefs with someone from outside. It is quite another for a self-declared outsider to adopt those practices in ways that are intentionally unpinned from religious histories, communities, and doctrines. A Christian could experience as mockery someone's wearing a cross as a fashion statement with no intention of accepting Jesus Christ as their savior.

Other religious traditions, such as Hinduism, have no such doctrinal imperative to convert others. Yet there may be political reasons for encouraging outsiders to borrow Hindu practices. When Anglo-Europeans and Anglo-Americans appropriate yogic practices associated with Hinduism as forms of "ancient Indian wisdom," for instance, it can help support the right-wing notion that Hinduism should be the basis of Indian nationalism. This is why Indian prime minister Narendra Modi is such a promoter of yoga. Its popularity helps consolidate his political power by reinforcing the association of Hinduism with India.

Finally, diversity within religious communities means that not all individuals experience religious borrowing as exploitation in the same way. For instance, some religious minorities welcome appropriation of their practices as a sign of mainstream acceptance. Others experience this as further marginalization. And since there are different opinions about what counts as correct practice, members of a religious community might find themselves accused of appropriating their own tradition.

Despite these challenges, there are advantages to using religious appropriation to think through the ethical implications of some common religious borrowings.

First, framing specific practices as *religious* appropriation makes them legible as part of what Malory Nye calls "religioning." Too often, appropriators claim that practices disconnected from "belief" or "institutions" are not religious. Calling these borrowings "religious" highlights that their connection to communities of devotion is what makes them desirable to outsiders in the first place. Using the example of yoga for a moment, an association with religion is why some people are attracted to yoga instead of, say, to Pilates; why they find it so valuable; and why they are unwilling to give it up.[49] My point is not to convince you that yoga is religious, but to ask you to consider that it might be, and certainly is for some, and how that changes the ethical implications of its mainstream popularity.

Second, framing these practices as religious *appropriation* brings their ethical implications to the forefront. If the practices we borrow have meanings rooted in devotional communities that we are not part of, we need to be aware of how our adoptions might affect those communities. In other words, classifying these borrowings as appropriation signals that they are potentially morally problematic and that we have culpability when we do them.

Thus my proposal is to use the term "religious appropriation" not as a diagnosis but as a framework of ethical analysis. The framework begins with the premise that ethically fraught forms of borrowing religious practices exist—and I'll call these religious appropriations. But that is only the starting point. The analytical work involves describing what these practices mean to religious communities, and why outsiders see them as attractive for adoption; identifying forms of exploitation and the profound offense that stakeholders experience from the appropriation; and finally, explaining how specific asymmetrical power dynamics make the appropriation exploitative. The label of "religious appropriation" is where our work begins, not where it ends.

I had many options for case studies I could have focused on. Meditation apps. Kabbalah. Zen home decor. Sweat lodges. Secular seders. SoulCycle. Lent as a cleanse. Burning sage at home. Vacations to religious sites. Wanderlust Festival. These are all examples of mainstream religious appropriation. The three cases I selected draw from areas of my research and teaching expertise: solidarity hijab as an example of political aesthetics, pilgrimage on the Camino as an example of educational tourism, and Kripalu yoga as an example of ritual converted to wellness routine.

These practices are all reasonably popular and appear morally neutral. All three are based on intended outcomes that liberals would consider "good," such as political solidarity, learning, and health. These intentions become reasons that these examples of religious appropriation avoid scrutiny: they are categorized as something else. When we look at them together, however, we see that liberal intentions do not prevent exploitation. In fact, illiberal results are common in cases of religious appropriation.

Most of the scholarly attention to what I call religious appropriation in the US context has been on Native American or South Asian traditions.[50] I wanted to think about a wide range of religious appropriation, so I intentionally selected some examples where the appropriation was of a so-called Western tradition. This allows attention to the ways in which forms of asymmetrical power dynamics exist even when the role of oppression is less obvious.

The case studies in this book focus primarily on Americans as agents of religious appropriation, a choice I made for several reasons. First, although conversations about cultural appropriation happen in other national contexts, they are particularly prominent in US culture wars. And yet as I mentioned earlier, cases of religious appropriation tend to avoid scrutiny entirely here. This provides an opportunity to investigate what features of the current US political and social landscape make forms of religious exploitation common and yet hard to see. Americans seem to feel entitled to appropriate from whomever we want. We don't care, or even hear, when religious practitioners object to our religious borrowings. If religion is messy, we are a nation of slobs.

Although the book focuses on the way Americans appropriate religion, it does not stop at the US borders. American religion is transnational, not only because of voluntary immigration, but also because of forced relocation and enslavement. And appropriation is a truly global dynamic. Yoga is attractive to Americans because yoga brands are created and marketed in the United States with explicit references to Indic lineages. Other countries required or banned Islamic headscarves, which contributes to how Americans understand the significance of this garment. Americans' appropriation of religion affects communities elsewhere, such as when increasing numbers of Americans walk the Camino in Spain.

The first case study is solidarity hijab—wearing an Islamic headscarf to signal opposition to gendered Islamophobia. Religious belief and practice often involve dress codes: Christian crosses, Buddhist monks' robes, and Jewish skullcaps. And certainly, religious clothing and accessories make their way into popular culture. The classic example is Madonna's use of the cross. But who, you might ask, would "appropriate" a hijab, the most politicized symbol of Muslim women's piety?

To answer this question, I focus on how hijab has recently been used as a symbol of progressive politics. Examples include Shepard Fairey's "flag hijab" image and the Headscarf for Harmony campaign in response to the 2019 massacre in a mosque in Christchurch, New Zealand. Of the three case studies in this book, solidarity hijab seems the most other-regarding. But we will see that a good intention toward a religious minority does not guarantee a good outcome. Solidarity hijab illustrates how appropriation can affect the perceived meaning of a religious practice, as well as how forms of religious appropriation can decenter actual practitioners from political discussions about their communities.

The second case study investigates the ethical implications of completing a Catholic pilgrimage for educational purposes when not Catholic. Pilgrimage is one of the most ancient religious practices, and it remains popular today: more than 130 million people embark on a religious journey each year. Pilgrimage is about reaching a sacred destination, and the journey itself allows the pilgrim to enter a different state of being, one in which some religious truth about the self, world, or divinity is revealed. Framed as a rite of passage, pilgrimages can be the occasion of a profound transformation, to knowing or becoming more.

Each year, approximately a quarter of a million people walk a section of the route in northern Spain known as the Camino de Santiago, or "the Way to St. James," to Santiago de Compostela, where legend has it the bones of St. James the Apostle are entombed. This is a Catholic pilgrimage, but Catholic pilgrims are in the minority. I have walked a section of the Camino five times as part of an experiential study abroad program I created and then led from 2013 to 2017. I draw on my experience as well as that of my students to explore why non-Catholics want to complete the Camino, what they hope to get out of the journey, and what exploitations the participation in a religious rite of passage might cause. Framing the Camino as appropriation allows us to see how it erases contentious political histories and involves the pilgrim in contestations over which Christians "own" the tradition. Through this case study, we discover how study abroad programs focusing on religion raise ethical concerns about the educational goal of achieving cultural competency.

The inclusion of the Camino case study is an opportunity to think about how powerful religions, such as Catholicism, might also be appropriated in problematic ways. In the case of European Catholicism, we have a religious tradition that has been responsible itself for so much global exploitation. And yet I suggest Catholic practices are also subject to appropriation, especially when they can be marketed as a part of self-transformation or used to prop up Christian nationalism. The Camino is also a helpful case study to explore the asymmetrical power relations that exist within the broad category of Christianity, such as between Protestants and Catholics, or between white and nonwhite Christian communities. Part of the attraction of the Camino to Americans is that it is a form of pilgrimage through western Europe, which allows us to experience "high" European culture. This is part of why the Camino joins Lourdes, France, and the Vatican as top pilgrimage destinations for American Catholics, instead of the Baclaran Church in Manila, Philippines; the National Shrine Basilica of Our Lady of Ransom in Kochi, India; or the Basilica of the Virgin of Guadalupe on the outskirts of Mexico City, Mexico.

Contemplative practices exist in all major world religions, but it isn't hard to notice that the mindfulness practices associated with Asian forms of ancient wisdom—such as meditation and yoga—are extremely popular in the United States. Apps, corporate wellness programs, and college minors all offer ways to create habits to help reduce stress, increase productivity, and improve health. A staggering one in three Americans has tried yoga at some point in their life, making it among the most widespread forms of religious appropriation. To explore how the ethical implications of yoga might be understood through the lens of appropriation, I take a deep dive into Kripalu yoga, at the Kripalu Center for Yoga & Health, the oldest school of yoga in the United States, located in Stockbridge, Massachusetts.

Formerly an ashram, Kripalu Center was reincorporated as an educational institution in 1994 as part of a radical reframing of Kripalu's mission, one that involved distancing itself from the aspects of devotional yoga more closely associated with Hinduism. Kripalu yoga is helpful for thinking about what aspects of religion are not appropriated because they are deemed too dangerous or incompatible with modern Western life, and how these choices are experienced as exploitation by those who feel some ownership of yoga's traditions, such as Hindu and South Asian Americans. It also raises questions about how best to adopt a devotional practice for a more secular context in ways that respect that heritage but do not colonialize it.

As research for this book, I intentionally engaged in religious appropriation to get an insider look into these phenomena. My analysis of solidarity hijab applies lessons on the politics of Muslim women's dress that I learned in Iran, Indonesia, and Turkey while researching my previous book, *Pious Fashion*. But as a white non-Muslim liberal feminist, I am also part of a community that has insisted solidarity hijab is an effective form of political protest. My exploration of pilgrimage draws on my experience walking the last 150 miles of the Camino in Spain five times with college students as part of an intensive study abroad program I designed that literally required religious appropriation for course credit. During those journeys, I was both a professor and a guide, but I was also a pilgrim in a foreign land, who walked thirteen to eighteen miles daily, often in rain and once in snow. My mother was a yoga teacher before that was cool, and I have practiced yoga myself for the last twenty-five years. As part of the research on yoga as appropriation, I became a 200-hour certified Kripalu yoga instructor. I then volunteered to teach a weekly class on my university campus and had to figure out how to do so in a way that did not feel like an exercise in colonialism.

I share many of the firsthand experiences in this book as auto-ethnography, but I am not presenting myself as a role model. In fact, my intent is the opposite. I share the ways I have appropriated religion because I am not proud of them, and I think we can all do better.

1

Solidarity Hijab

By the spring of 2019, two front-runners emerged from the pool of candidates hoping to secure the Democratic nomination for the 2020 US presidential election: the eventual nominee, former vice president Joe Biden, and Senator Elizabeth Warren. Both campaigns made combatting Islamophobia part of their platforms and criticized Donald Trump's anti-Muslim rhetoric and policies in their stump speeches. They also attempted to visually signal their commitment to the Muslim community by including Muslims in their promotional materials. As part of these efforts, both campaigns ran ads featuring images of Muslim women in headscarves. But the women featured were not always asked for permission to use their image in these aesthetics of solidarity. This was, I want to suggest, a form of symbolic religious appropriation.

Sabirah Mahmud, a teenage Bernie Sanders supporter, attended Biden's Philadelphia kickoff rally in May 2019. Shortly after she was surprised to see herself featured in a campaign promo video and tweeted, "was just used as hijabi clout for the @JoeBiden campaign, too bad i'm #hotgirlsforbernie."[1] In an interview with *Jacobin* magazine, Mahmud explained in more detail what she meant by "hijabi clout." "It's not like I was chanting, it's not like I was clapping or smiling," she said. "I had a stern face . . . it doesn't really make sense at all why I'm in that video other than for purposes of, like, profiting off my hijab."[2] In much the same way, Ayanna Lee discovered herself in an ad for Warren after attending a rally in Milwaukee to protest the candidate. Lee told the *Guardian* that the Warren campaign was not aware she was not supporting Warren, but nevertheless she felt "they took advantage of who I am. It made me upset that I was being used for a campaign."[3] And 2020 was not the first time Democratic presidential hopefuls used the image of a Muslim woman in hijab. In 2016, after Nida Allam attended the Democratic National Convention, an image of her crying on the delegate floor went viral after it was tweeted by the Hillary for America account with the tagline "We made history." "It was the moment Senator Sanders had conceded," Allam told the *Guardian*. "I was crying because I was working on the Sanders campaign."[4]

To explore the ethics of appropriating hijab, I consider in this chapter what I call solidarity hijab: political campaigns initiated and adopted for the most part by non-Muslims with the intention of combatting gendered Islamophobia. I focus on two high-profile examples: the adoption of Shepard Fairey's "flag-hijab" image during the 2017 Women's March and the 2019 #HeadscarfForHarmony campaign launched in the wake of the Christchurch massacre in New Zealand. The first was a feminist protest that utilized the image of Muslim women in hijab. The second encouraged non-Muslim women to wear hijab to protest violence against Muslims. By highlighting the ways some Muslim women experienced these well-meaning acts as exploitation, I show that these expressions of liberal inclusion did not always have the effect of supporting Muslim women. In fact, just the opposite: in some cases, solidarity hijab contributed to the further racialization and subjugation of Muslim women.

We are used to thinking about clothing in the context of discussions of cultural appropriation. Indigenous, African, and Asian aesthetics are often adopted and marketed as high fashion or hipster cool in ways that communities experience as exploitation because clothing also creates and expresses racial and ethnic identity. But appropriating religious clothing raises additional ethical issues because of its specific religious functions. Religious leaders wear liturgical vestments to be visually identified as a representative of God on earth. Ordinary practitioners wear religious clothing during ceremonies to sanctify the body by sartorially orienting it to the divine. Other items, such as hijab, are meant for everyday use not only to communicate commitment to religious identity and values, but also to create a specific social space and cultivate an individual's character.

Religious clothing and accessories enter popular culture in ways that look like appropriation. In the Introduction, I discussed Madonna's—and my—appropriation of cross jewelry. A more recent example was Gucci's decision in 2018 to send a model wearing a bright blue turban down the runway during Milan Fashion Week. Although the turban is a common item of clothing in many cultures, to the Sikh community it was clear the style of the Gucci headpiece referenced a *paghri* or *pagh*, a Sikh turban neatly tied to produce a slightly angular shape. For Sikhs, this head covering is a religious practice, an expression of religious identity but also a form of devotion. According to the Sikh Coalition, wearing a turban "asserts a public commitment to maintaining the values and ethics of the tradition, including service, compassion, and honesty."[5] As a sign of Sikh identity, turbans have made Sikhs a target of violence in the United States. But Gucci's "Indy Full Turban" was, according to the department store Nordstrom, "ready to turn heads while keeping you in comfort," and available for purchase for $750.[6]

A model walks the runway in Gucci's "Indy Full Turban" during the luxury brand's Milan Fashion Week show on February 21, 2018. (Venturelli / WireImage / Getty Images)

No item of religious dress is as politically charged in the West as the hijab, so the case of its appropriation might seem unlikely. Nevertheless, speaking as someone who has studied the politics of Muslim women's clothing for the last fifteen years, it is clear that instances of appropriated hijab have become more frequent recently. When this occurs without an understanding of how hijab functions as a religious practice for some Muslim women, such adoption can cause profound offense.

Most Muslim women who wear a head covering claim they are following a written directive in the Quran. Three verses are commonly cited as Quranic evidence — 24:30–31, 33:53, and 33:59–60 — but there are enormous variations in what these verses say. Different Arabic terms are used (only 33:53 uses the word "hijab"). Who is asked to veil (the Prophet's wives versus all believers) and for what reasons (privacy, security, modesty) differs in these verses, which complicates how to interpret these directives to cover. As I have argued in detail in *The Islamic Veil*, a Quranic justification for hijab is only possible through a holistic reading of this sacred text, one that links these verses and semantically expands the meaning of each.[7]

Because the Quran can support multiple interpretations, and different readers bring different questions, concerns, and assumptions to the text, there are different beliefs about what, if any, form of clothing the sacred text requires. This is why adoption of hijab within the Muslim community is not universal. In the United States, for instance, a 2017 Pew Survey found that a little over of half of Muslim women wear a headscarf. Thirty-eight percent wear it all the time; another 5 percent, most of the time; and 15 percent, some of the time. That means 42 percent of Muslim women living in the United States never wear a headscarf.[8]

That there is no consensus over hijab doesn't take away from the fact that it is an important religious practice for many Muslim women.

To assume otherwise would be like saying keeping kosher is not a religious practice because some Jews don't observe it. My rule of thumb
is to defer to religious practitioners who claim a practice is devotional.

A good beginning question is, what do Muslim women say about
the religious function of hijab? A 2012 study that interviewed 1,733
American Muslim women was designed to answer just that. The researchers asked these women, "Why did you decide to wear a Muslim
head covering?" then invited participants to select from among multiple provided reasons. Popular responses included "expression of personal identity" (45 percent) and "to spread the word about Islam"
(24 percent).[9] But the overwhelmingly most popular response—
selected by 82 percent of the participants—was "personal piety."

The piety associated with hijab operates on several levels. There is
corporate piety, insofar as the hijab creates a gender-segregated social
space. There is interpersonal piety, whereby hijab organizes the interactions of unrelated men and women. And there is personal piety:
hijab has moral implications for the wearer herself. This makes the
"personal" of the response "personal piety" an important modifier. It
means for 82 percent of the study's respondents, hijab is about their
own character, and not necessarily about establishing public gender
norms of dress or creating visual separation between men and women.
Or put differently, the researchers found that for the majority of
American Muslim women who wear a hijab, the garment is about
becoming a good Muslim.

As I have written about elsewhere, I find the concept of virtue
helpful for understanding the way hijab creates personal piety.[10] Virtue
ethics is an ethical theory that sees the cultivation of moral excellences
as important to living a good life. In many formulations, including
the work of influential Islamic philosopher Miskawayh (d. 1030), belief, understanding, and instruction are not enough to transform a
person into a good Muslim: specific actions—repetitive behavior and

physical habits—are also part of moral development.[11] A pianist's physical practice creates dexterity, muscle memory, and a good ear—all necessary to become a good musician. In the same way, religious practices transform the person who does them by creating virtues or dispositions to behave a certain way: daily prayer cultivates humility and submission, and fasting during Ramadan cultivates devotion.[12] Some Muslims believe wearing hijab builds the habits necessary to cultivate the virtues of modesty, shyness, humility, or obedience. That makes its wearing part of a program of moral training, much as musicians use hours of daily practice to hone their craft.

Even though we often consider the cultivation of character to be a personal task, it is also acutely social. The moral development of wearing a hijab, for instance, relies on learning social norms about what to wear and then having an audience for the sartorial practice. For a faithful Muslim woman, choices about appropriate dress are shaped by discussions with family, peers, and religious leaders about what it means to be a good Muslim woman. And then, wearing a hijab publicly depends on a particular readability of this head covering. This means that how non-Muslims think about and use hijab can change the practice for Muslims, including, as we will see, its ability to cultivate personal piety. Since hijab is not merely a symbol of Muslim identity but also how some Muslim women make themselves into a particular sort of religious subject, the stakes of its appropriation are high.

Before considering prominent examples of solidarity hijab in the United States, it is helpful to understand the other ways this head covering has been politicized. I'll focus on how hijab became an important symbol of Islam, the marginalization and discrimination of Muslims in the United States, the increased popularity of Muslim fashion, and the role of misogyny and feminism in gendered Islamophobia.

In her classic text *Women and Gender in Islam*, Leila Ahmed argues that the Islamic veil is "pregnant with meaning" because of a relatively recent political process that began in the late nineteenth century. This was when European colonizers decided Islam was the defining feature of Indigenous populations, the characteristic that made those peoples very different from the Europeans (a "them" vs. "us" approach). At the same time, women came to be seen by both the colonizers and the colonized as the repository of all culture and religion. Within this context, the significance of Muslim women's head and face coverings increased. Colonists tried to unveil Muslim women to make them more "modern" and Western. Local Muslim elite reacted by promoting the veil as a practice central to the survival of the Muslim community. As both the target of colonial reform and the method of resistance to occupation, Muslim women's covering suddenly became *the* symbol of Muslim identity and difference.[13]

The politicization of hijab endures today, when 3.45 million Muslims living in America make up 1.1 percent of the total US population.[14] As one of the most diverse religious groups in the United States, Muslims differ in terms of race, culture, class, ideological commitments, education, and language. And yet a hijab is the most widely accepted symbol of this community.

The Muslim presence in North America predates the founding of the republic; the first significant wave of Muslims to the continent came as part of the slave trade from Africa. However, the majority of non-US-born Muslims arrived after 1965, when the national quota system was replaced with other criteria for immigration, such as reuniting families and growing the US economy. Over half of the US Muslim population comprises South Asian, Persian, and Arab immigrants, and African Americans make up another quarter.

A generation ago, scholars predicted that second- and third-generation Muslim immigrants would gradually lose the commitment to specialized clothing in attempts to appear "more American." But the opposite has turned out to be true. For many Muslim Americans, it was after they emigrated from Muslim-majority countries, such as Pakistan, Saudi Arabia, Iran, and Bangladesh, to the United States, that they began to adopt visual symbols of Muslim identity like the hijab.

Suspicion of Muslims existed in the United States prior to 9/11, influenced by the Iranian Revolution, the first Persian Gulf War, and various terrorist bombings attributed to Islamist groups. But it is undeniable that 9/11 made this situation much worse by linking terrorism and Islam for many Americans. The Bush administration used this fear to help garner support for a military campaign in Afghanistan against the Taliban, describing it as a way to liberate Muslim women from Muslim men. Note that this same tactic was used to justify the colonialization of Muslim-majority regions.

The so-called war on terror, because it entailed a propaganda campaign that associated Islam with extremism and violence, increased harassment of American Muslims.[15] The Council of American Islamic Relations (CAIR) reported over 1,500 cases of backlash discrimination against Muslims in the six months following the 9/11 attacks.[16] Veiled Muslim women, as the most easily recognizable American Muslims, found themselves especially vulnerable to public harassment and the potential victims of hate crimes. Some Muslims supported abandoning the hijab, arguing that it was too dangerous in the post-9/11 climate. However, scores of women, particularly young women, put on a hijab for the first time as an act of defiance against increased expressions of Islamophobia. While a powerful act of resistance, it also reinforced the idea of hijab as the presumptive sign of Muslim American identity in the US context.

After a reduction in assaults against Muslims in 2002, cases of anti-Muslim harassment and violence in the United States have been steadily rising. According to the FBI, the number of Muslims assaulted in 2015 through 2016 reached and then surpassed the 9/11-era level.[17] Things got even worse under President Donald Trump, as his administration not only set anti-Muslim policy but also constantly framed Muslims as foreign and dangerous.

Muslim women, especially those who are visibly Muslim because of hijab, continue to be disproportionately affected by Islamophobia. In the United States, Muslim women have been fired from jobs for wearing hijab. Muslim girls who wear hijab have been assaulted at school and prevented from participating in sports. There are cases of Muslim women being barred from public places, such as sports arenas, amusement parks, and shopping malls, for their attire.[18] Muslim women have been denied the right to wear a headscarf while in jail or detention. They have had their headscarves removed by police for mug shots with such frequency that several civil cases have been filed against police departments.[19]

Feminism was co-opted in the colonial context to rationalize controlling Muslim populations and more recently to justify US military interventions in Muslim-majority countries. As feminist critic Gayatri Chakravorty Spivak famously put it, these interventions were presented as necessary to save brown women from their brown men.[20] This tactic continues today. For most of the twentieth century, Western liberal feminists were more likely than not to hold up hijab as a symbol of Muslim women's oppression. Secular or nominally Christian feminists had difficulty with the gendered practices of religious minorities, and instead of allying with religious women, they merely asserted that some religions, such as Islam, were patriarchal.[21]

American feminism's relationship to hijab changed as part of what Yvonne Haddad describes as a shift in the meaning of hijab from a stigma to an icon.[22] Muslim women's articulation of hijab as a choice combined with liberalism's commitment to autonomy and inclusion created conditions in which hijab could be reframed as an icon of resistance. As seen in the symbolic politics of the 2017 Women's March to be discussed in this chapter, liberal non-Muslim feminists began to locate the oppression of Muslim women within the wider social context of gendered Islamophobia instead of the religious tradition itself. As conservatives framed hijab as a marker of Islam's incompatibility with the American way of life, hijab became adopted by liberals as a symbol of how Muslim women resist this narrative.

There is one more development that helps ease the way for recent acts of solidarity hijab: like cross jewelry, hijab became part of mainstream fashion. My last book, *Pious Fashion*, was a global study of Muslim women's style. Muslim fashion had been of interest to Muslim women for some time, but for the decade I worked on this topic, non-Muslims all but ignored it. Then suddenly, as *Pious Fashion* was going to press, modest clothing was becoming all the rage. In 2016, as I was reading page proofs, Dolce & Gabbana released a collection of headscarves and coordinated *abayas* and Uniqlo released a modest collection by the UK-based Muslim designer Hana Tajima. In 2017, as the first copies of my book were printed, Nike announced plans to sell a sports hijab, and a Muslim modest designer, Ayana Ife, made *Project Runway*'s finale. Surprising no one more than me, a literal expert on Muslim women's fashion, by 2017 Muslim clothing had gone mainstream in America.

This was spurred in part by the realization of the buying power of Muslims, the success of Muslim entrepreneurs, as well as increased visibility and acceptance of minority populations. But it is also the sign of something else. Companies that promoted modest lines or hired hijabi brand ambassadors were not just targeting Muslim women, but also hoping that by visually incorporating Muslim women into ad campaigns, they would appeal to liberal non-Muslim women who value diversity and inclusivity in the marketplace.

By 2017, Shepard Fairey's image of a woman in flag hijab was adopted as the symbol of feminist politics, and the #HeadscarfForHarmony campaign convinced thousands of non-Muslim women to wear a hijab to support victims of the 2019 Christchurch massacre because of the ways hijab had already been politicized. Specifically, Americans were ready to embrace headscarves as a sign of progressive politics because they already associated hijab with Muslim identity, already thought head coverings could signal allyship, and already believed Islamic headscarves could be worn in ways disentangled from Muslim communities.

Dressing Up to Fight Islamophobia

Many examples of activism use hijab to signal support for Muslim women. Some are initiated by Muslim women themselves. For instance, in 2013, Nazma Khan launched World Hijab Day, which encourages wearing a headscarf as an act of solidarity with Muslim women. The campaign's slogan is "Before you judge, cover up for a day." Millions of women participate annually, according to the event's website. But World Hijab Day is not without controversy. In 2015, an opinion piece titled "As Muslim Women, We Actually Ask You Not to Wear the Hijab in the Name of Interfaith Solidarity," by journalists Asra Nomani and Hala Arafa, ran in the *Washington Post*.[23] The authors argued that using hijab to increase public understanding of Muslim life is itself a claim about Islamic orthodoxy, mainly that good Muslim women wear hijab, and thus the campaign erases Muslim women who don't cover their heads. Because it exploits the hijab in ways some Muslim women find offensive, World Hijab Day could be framed as a case of appropriation, albeit by religious insiders.

Other forms of solidarity hijab involve an individual's wearing a headscarf as a way to make a public statement, such as professor of politics Larycia Hawkins's decision to post on social media an image of herself in a hijab, for Advent. At the time, Hawkins was a tenured professor at Wheaton, a prominent Christian liberal arts college. Herself a Christian, she wore hijab to draw attention to the fact that, in her words, Muslims and Christians "worship the same God." Most of the criticism of Hawkins came from Christians, not Muslims, particularly over her theological statements. Hawkins eventually left Wheaton over the controversy her solidarity hijab created, after accepting terms that are subject to a confidentiality agreement with the college.[24]

The two high-profile cases of solidarity hijab that I focus on differ from World Hijab Day and Hawkins's hijab protest because they were both initiated by non-Muslims as part of a coordinated political protest: the adoption of Shepard Fairey's iconic "flag hijab" image as a symbol of the Women's March, and the #HeadscarfForHarmony social media campaign in response to the Christchurch massacre in New Zealand.

Fairey's flag hijab portrait is arguably the most widely known example of what I call solidarity hijab, and one that many people still consider a successful case of allyship with Muslim women. As I was working on this case study, for instance, my daughter, who attends a public school in Brookline, Massachusetts, said, "Hey mom, I know that image, my art teacher and my literature teacher both have it up on the wall of their classrooms."

The #HeadscarfForHarmony campaign, in which non-Muslim women physically put on a hijab as a sign of solidarity, was created, promoted, and then critiqued on social media. It allows us to explore religious appropriation in digital spaces.

Both examples of solidarity hijab aimed to build a coalition that acknowledged the diversity of women's experiences. And yet both campaigns were experienced as exploitative and profoundly offensive by some Muslim women. Let's look at each case more closely.

In winter 2017, like many white liberal feminists, I was reeling over Trump's election. Still furious that I had had to explain to my then eight-year-old daughter what "grab them by the pussy" meant, I was trying to figure out how my country had elected a president who had made explicitly misogynist, racist, and Islamophobic statements during his campaign. And Trump's comments equating Islam with terrorism were a particular red flag to me, including his promise to ban Muslims from entering the United States entirely, which he tried to make good on within weeks of taking office by a series of executive actions suspending travel from Muslim-majority nations. It seemed clear to me that Trump's promise to "Make America Great Again" would mean increased discrimination against women and Muslims.

This was the backdrop for the 2017 Women's March on Washington, a protest timed for the day after the inauguration of President Donald Trump. Modeled after the nonviolent marches of the civil rights movement, the main march in Washington, DC, drew almost half a million people—over three times the number who had attended the inauguration itself.[25] Approximately four million people participated in marches around the country, leading some political scientists to call this the largest single-day protest in US history.[26] I wasn't able to travel to DC because of childcare responsibilities, but many of my friends and colleagues marched, and I followed the day through their postings. It was the first time since the election that I was hopeful about the future of US politics. But, in hindsight, I can see that organizers used religious appropriation to mobilize liberal white women.

The Women's March attempted to enact a form of intersectional feminism. Intersectionality—a mode of analysis named by critical race scholar Kimberlé Crenshaw and theorized most notably by sociologist Patricia Hill Collins—demands acknowledgment of overlapping modes of oppression based on such things as class, gender, sexual preference, and race. The march's commitment to intersectional feminism was reflected in its leadership, which included activists Tamika Mallory, Carmen Perez, and Linda Sarsour, who had all been leaders in Black Lives Matter protests, as well as on other civil rights issues, such as immigration and mass incarceration reform.

There was also an attempt to get women who had never been politically active to participate in the march. The Pussyhat Project was part of this effort. Initiated by Los Angeles–based Krista Suh and Jayna Zweiman, the project aimed to have one million pink hats worn at the march for visual impact. The hats, as feminist scholar Holly Derr put it in a piece in *Bitch Media*, were meant "to reclaim the word 'pussy' from our president-elect and his crotch-grabbing tiny hands."[27] But they were also cute, fun, crafty, and appealed to even hesitant activists. As co-organizer Zweiman put it, the hats were a way to say "no matter who you are or where you are, you can be politically active."[28]

And yet if white cis women saw themselves represented in the pussy hats, other women did not. Dubai-based writer Amiya Nagpal explained how the project's imagery was exclusionary because it "conflated womanhood with having a vagina," which leaves out trans women, and implied that women have a pink vagina. "My vagina is not pink" Nagpal pointed out.[29]

Adoption of Shepard Fairey's flag hijab portrait by participants was also an attempt to be inclusive, specifically by showing support for and allyship with Muslim women who stood at the intersection of Trump's misogyny and Islamophobia. But when the Women's March used religious appropriation as a tactic to visually communicate a commitment to Muslim inclusivity, the result was alienating and offensive to some Muslim women.

The flag hijab portrait is part of a series of three posters released in 2017 by Fairey, an American street and graphic designer who became widely known for his iconic Barack Obama "Hope" portrait. Commissioned by the nonprofit Amplifier Foundation, which describes itself as an "art machine for social change," the posters were part of a series called "We the People," designed to protest President-elect Donald Trump. The three portraits—a Muslim woman, a Latina woman, and an African American boy—represented groups Fairey predicted would be the most adversely affected under a Trump administration.[30] The series is meant to convey an alternative to Trump's America, one that centers marginalized populations—Muslim, Indigenous, and Black.[31] Funded by a Kickstarter campaign that raised over one million dollars, the images were free to download. Copies were also distributed at DC Metro stations and printed in full-page color ads in the *Washington Post* and *New York Times* on the day of Trump's inauguration to provide protest art for marchers that fit the size restrictions of posters allowed at public inauguration events.

The three images have a similar aesthetic, but each portrait is styled differently to visually communicate the identity of the subject. The African American boy sports long dreadlocks. The Latina woman wears a red T-shirt printed with a Mexican eagle graphic, her loose, wavy, shoulder-length hair pinned at her ear with a large red rose. The Muslim American woman has red lips and strong brows, but her image is dominated by one item of clothing: a headscarf made of the American flag, with stars draped on one side, and stripes on the other.

Although part of a series of three, the "flag hijab" image was the most widely circulated as a sign of feminist protest against Trump. There were aesthetic and political reasons for this: The flag hijab portrait was a gorgeous image. Fairey's portrait, based on a photograph of Munira Ahmed, a Bangladeshi American who grew up in Queens, New York, felt both timeless and of the moment. The woman represented in the poster was attractive, and his graphic interpretation of her was like the best filter you could put on a photograph: high contrast, vivid color, and sharp. It was an image you would want to display in your office, or post as your social media profile picture, because

One of the posters from Shepard Fairey's "We the People" series, made
available by Amplifier, a nonprofit design lab. (Shepard Fairey/Amplifier)

it was pleasant to look at. I confess that I did both of these things, as did many of my feminist colleagues.

But all three images had strong aesthetics, so there were also political reasons the flag hijab portrait became the most popular of the series.

Trump had his own political aesthetic—white Evangelical masculinity—focused on his body, which he considered a sign of male virility, strength, and success. When Trump focused on the bodies of women, religious minorities, and people of color, he framed these bodies as inferior to his own white male Christian one. This made Fairey's flag hijab portrait readable as a protest of Trump. It was a pictorial celebration of religious and ethnic diversity and women's role in America. Being female, brown, and Muslim was the visual antithesis of Trump.[32]

Although adopting the flag hijab image was motivated by a desire to demonstrate solidarity with the Muslim community, the effect was to alienate some Muslim women. Zainab Khan, a Muslim community organizer based in Atlanta, attended the Women's March in 2017, but said that she didn't feel that her values were represented. "I remember there were these posters of a Muslim woman in an American flag hijab," she continued. "That is all I needed to know."[33]

I want to highlight Iranian American activist and writer Hoda Katebi's critique in "Please Keep Your American Flag Off My Hijab," which she posted on her website two days after the Women's March. This short piece summarized several concerns raised about Fairey's flag hijab by Muslim women at the time.

One set of Katebi's critiques had to do with the image's production. Fairey was a white man depicting a Muslim woman, and Katebi questioned why the work of Muslim women artists could not have been promoted by the Women's March. "Know that if the only time you are comfortable uplifting Muslim woman is when her image has been crafted by a white man," she wrote, "I cannot call you my ally."[34] In an interview with the *Guardian*, Fairey brushed off this concern in comments reminiscent of Shriver's sombrero speech, which I discussed in the Introduction. "That I wouldn't be qualified to paint someone from another race or religion would be as absurd as me telling someone from another race or religion that they can't paint JFK." He added that minorities must understand that "artists won't always get it right" and that he would not "be intimidated by people or identity politics."[35]

In every interview I've ever read with Munira Ahmed, the woman in the photo Fairey's portrait is based on, she claimed to be pleased with the likeness. But since the image was not circulated as a portrait of Ahmed, but rather as a representation of all Muslim women, her approval is not enough. Any Muslim woman has a right to potentially be offended by this depiction, given the way it was deployed. It is also important to note that Ahmed does not herself wear a headscarf, and the original picture was composed by Ridwan Adhami, a New York–based photographer. We could say that Ahmed and Adhami were themselves involved in a form of religious appropriation, and thus not the best judges of whether any moral harm resulted.

For Katebi, Fairey's decision to use a hijab as a prop was strategic and problematic. Much the same as the African American boy's dreadlocks or the rose tucked behind the Latina woman's ear, the hijab was supposed to make the woman in Fairey's portrait immediately readable as Muslim. But not all Muslim women cover in this way. As already mentioned, 42 percent of Muslim women living in the United States never wear a headscarf, a clear indication that opinions over the importance of the religious garb differ among Muslims.[36] To politically represent all Muslim women with a hijab erased Muslim women who do not wear one. In this way, solidarity hijab took a side in an intra-Muslim debate, allowing non-Muslim women to define a proper Muslim woman as one who covers.

To make things worse, Ahmed was not just wearing a hijab, she was wearing one made of an American flag. Sartorially, this is ridiculous. Muslim women do not go around wrapping national flags on their head. The other two images in the series did not incorporate such blatant symbols of patriotism. The message implied in Fairey's portrait of Ahmed was clear: for Muslim women to belong, they have to be literally cloaked in the fabric of America.[37]

For many Muslim Americans, Katebi pointed out, the US flag is associated with US military operations in Muslim-majority nations and acts of anti-Muslim legislation. "The American flag represents oppression, torture, sexual violence, slavery, patriarchy, and military and cultural hegemony for people of color around the world," she wrote. Placing a Muslim women in a flag hijab was forcing her consent to this violence and discrimination, literally folding her into the national narrative despite the fact that her voice and community had often been excluded from it.[38] As Katebi put it, "My liberation will not come from framing my body with a flag that has flown every time my people have fallen."[39]

The second example of solidarity hijab I want to discuss was a response to a specific violent hate crime against a Muslim community. In this case, large numbers of non-Muslim women not only carried an image of hijab, they physically put on a hijab. And this raised the stakes of the appropriation considerably.

On Friday, March 15, 2019, Brenton Tarrant entered Al Noor Mosque and then Linwood Islamic Centre in Christchurch, New Zealand, during Friday prayer, and opened fire. Fifty-one Muslims lost their lives in the mass shooting. The event was made more violent by the fact that Tarrant wore a body camera, filmed the entire rampage, live streamed it, and published an online manifesto making it clear that the act was motivated by white nationalism.

New Zealand's leaders and citizens responded to this mass shooting in very public ways that, to an American like myself, were particularly striking, since they were so different from our own anemic response to violence against religious minorities. Spontaneous performances of *haka*, the Māori war dance, went viral on social media. The *adhan*, the Muslim call to prayer, was broadcast across New Zealand. A prayer vigil attended by over five thousand people was held in the park adjacent to the Al Noor Mosque. The *Press*, a Christchurch-based daily, printed the words "Salam" and "Peace" in both English and Arabic on its front page with the names and ages of all victims of the massacre. In the context of these public displays of support for the Muslim community, non-Muslim women began to wear a headscarf as a "sign of solidarity."

New Zealand prime minister Jacinda Ardern was the first. She wore a simple black headscarf when she visited the Muslim community on the Monday after the shootings. Female news broadcasters in New Zealand wore hijab on air the following Friday, to commemorate the one-week anniversary of the event. That same day, my social media feeds became overrun with selfies of non-Muslim women in hijab with the hashtag #HeadscarfForHarmony.

Thaya Ashman, a doctor in Auckland, launched the campaign Headscarf for Harmony in response to hearing from a Muslim woman that she feared her hijab would make her a target for violence after the terrorist attack. Ashman's goal for the campaign was to have a concrete way for non-Muslim women to protect Muslim women.

The Headscarf for Harmony campaign quickly expanded beyond New Zealand, with non-Muslim women from around the world posting selfies, in hijab, on social media with the hashtag #Head-scarfForHarmony. Annie Messing was among the young women who participated. On March 21, 2019, one week after the shooting, Messing posted a selfie, mouth pursed, a white scarf draped loosely over her chestnut hair. "It's amazing what a small piece of cloth can do," she wrote. "I actually believe that this experience will help me to have a better understanding of women who choose to dress modestly." Another young woman posted a photo of herself in hijab on Facebook with the comment "Guys, this is so cool. I got more than 500 likes for my hijab pic. How crazy is that?"[40]

It was impossible not to notice that, unlike the austere head covering of the prime minister and on-air journalists, many of the women who posted selfies of solidarity hijab wore heavy makeup. Some wore the headscarf over tank tops and supertight jeans. Others displayed cleavage or posed coquettishly. This was decisively not a hijab of modesty. It was performed to get attention.

The first question I had was, How did the local Muslim community feel about this gesture—did it make them feel safer? Outside New Zealand, this was something we heard very little about because, when covering the campaign, the media focused most of their attention on the non-Muslim women who were wearing hijab in solidarity: the prime minister, the journalists, the brave ordinary citizens. The gesture ended up centering non-Muslim women rather than Muslim women in the public conversation about gendered Islamophobia.

A notable exception was a pair of opinion pieces published in New Zealand's popular online news site *Stuff*. On March 21, Mehrbano Malik, a twenty-one-year-old recent graduate of the University of Otago, wrote about how the #HeadscarfForHarmony campaign reflected orientalist ideologies that Muslims were foreign. She explained that as a Muslim woman who does not wear hijab, a campaign of solidarity that relied on the hijab excluded her.[41] In another strongly worded March 22 *Stuff* opinion piece, an author who identified herself only as Muslim woman wrote, "I think this is nothing but cheap tokenism. It's a gimmick and pretty distasteful. . . . Support does not look like this." The anonymous writer also pointed out how temporary the gesture was. "You can't help a Muslim woman with a photo," she wrote. "Most people will remove their scarves when Friday ends whilst my mother and sisters continue to be abused—as it's their religious outfit and not a costume."

The anonymous writer acknowledged that some older Muslims she knew personally supported the idea as a way "to pacify non-Muslim Kiwis and make them feel good about themselves." But for the writer, this support was not a sign that solidarity hijab was effective, but rather, symptomatic of just how marginalized Muslims feel in New Zealand. "Muslims here have been so deprived of support that they are willing to accept any and every kind, whether it is racist, culturally appropriating or just misplaced and misinformed."[42]

There were Muslims beyond New Zealand who posted their appreciation for the campaign as well. They accepted solidarity hijab as a well-intentioned symbol of support. But not everyone was pleased, including some of the most active American women on Muslim Twitter. The #HeadscarfForHarmony campaign spurred an online debate within the Muslim community about the effectiveness of solidarity hijab as a strategy of allyship. This debate got quite heated, and because it occurred in corners of Muslim social media, it was a debate most Americans did not see.

Some estimates put current active users of Twitter, a micro-blogging media platform that launched in 2006, at over 300 million. One of the distinctive features of Twitter is the way it creates a community of users, what the authors of #HashtagActivism call a counterpublic: a digital space where marginalized people can make ethical demands on those with more power.[43] This occurs when discrete users regularly post on a given topic and use hashtags to create digital discussions. This means Twitter can be a place to find critical engagement with current events from minoritized groups, groups I suggested in the Introduction are more vulnerable to exploitation from forms of religious appropriation. "Listening in" to these discussions is easier if one follows users who are part of an online counterpublic. For instance, when #HeadscarfForHarmony went viral, I was already following several Black Muslim thought leaders on Twitter who regularly post about gendered Islamophobia and anti-Black racism. My feed made clear when a shared critique of the campaign emerged from this group of activists and scholars.

The first comment I saw on Twitter that was critical of #HeadscarfForHarmony was from Kayla Wheeler (@krw18), a scholar of Black Islam and Muslim fashion, whom I have followed since I joined Twitter in 2018. Wheeler described solidarity hijab as erasure. "Non-Muslim women who wear hijab out of solidarity erase Muslim women who don't cover and de-center Muslim who do cover, who face the brunt of the Islamophobic violence."[44] Wheeler also called out the campaign as liberal virtue signaling. "People get to pat themselves on the back," she tweeted, "without actually doing anything meaning/helpful. I think it's harmful."[45]

As I watched my feed over the next few days, other comments popped up from female Black Muslim thought leaders. Layla Poulos (@LaylaAPoulos), an author and activist, pointed out how temporary the gesture was. "Keep in mind," she tweeted, "many of the non-Muslim women wrapping in a headscarf for a day of 'solidarity' will take it off and cuddle up with the same ideologies and men that make us unsafe."[46] Journalist Vanessa Taylor (@BaconTribe) criticized the campaign for relying on shallow performances that reinforced rather than reduced gendered Islamophobia because they relied on a "fixation and reduction of Muslim women to hijab."[47] Similarly, anthropologist Donna Auston (@TinyMuslimah) tweeted, "solidarity requires skin in the game."[48]

The critiques of the #HeadscarfForHarmony campaign had some overlap with Katebi's critique of Fairey's flag hijab image, including that it neglected the diversity of the Muslim community, co-opted inclusivity in a form of superficial allyship, and functioned as virtue signaling rather than addressing actual injustice. And worst, #Head-scarfForHarmony decentered the actual Muslims affected by the massacre, since non-Muslim experience with and performance of the hijab was at the center of the #HeadscarfForHarmony campaign.

In part because these critiques of solidarity hijab occurred on Twitter, a format that encourages volatile interactions, they were met with harsh rebuke. Some of this pushback was from other Muslim women. Natasha Rahman (@fizzydizzy) replied to Kayla Wheeler with an eye-rolling tweet: "Oh please. There are a billion ways to do a billion things. For now however can't we just be grateful for the support given to one horrible act of violence?"[49] Sana Saeed (@SanaSaeed), the high-profile Canadian producer and host at AJ+, tweeted, "Can American Muslims for a few minutes not make themselves the arbiter of these things all the time and everywhere?"[50] This was a classic passive-aggressive subtweet: instead of responding directly to any specific American Muslim woman, Saeed indirectly ridiculed them to her more than 90,000 followers.

The Muslim women who spoke out the loudest against the #Head-scarfForHarmony campaign on Twitter were Black, and those who tried to silence them were not. This was not a coincidence. Black Muslim women saw something different because, existing amid overlapping modes of oppression (Islamophobia, misogyny, and white supremacy), they are used to being erased, tokenized, and exploited. And when Black Muslim women raised concerns about solidarity hijab, they were offering their intellectual labor to the public by explaining how gendered Muslim experience was not necessarily the same for everyone. But things took a turn when non-Black Muslims told these Black Muslims to "get over it," accusing them of being irrational and overly sensitive about #HeadscarfForHarmony. Kameelah Rashad (@KameelahRashad), a mental health activist and educator, summarized this dynamic in a tweet: "they're all 'Listen to Black women!' until we say some ish that complicates their aspirational whiteness and proximity to privilege. Then it's 'be quiet, you don't have a comment, just be grateful the *whites want to be kind to us!'"[51] As Layla Poulos put it, "Many NB Muslims become condescending, dismissive, and combative once Black Muslims stop sounding the way they want."[52] Put differently, the intracommunity debate over solidarity hijab became an occasion for reinforcing asymmetrical power dynamics within the Muslim community itself. It was another level of erasure of Muslim women: this time, the erasure of Black Muslim women's voices by non-Black Muslim women.

This Twitter debate illustrates how the religious appropriation of #HeadscarfForHarmony was not experienced the same by all Muslim women. For the Black Muslim scholars and activists I have highlighted, solidarity hijab, especially when practiced by white non-Muslim women, was a form not only of gendered Islamophobia, but also of white supremacy. As Donna Auston explained on Twitter, "white supremacy doesn't only look like spectacular acts of hatred and violence. White supremacy is also what compels us to protect white people from ever feeling discomfort in conversations about anti-racist solidarity."[53] When non-Black Muslims tried to silence this critique, they proved Auston's point.

Tokenizing, Silencing, and Virtue Signaling

The authors of #HashtagActivism could have predicted that #HeadscarfForHarmony would be ineffective. Allyship hashtags, they argued, can be "relatively superficial" and often counterproductive because they "shift the attention away from the incident and engender a level of self-centered reflection that does not contend with the systemic nature of the problem."[54] This was certainly the case with solidarity hijab campaigns. Muslim women experienced them as forms of distracting symbols that were reductionistic, prematurely assumed kinship, decentered Muslim women, and served as virtue signaling for non-Muslim women. To make things worse, solidarity hijab risked undermining the religious meaning of hijab for Muslim women who chose to wear it. A good intention—combating gendered Islamophobia—did not prevent these negative outcomes.

The first problem is that any form of solidarity hijab relies on the idea that Islam can be represented by one practice—a hijab—whose meaning and importance is debated by the community itself. As already discussed, not all Muslim women agree that hijab is obligatory or even recommended. This means the symbolic politics of Fairey's flag hijab erased the 42 percent of US-based Muslim women who don't cover. Similar essentializing occurred with the #HeadscarfForHarmony campaign, which tried to embody solidarity in the act of wearing a hijab for one day, thus reducing an entire tradition and community to one piece of cloth. Advocacy for all Muslims is impossible with a symbol that makes some Muslims feel left out.

Just because Fairey's image was not negative—the woman was presented as attractive and entirely American—doesn't mean it was not reinforcing stereotypes. It was no accident that Fairey's image was based on a photograph of a brown, not Black or white, woman. Most American non-Muslims associate Muslim identity with Arab or Asian ethnicity, even though 20 percent of Muslims in America identify as Black and 41 percent as white.[55] Fairey's image reinforced the stereotype that all US Muslims are brown.

The fact that Fairey wrapped the Muslim woman in the series, and only the Muslim woman, in an American flag implied this was necessary to make her readable as American. This, Katebi pointed out, was profoundly offensive. "Know that Muslims are tired of having to 'prove' they are American," Katebi wrote. "But also, know that one does not need to be American to deserve respect, humanity, dignity, equality, rights, and freedom from hate and bigotry."[56] In fact, even if Fairey's image was produced and adopted as a protest against Trump's anti-Muslim rhetoric and politics, its aesthetics emphasized "being American as a prerequisite of deserving respect," which "is only pushing [the Trump] agenda further."[57]

Adopting hijab as the symbol of Islam also reinforced the presumption that religious otherness is literally held in the bodies of women. When Muslim women are assumed to be the receptacles and conveyors of religion, their sartorial choices take on excessive political meaning. But even worse, rather than recognizing Muslim women as agents, solidarity hijab frames them as passive victims. As Amaney Jamal, a scholar of Middle East politics, put it, the symbolic use of Muslim women in protests imagined them as subjects who, in the current political situation, require even "more protection, more support, and more help."[58] This is similar to the rationale Anglo-Europeans provided for colonializing Muslim-majority territories. But instead of saving Muslim women from Muslim men—by banning a veil—solidarity hijab adopts headscarves as way to save Muslim women from the white men of the alt-right. Both cases assume Muslim women are so oppressed that they need outsiders to save them.

In her recent book *White Feminism*, the former editor in chief of *Jezebel*, Koa Beck, describes how flag hijab was part of an overall feminist lifestyle brand cultivated by women after Trump's election. "Someone who made sure to wear their NASTY WOMAN shirt from Etsy and pack their FEMINIST water bottle from Amazon and take lots of selfies with trending hashtags," these same women adopted the flag hijab image as part of "positioning themselves as activist chic."[59] But even as protesting became "the new brunch," the tactics of liberal feminism did little to change systemic injustice. In this way, solidarity hijab made the gendered dimension of Islamophobia worse, not better, by trading on an image of Muslim women as subjects to be saved by feminists instead of agents of feminist intersectional change.

This means hijab was domesticated for non-Muslim politics without any engagement with its actual religious meaning.[60] Such engagement would have likely prevented adopting a hijab as a symbol of any progressive agenda. Instead of fostering religious literacy or a nuanced understanding of hijab, solidarity hijab allowed Muslim women's head covering to remain an exotic sartorial practice.

A second type of exploitation caused by solidarity hijab stems from its implied kinship and familiarity, a feeling that "we're all in this together." That assertion was false, premature, and profoundly offensive.

The temporary nature of the act was one barrier to its ability to foster kinship. Wearing or displaying a hijab for a single day could never capture the enduring nature of anti-Muslim racism, which is not felt as a moment, but as the culmination of experiences through a lifetime. In addition, participating in a coordinated campaign like #HeadscarfForHarmony made the act less risky: when so many non-Muslims were wearing hijab, there was little danger of being read as a "real" Muslim.

In some cases, solidarity hijab was worn by non-Muslim women to know what it is like to be Muslim. As Annie Messing, one of the participants in #HeadscarfForHarmony, put it, "I actually believe that this experience will help me to have a better understanding of women who choose to dress modestly."[61]

When non-Muslim women like Messing veil temporarily to try to understand Muslim experience, they assume they have a right to firsthand experience of Muslim oppression. Philosopher Shannon Sullivan has a term for this: "ontological expansiveness."[62] With so many testimonies from Muslim women about the discrimination they face, non-Muslims' insisting on a personal, firsthand experience is part of a broader colonial gesture. It implies a distrust of the native informant that, as philosopher Helen Ngo argues, "reproduce[s] the very structures of the racism and white privilege they set out to challenge."[63] As the author of the *Ms. Muslamic* blog put it, "The veil is an ~*exotic foreign country*~, and you can't trust the locals to tell you what it's all about."[64]

And yet, there are some things we can't know because we don't have the catalog of past experiences to understand them or because our motivation is simply not the same. The author of *Ms. Muslamic* explained, "As a non-Muslim, you can never really 'wear hijab,' because it will never be about publicly declaring yourself to be a Muslim or consciously connecting to the traditions of our pious predecessors or striving for deeper spiritual connection with the divine." Instead, she reminded her readers, "You are just playing dress-up."[65]

Put in the terms I used to define appropriation in the Introduction, solidarity hijab created the illusion that religious outsiders could safely participate as religious insiders in the name of progressive feminist politics. In other words, even though solidarity hijab was an attempt at intersectional feminism, it did not truly respect Muslim women's diverse experience because it allowed liberal politics to supersede any claims made by religious group members.

This leads us to a third form of exploitation: both of the cases of solidarity hijab discussed here decentered Muslim women. When the media covered the Women's March, they circulated images of non-Muslim women carrying posters with Fairey's portrait, reinforcing the idea that non-Muslim women can combat misogyny on behalf of all women. The same is true for the response to #HeadscarfForHarmony. When this campaign gained momentum, the media was suddenly celebrating politicians, journalists, and ordinary non-Muslim citizens wearing hijab as a sign of support for the New Zealand Muslim community. The community affected by the massacre was no longer the focus of anyone's attention. Both attempts at solidarity contributed to the marginalization of Muslim women.

Efforts by Muslim women to combat gendered Islamophobia are rarely given the same attention as those by non-Muslims working toward the same goal. For example, during the 2019 Women's March, a group of Muslim women formed the "Muslim Women's Wave." Participants wore blue hijabs or neck scarves. They marched together chanting loudly for an end to the Trump Muslim ban and carried signs to express solidarity with the Rohingyas and the Uyghurs, Muslim minorities who have suffered religious persecution.[66] But the media for the most part ignored the Muslim Women's Wave.

The media coverage of the funeral for victims of Christchurch massacre didn't even focus on Muslims. Instead, the news that day was dominated by an image of Whanganui police constable Michelle Evans, a blond woman who wore a black hijab as she stood guard outside Christchurch's Memorial Park Cemetery. Headlines included "Meet the Hijab-Wearing Police Constable Who Stood in Solidarity with the Muslim Community'" and "Hijab Wearing Police Officer's Photo Makes Powerful Statement in Wake of Christchurch Mosque Shootings."[67] Almost identical photographs of Constable Evans taken by *Stuff* photographer Alden Williams and AP photographer Vincent Yu were picked up by major news outlets around the world. Williams posted the photo on Instagram and within a couple of hours, it had more likes than any previous post.[68]

Decentering religious individuals and communities in this way is rooted in inequities about who gets to claim expertise and authority. When non-Muslim protesters wearing hijab are allowed to be the experts in naming, defining, and combating gendered Islamophobia, they are enjoying an "excess of expertise." And this has a direct effect on Muslim women who themselves already have trouble being acknowledged as experts, even of their own marginalization. As the

Police Constable Michelle Evans stands guard at the Memorial Park Cemetery in Christchurch, New Zealand, March 21, 2019. (AP Photo / Vincent Yu)

anonymous author of *Ms. Muslamic* wrote, "We have many Muslim sisters . . . all of them deserve to be heard. . . . Our empowerment must come through uplifting the voices of Muslim women."[69] By decentering Muslim women and contributing to their "deficiency of expertise," solidarity hijab worked against its own goal to combat gendered Islamophobia.

One of the reasons hijab has become a common symbol of solidarity politics is that it has been successfully rebranded from "stigma of minoritized religion" to "icon of liberal inclusion." Let's think again about the flag hijab portrait. It was not just the beauty of Fairey's design that made a covered Muslim woman adoptable as a sign of protest; it was the popularization of the visual politics of Muslim difference that surrounded its release. Fairey's image was "pushed" out into the world by organizers of the march, but it was well received by American liberals because hijab had already become a mainstream symbol of religious diversity.

We can see this from the ways hijab has continued to be incorporated into the ad campaigns of major apparel and beauty brands. CoverGirl hired its first hijab-wearing brand ambassador in 2017. The Gap's 2018 back-to-school ad featured a preteen in a headscarf. The 2019 *Sports Illustrated* swimsuit issue featured Halima Aden in a *burkini*. To be sure, many Muslim women welcomed these examples of increased representation. But there was another part of the story. In all three of these cases, the target audience was not only Muslims, but consumers who wanted to associate themselves with a company or brand that valued inclusion. My liberal Gen Z students tell me they are more likely to support a cosmetic brand that shares their values. As a mom, I'd rather purchase clothing for my daughter from a company that supports marginalized communities. The burkini issue of *Sports Illustrated* got an enormous amount of positive press for being groundbreaking. What these examples have in common is that they demonstrate the extent to which the hijab has become a way to signal liberal wokeness to non-Muslims. This is why headscarves were so easily adopted as a sign of progressive politics in 2017, and then again in 2019 after the Christchurch massacre: hijab had already been used to communicate commitment to difference.

But while solidarity hijab might have boosted the protesters' public image, it was not accompanied by tangible improvements for the Muslim community. One of the most visceral examples I have seen of this dynamic is an image of two NYPD officers wearing American flags as headscarves on World Hijab Day in 2018.[70] World Hijab Day is a coordinated day of worldwide solidarity hijab, so wearing a flag hijab on this day was an action that combined the missteps of both Fairey's image and the #HeadscarfForHarmony campaign. But there was an additional layer of exploitation in this example because the NYPD was involved. In a series of class-action lawsuits filed against the city in the last few years, Muslim women have sought damages for having their head coverings removed for mug shots. That means this photograph shows NYPD officers wearing solidarity hijab while the NYPD was being sued for harassing Muslim women for wearing devotional hijab. Here we have a clear case of hijab adopted as a symbol of inclusion without the work of making structural change to prevent abuse of Muslim women.

Non-Muslim women carried hijab images during the Women's March and put on a hijab in the #HeadscarfForHarmony campaign because the meaning of hijab as a symbol of solidarity has begun to replace its meaning as a form of religious practice. That is, it is only when there is no danger of being mistaken for a Muslim woman that non-Muslim women adopt hijab as a sign of solidarity. And this sort of shifting of the public meaning of hijab can be understood as a fourth form of exploitation, one that is arguably profoundly offensive because it interferes with hijab as a devotional practice.

Remember that most Muslim women who wear hijab in the United States do so for personal piety. Adoption of the hijab for a political agenda is a blatant disregard for this religious meaning. The author of *Ms. Muslamic* argued that solidarity hijab is in fact "based on the false premise that you can lift hijab out of its religious and cultural context, turn it into a fancy-dress costume, and then invite non-Muslims to take a tour of the experience." This hijab tourism is offensive, she continued, because "hijab simply isn't the same without its religious context."[71] Put differently, appropriating religious symbols to support a religious community demonstrates a willful lack of understanding of the way these symbols matter. Solidarity hijab is an act of ignorance, not support.

But there is more at stake. Even as donning piety hijab is a personal practice, it requires a public that interprets this head covering as an act of Muslim ethics. When the public changes its mind on what it thinks hijab means, it also affects a woman's ability to use it to cultivate her character. In other words, a Muslim woman who wears hijab for personal piety assumes others will see her as enacting a public expression of Muslim identity and modesty. When the public readability of hijab changes, its religious meaning is affected as well.

Let's take an example from a different national context. While I was conducting research in Iran, many Muslim women told me that compulsory hijab was not just a problem for Iranian women who didn't want to wear hijab, it was also a problem for those who did. Prior to that mandate, hijab was something Iranians could choose to wear because of a sincerely held religious belief. After the mandate, every woman had to wear it to abide by the law. This meant it became impossible for observers to distinguish between the hijab that I wore to follow the law while conducting fieldwork, and a devotional hijab. The Iranian government undermined hijab as a personal religious choice when it legally mandated that all women, regardless of their faith, wear it in public. But it also changed its public readability.

A different shift in the hijab's meaning is taking place in the United States, but this one is also animated by political agendas that instrumentalize the head covering. As this form of religious clothing is increasingly used in US politics as a symbol of inclusion, it becomes less readable as a symbol of personal piety. And this means that the religious purposes of hijab are in jeopardy. Much as what happened to a cross necklace once Madonna made it an icon of pop culture, solidarity hijab is defining the public meaning of hijab in ways that undermine its ability to function as a religious practice.

Orientalism, White Feminism, Anti-Black Racism, and American Nationalism

Solidarity hijab is well intentioned—it aims to combat gendered Islamophobia. And yet, since it uses the religious practice of a community, the intention motivating the gesture is not the primary way to assess its ethical implications. We must also consider how Muslims experienced solidarity hijab, and some Muslims, importantly those from the most marginalized communities, experienced it as a reductive, erasive, presumptive, and co-optive act. The takeaway is simple: solidarity hijab is not as violent as other prevalent forms of anti-Muslim racism, but it is not the antidote either. Non-Muslims adopting hijab for the day did not dismantle the underlying systems of structural injustice that disproportionately affect Muslims, especially Muslim women of color. Those underlying structures include orientalism, white feminism, anti-Black racism, and nationalism.

In 1978, Edward Said defined orientalism as "a style of thought based upon an ontological and epistemological distinction made between 'the Orient' and (most of the time) 'the Occident.'"[72] He documented how orientalism framed Islam as Eastern and judged it inferior to the West, which in contrast was defined geographically as North America and Europe and philosophically by secularism and Christianity. Put differently, orientalism becomes the intellectual framework of hierarchy behind an enduring discourse that there exists some "us" versus a "them," with Muslims framed as always already foreign.

Adopting hijab as a symbol of solidarity is orientalist in a way that is both gendered and romantic. During the colonial period, the veil became enmeshed in gendered orientalism, resulting in Muslim women being designated the bearers of Islamic tradition. Today, using gendered aesthetics to symbolize Islam in political movements relies on that same framing.

What is tricky about the orientalism of solidarity hijab is that it is not blatantly negative. In fact, even as protesters deployed hijab as a sign of Muslim difference and identity, they also insisted that they were interested in a positive portrayal of that symbol. Minh-Ha Pham, a scholar who has written about the exploitation of Asian design in the West, has a helpful term that applies here: romantic orientalism. Pham uses this term when discussing so-called positive presentations of Eastern aesthetics that are nevertheless orientalist insofar as they are justified by assumed Western superiority, entitlement, and a liberal political agenda.[73] The anonymous author of *Ms. Muslamic* described solidarity hijab in terms that echo Pham's concept of romantic orientalism: "Whether you're upholding the veil as symbolic of oppression or purporting to 'challenge assumptions' about it," the blog reads, "this is still a reductive, one-dimensional and over-simplistic view of how Muslim women experience their faith, their identity and their bodies."[74]

The cases of solidarity hijab discussed here were engaged in as forms of feminist action that tried to take intersectionality seriously. And yet, feminism is another form of structural injustice that contributes to the exploitation of this political gesture. Solidarity hijab failed because it assumed sisterhood was possible without taking difference — particularly in terms of religio-racialized experience — more seriously. This failure is an indication of how challenging it is to implement intersectionality in symbolic politics, which by nature depend on aesthetics that are often reductive and exclusionary. But it also points to a particular problem mainstream feminism has had: understanding how religious identities contribute not only to women's marginalization and vulnerability, but also to their empowerment and flourishing.

The problem is not feminism per se, but the dominance of a type of feminism that women of color have increasingly named and critiqued publicly: white feminism. White feminism is not only about white women. It is an ideology that anyone can subscribe to. Rafia Zakaria, the author of *Against White Feminism*, defines a white feminist as "someone who refuses to consider the role that whiteness and the racial privilege attached to it have played and continue to play in universalizing white feminist concerns, agendas, and beliefs as being those of all of feminism and all of feminists."[75] This may be unintentional, Zakaria continues: "A white feminist may be a woman who earnestly salutes the precepts of 'intersectionality' . . . but fails to cede space to the feminists of color who have been ignored, erased, or excluded from the feminist movement."[76] Koa Beck, author of *White Feminism*, explains white feminism in terms of its tactics. "It's a type of feminism," she writes, "that takes up the politics of power without questioning them — by replicating patterns of white supremacy, capitalistic greed, corporate ascension, inhumane labor practices, and exploitation, and deeming it empowering for women to practice these tenets as men always have."[77] That is, white feminism is about increasing the power of particular women, through increased autonomy, wealth, and self-actualization, instead of redistributing power. It plays by the rules of patriarchy and white supremacy instead of dismantling them. In white feminism, women advocate for themselves to be treated like white men.

At the time of the 2017 Women's March, I thought it was extraordinary that my secular feminist colleagues and friends would adopt a hijab as a symbol of their liberal commitments. I knew they had long considered this sartorial practice an example of how religion oppresses women, so I thought their solidarity hijab was a sign of a major shift. But I was naive. I thought using hijab as a symbol of feminist protest was only possible with a level of religious literacy as well as the understanding that Muslim women do not need to be saved from their faith commitments. But the symbolic gesture was just that, a gesture. My secular colleagues had not needed to learn anything about Islamic practice or Muslim women to replace their Facebook profile picture with Fairey's flag hijab image. They still thought of religious affiliation primarily as a barrier to women's empowerment. They never considered thinking about religion as a resource for dismantling patriarchy. They wanted to show support for their marginalized Muslim sisters, not learn from them how feminist politics might be contributing to that marginalization.

When white feminism employs a tactic of protest that involves religious appropriation, it reduces religious women to a token of diversity. This means that the appropriation of hijab recruited Muslim women, or at least their image, in the perpetuation of their own marginalization. Religious appropriation makes religious inclusion possible.

When I say white feminism is contributing to gendered Islamophobia, I do not intend to erase white Muslim women, because of course they exist. Instead, I mean that an ideology of whiteness supports the use of hijab as a sign of universal feminist protest, and that not only white women—but also a lot of white women—participated in solidarity hijab campaigns as an expression of whiteness.

At the same time, the support we saw for solidarity hijab within the Muslim community might itself be an expression of internalized white feminism. Accepting the tactics of white feminism—such as thanking non-Muslim women for acts of solidarity hijab—is a way to be an insider in the dominant expression of feminism today. But as Rafia Zakaria pointed out, participation in white feminism requires "feminists of color to denounce their racial or cultural communities to participate in feminist discourse."[78] We saw this dynamic play out when some Muslim women censured members of their community who criticized the #HeadscarfForHarmony campaign.

This brings us to a third form of existing structural injustice solidarity hijab illuminates: anti-Black racism, which in the United States touches almost every part of life, from police violence and health disparities to access to employment and education.

Activists have noted that anti-Black racism affects who is invited to represent the Muslim community in public events or in leadership positions. Namira Islam Anani is a lawyer and cofounder of Muslim Anti-Racism Collaborative (MuslimARC), an educational organization that works to raise awareness about anti-Blackness in the Muslim community. In a commentary titled "Soft Islamophobia," she pointed out that since the 2016 presidential election, Muslim perspective in panels, media appearances, or reports has been offered predominantly by South Asian or Middle Eastern representatives.[79] Ignoring Black Muslims is a glaring omission, since 20 percent of Muslims in the United States today are Black and the first Muslims in North America were enslaved Africans.

The American Muslim community, even as a religious minority, is not immune from internal racism. MuslimARC published a survey in 2015 of 400 Muslims living in the United States. Eighty-two percent reported experiences of ethnic or racial discrimination from society at-large, which is perhaps not surprising. But 59 percent reported similar discrimination from other Muslims in various forms: hostility in Arab- or South Asian–predominant mosques, being referred to as *abeed*, a derogatory term in Arabic that means "slave," and fragmentation along racial lines of Muslim student associations on campuses.[80]

We can see the effects of anti-Black racism in the cases of solidarity hijab discussed. Fairey chose to create an image based on a photograph of a brown woman in part because of the way Islam is racialized. He assumed that an image of a white or Black woman would be less readable to the majority of Americans as Muslim. He was likely correct. And it was also significant that the woman in the flag hijab image is South Asian, not Arab. Scholars have argued that South Asian Muslims are viewed as the "model minority" within the American Muslim community, as not quite white but also avoiding negative associations of Arab Muslims.[81] The image of a South Asian Muslim woman was "easier" for non-Muslims to adopt as symbol of protest.

Anti-Black racism explains why the exploitations associated with solidarity hijab were experienced differently by members of the Muslim community. We saw this in the heated debates over the #HeadscarfForHarmony campaign on Twitter. The loudest US critics of #HeadscarfForHarmony were Black Muslim women who saw this campaign as shallow virtue signaling that decentered Muslims. Non-Black Muslims questioned this experience and tried to silence Black Muslims, demonstrating racial tensions within the community. This dynamic meant that "religious insiders" contributed to the exploitative effects of the appropriation: when non-Black Muslims ridiculed and undermined Black Muslim women on Twitter, they exacerbated the offense that Black Muslims experienced as part of the original form of religious appropriation.

Coined by Moya Bailey, the term "misogynoir" points to one form of intersectionality: the ways anti-Black and misogynistic representations shape broader ideas about Black women. However, discussions of gendered Islamophobia often ignore race, and discussions of misogynoir often ignore religion. As Kayla Wheeler has pointed out, the experience of Black Muslim women deserves particular attention. "Not only do Black Muslim women face intersecting misogynoir and gendered Islamophobia from non-Muslims," Wheeler writes in an essay for *Maydan*, "they often face misogynoir from other Muslims. Struggles over who gets to represent Islam to the non-Muslim public are often rooted in anti-Blackness." Wheeler suggests that taking race more seriously "would mean simultaneously recognizing that race is a master category in the United States—it plays a fundamental role in shaping history, culture, and economics—and that Black Muslim women cannot separate their multiple intersecting identities: woman, Black, Muslim."[82]

Race is also important in the final form of structural injustice I want to discuss, namely American nationalism. Islam has been racialized throughout the American experiment as part of how Muslims have been cast as not (fully) American.[83] I discussed this briefly when setting the context for solidary hijab, but it is worth repeating here as a form of structural injustice. The idea of Islam as anti-American predates 9/11, but it has become explicitly part of US domestic and foreign policy since that event. George Bush's military campaign in Afghanistan and Donald Trump's framing of Muslims as threats are obvious examples of American nationalism deployed against Muslim-majority populations. But recent liberal presidents relied on similar problematic narratives of Muslims as outsiders. As egregious as Trump's Muslim travel ban was, the Obama administration had already restricted travel to the seven nations—Iraq, Syria, Iran, Sudan, Libya, Somalia, and Yemen—over concerns about terrorism. Former president Bill Clinton talked about how Muslims could be recruited to help identify extremist factions, reinforcing the idea that good Muslims were patriotic ones. Hillary Clinton repeated this idea during her 2016 presidential campaign. Sociologist Neda Maghbouleh explained to a *Vox* reporter that "for Muslims to be 'good' and worthy cultural and political citizens of America, they have to pledge fealty to the same law enforcement, media, and politicians that have been surveilling, jailing, and abusing them based on their names, their faith, and their physical appearances."[84] This holds Muslims to a different standard than people in other religious communities, who can have a range of political views without being labeled unpatriotic. But the only acceptable Muslims are the ones who pledge complete fidelity.

Adopting hijab to combat gendered Islamophobia fails because of existing asymmetrical power relations, relations that are easier to see once we understand how this gesture is experienced by some Muslim women as exploitation and profound offense. While neither Fairey's flag hijab image nor the #HeadscarfForHarmony campaign created the injustice of orientalism, white feminism, anti-Black racism, or American nationalism, they did depend on the logics of these ideologies and the systems of inequality that they produced.

Beyond Allyship

Part of the difficulty with assessing the ethics of religious appropriations is that they are often defined as something else. For instance, framing solidarity hijab as progressive politics makes it harder to see the ways it functions as appropriative harm. And yet by paying attention to concerns raised by Muslim women about both campaigns, we saw that many Muslims experienced them as reductionistic, prematurely assuming kinship, decentering Muslim women, and exhibiting virtue signaling. Identifying these exploitations allowed us to see broader systemic forms of injustice that were drawn on and reinforced through solidarity hijab, mainly orientalism, white feminism, anti-Black racism, and a particular form of American nationalism that presents itself as neutral but is acutely Christian, white, and masculine.

By applying the framework of religious appropriation to solidarity hijab, we learned that intentions do not predict outcomes. The cases I considered were initiated by non-Muslim women—self-described outsiders of the Muslim community—who intended to use hijab's aesthetics to fight against Muslim hate and discrimination. And for many non-Muslim women who participated, this was the first time they conceived of hijab as an icon of feminist politics instead of merely a stigma of religious extremism. They thought solidarity hijab communicated that they saw themselves as "on the same team" as Muslim women. But not all Muslims agreed; in fact, for many solidarity hijab felt more like an assertion of privilege of non-Muslim feminists than meaningful support. Instead of fighting gendered Islamophobia, solidarity hijab contributed to it.

Part of what makes solidarity hijab so ethically fraught is that this head covering has a particular religious function. For some Muslim women, it is a marker of Muslim identity, or put in terms of the idea of group intimacy discussed in the Introduction, hijab is a practice that creates a sense of group membership. When the headscarf is used by non-Muslims, that group intimacy is in jeopardy not only because kinship is assumed where there is none, but also because hijab can no longer function in the same way. How can something be the basis of group identity when outsiders so easily adopt it?

Solidary hijab also contributes to a cultural shift in the meaning of the head covering: away from an embodied sartorial practice to cultivate a particular religiously informed character to a symbol of liberal wokeness. For the Muslim women who depend on hijab to be readable as a demonstration of personal piety, their ability to cultivate their own character is thwarted when it is used to signify a commitment to some vague notion of inclusion.

Even though the meaning of hijab is the subject of ongoing debate within the Muslim community—for example, whether a headscarf is obligatory, recommended, or unnecessary for a modern Muslim woman—this does not diminish the stakes when outsiders appropriate it. On the contrary, it makes the appropriation of hijab as *the* sign of Muslim womanhood even more fraught because it takes a side in an ongoing intrareligious debate. When outsiders weigh in on Muslim discussions in this way, they are both asserting what I have described as an "excess of expertise" and contributing to a "deficiency of expertise" of Muslim women who might already have trouble claiming space as sources of religious knowledge and feminist insight.

This is all to say that solidarity hijab does not just borrow the aesthetics of Islamic head covering, which would be objectionable from the point of view of cultural appropriation. It also gets involved in the inner workings of religious practice in a very substantial manner. Solidarity hijab erases the religious values and purposes associated with hijab. It ignores internal religious diversity. It replaces religious meanings with pedestrian ones. It is not just exploitative; it is profoundly offensive.

Acts of allyship often do more to alleviate the guilt of the protesters than enact meaningful change for the communities they are trying to support. This is exacerbated when allyship with a religious community involves borrowing a religious practice and redeploying it for political agendas. In the case of solidarity hijab, appropriation made the goal of allyship impossible for at least two reasons: the superficiality of symbolic politics and the limitation of tolerance as a strategy to address religious difference.

Symbolic politics occurs when items, images, or motifs are used to represent a political standpoint. In the cases of solidarity hijab just discussed, the symbol was of course hijab, based on the idea that it would be readable as "Islam" even when unlinked from actual Muslim practice and belief. The intent of appropriating this religious symbol was to combat Islamophobia.

Not only were the symbolic politics of hijab not enough to create substantial change, but they allowed participants to pretend that things were better than they were by distracting from violence against Muslims.[85] Like other forms of symbolic politics, solidarity hijab alleviated the protesters' guilt, making them less likely to feel an urgency to engage in more concrete forms of action.

That does not mean engagement with hijab could not be the basis of more effective political action. In fact, I have spent quite a bit of time writing for the mainstream media about the sartorial practices of Muslim women, to educate non-Muslims about diversity within the Muslim community and about the creativity of Muslim women. But in this work, the goal is to let the everyday lived experience of Muslim women animate the narrative, to highlight their experiences as examples of feminist understanding and action, not just examples of suffering.

Here is another way to think about this: The goal of solidarity hijab is tolerance for religious difference. But that bar is too low. "Tolerance" is defined in *Merriam-Webster's Collegiate Dictionary* as "sympathy or indulgence for beliefs or practices differing from or conflicting with one's own." Tolerance thus reinforces a firm distinction between "us" and "them." We (the majority) tolerate them (the religious minority). That doesn't require much of the "we." Intellectually, we don't need to understand the religious other. Politically, we don't need to create space for their freedom by giving up our privilege. We merely bear the existence of the other, a stance that reinforces division and hierarchy and does very little to fight the problem of hatred.[86]

A feminist form of religious engagement that takes intersectionality and difference as generative would ask more of us than tolerance. It would see Muslim women and their religious practices as resources for constructing a feminist outlook, instead of merely evidence of oppression. For example, modest clothing practices can encourage an examination of the hypersexualization of women, as well as a broader discussion of the politics of gendered clothing globally, and the ethics of how clothing is produced and marketed. The politicization of hijab is an opportunity to think about the role of gendered and racialized bodies in forms of religious representation. Intersectional feminism would acknowledge that Muslim women's insight into social justice is not reducible to their sartorial practices.

Taking intersectionality seriously cuts both ways. It is not only acknowledging the expertise of minoritized women, but also the privilege some of us unjustly wield as white, secular, or in the US context, Christian. Intersectional feminism requires a willingness to renounce that privilege.

The solidarity hijab campaigns insisted that the aesthetics of hijab could be easily disentangled from their devotional meanings. Missing was any meaningful attempt to educate participants about the religious meaning of hijab. Indeed, I think solidarity hijab is a case of appropriation that depends on willful ignorance: someone who understands the significance of this sartorial practice, how its obligation is debated within the community, and its history of being adopted for political agendas that are harmful to Muslim women, would be uncomfortable participating in a solidarity hijab campaign merely to increase their feminist brand.

2

Playing Pilgrim

In 1853, British explorer Sir Richard Francis Burton embarked on his riskiest undertaking, completing the hajj to Mecca. Only Muslims are allowed to participate in this Islamic pilgrimage to the birthplace of the Prophet Muhammad, the location of early revelation, and the home to the Kaaba, a cube-shaped building inside the Masjid al-Haram, considered the holiest Islamic site. In 1853, the penalty for a non-Muslim caught performing hajj would certainly have been death. Burton was aware of the danger. He wrote in a letter to his wife, Lady Isabel, "A blunder, a hasty action, a misjudged word, a prayer or bow, not strictly the right shibboleth, and my bones would have whitened the desert sand."[1]

In preparation, Burton learned Arabic and studied Islamic rituals. He took the name Abdullah, posed as a Sufi ascetic, and created an elaborate fictional backstory for himself: born an Afghan Muslim, raised in India, and educated in Burma. Knowing that the safest way to travel to Mecca was by joining a caravan, Burton got circumcised at the age of thirty-two so that a roadside pit stop would not blow his cover. When he made it to Mecca, he donned the traditional white pilgrim's garment and completed all the rituals of hajj, including praying at the Kaaba.

Illustration of Richard Burton dressed as "Abdullah" en route to Mecca during his pilgrimage in 1853. (Alamy)

Burton was not the first non-Muslim to complete the hajj—the Italian aristocrat Ludovico di Varthema's trip was documented centuries earlier in 1503. But Burton's pilgrimage was among the most well known because he recorded every juicy detail in a three-volume book that delighted Victorian readers in the West. For many Europeans, Burton's account of his hajj was their first "insider" look into this Islamic rite of passage.

Burton could have completed this pilgrimage with much less risk had he converted. In his book, he explained his reasons for rejecting this option. First, he did not want to become an object of contempt for his fellow Europeans. Playing a Muslim was one thing; becoming one would have barred him from high society. Second, he believed a recent convert would raise suspicion among Muslims and prevent him from gaining the trust necessary for potential informants. In other words, his goal was to experience true Islamic pilgrimage without becoming polluted by Islam. "Curious to see with my eyes what others are content to 'hear with ears,'" he wrote, "namely, Moslem inner life in a really Mohammedan country" and "to set foot on that mysterious spot which no vacation tourist has yet described, measured, sketched and photographed."[2] To achieve his objective, he had no choice, he thought, but to pose as a born believer.

It is easy to see why Burton's hajj was problematic—his journey entailed an intentional deception—and yet some forms of experiential learning about religion have much in common with his adventure: designed to be temporary, entailing no danger of conversion, and providing a firsthand experience of the religious practice of others for personal enrichment.

I have experience with my own version of Burton's hajj: traversing a section of the 500-mile pilgrimage to the Cathedral of Santiago de Compostela in northwestern Spain where, tradition has it, the remains of St. James the Apostle are buried under the cathedral. A network of

routes developed across Europe as the faithful traveled by foot to perform a set of rituals at the shrine of St. James. These routes are known
today as the Camino de Santiago de Compostela, or St. James's Way.
The most popular path, called the Camino Frances, begins in the
French Pyrenees, passes through the vineyards of La Rioja to the vast
plains of the Meseta, and finally crosses over the mountains of Galicia.
For Catholics, Santiago joins the Vatican, Jerusalem, and Lourdes as
an important devotional pilgrimage site. Today, an estimated quarter
of a million pilgrims enter Santiago each year. And only about half
are Catholic.

I have walked the last 150 miles of the Camino Frances five times
with college students, most of whom are not Christian, much less
Catholic, as part of an intensive study abroad program I developed
for Northeastern University. Dozens of US colleges offer programs
for course credit on the Camino, to study everything from Spanish
language to medieval art to European history. My program focuses
on religious practice. It is based on the premise that participation in a
religious pilgrimage, even as someone outside that faith, can be a valuable way to learn about the power and meaning of that practice. It is
religious appropriation for course credit.

Beyond the enticing distributional credits my program offers, my
students tell me the attraction of the Camino walk is that it offers
"meaning," "transformation," or the opportunity to discover something
"authentic." Simply put, my students enroll because, much like Burton,
they are interested in experiencing the adventure of pilgrimage for
themselves. In this chapter, I will think through my students' motivations, takeaways they gained from their journey, forms of exploitation
they unintentionally participated in, and what this tells us about how
study abroad programs may tread into underlying systems of structural injustice. I will problematize the idea of an "authentic" pilgrim
experience and theories of learning that promise cultural mastery

and will suggest alternative approaches to study abroad that focus on productive anxiety and humility.

Solidarity hijab provided a clear case of appropriation from a religious minority. The case of the Camino, in contrast, allows us to think through the ethics of religious appropriation from a majority, even hegemonic, religious tradition—namely, Christianity. To be sure, Catholics are themselves a religious minority in the United States, something I discussed in the Introduction, so part of what we will see is how Americans' presumptions about Catholicism influence their experience of the Camino. The Camino will also force us to think about forms of exploitation and profound offense that occur when it is not immediately clear who the victim is. For example, asserting that personal bodily experience, whether wearing hijab for a day or completing a pilgrimage, is necessary to achieve a sense of mastery—of either gendered Islamophobia or a religious ritual—is itself an assertion of privilege and superiority.

Pilgrimage is one of the oldest religious practices. Ancient Greeks and Romans traveled to sacred places for healing or to contact the gods. Buddha prescribed four places of pilgrimage to his followers. Journeys of veneration to Jerusalem have significance for Jews. Pilgrimage to the places associated with Christ's life and death have been prominent within the Christian tradition. The hajj is one of the five pillars of Islam and a central element of the Muslim faith. What these practices have in common is the idea that sacred journeys can be the occasion of significant religious transformation.

In a recent contribution to the field of pilgrim studies, Hillary Kaell argues that for American Christians, pilgrimage entails several juxtapositions that make the journey uncomfortable, such as material evidence/transcended divinity, religious/secular forms of authority, and commodification/anti-consumption drives.[3] The working out of these competing claims is why the meaning of a specific pilgrimage can differ radically among religious practitioners. For instance, some Catholics believe the water from Lourdes has miraculous physical healing properties. For others, Lourdes is merely a place for focused prayer. And Protestants might consider Lourdes a problematic pilgrimage site altogether, given that it is promoted by the Catholic Church. To put it simply, the religious meaning of pilgrimage is not singular. As a practice, pilgrimage allows for religious contestation and conflict, and it both reinforces and reforms various religious norms.[4]

Despite these variations, we can say a few things about pilgrimage. It is a dual experience of moving toward a sacred space and through an unfamiliar land. The journey ends in a specific location: a temple town, a mountain shrine, a cathedral city. Often the destination is associated with foundational narratives of a tradition and is significant to remembering, re-creating, and reinforcing these stories. But Burton's caravan adventures were just as much a part of his hajj as was his performing of rituals in Mecca. Pilgrims to Santiago often describe their journey, rather than their arrival, as the aspect of their pilgrimage that has the most meaning. In fact, the modern reworking of Camino described later links the authenticity of the pilgrim's experience to the journey itself, not the purported existence of St. James's bones in a cathedral's tomb.

Pilgrimages can be classified as a rite of passage, an experience that has the potential to fundamentally change the participant. The specific goal of a pilgrimage might be a closer relationship to God, penance for past sins, or moral development. What these all have in common is the assumption that pilgrimage can be transformative for the individual pilgrim because of a multidimensional experience that includes performance, spectacle, displacement, and community.

The performance of pilgrimage is the doing: the physical exertion required to complete the journey. Burton's performance entailed traveling with a caravan, wearing special clothing, and completing a series of rituals once he arrived in Mecca. Completing the Camino on foot, as my students do, requires a lot of walking, adopting certain accessories, such as a scallop shell, and stamping a pilgrim passport.

It might seem weird to say that pain is part of the Camino journey, but it is more understandable when we realize that a Christian pilgrim's suffering was traditionally understood in theological terms as a way to bring new appreciation for life and understanding of God's plan. The pilgrim who suffers is the pilgrim who is performing the pilgrimage correctly. Even forms of pilgrimage that do not valorize pain do promote the idea that physical experiences can disclose existential or ethical insights.

The second element of pilgrimage involves spectacle, the aesthetic experience of seeing and touching forms of material culture. On hajj, this includes seeing the Kaaba. Christian pilgrimage to the Holy Land is motivated by the idea that a better grasp of biblical events is possible by seeing with our own eyes the locations of those events. The spectacle on the Camino includes the experience of standing in the final shrine of Santiago, as well as visiting churches and relics that dot the routes through northern Spain.

A third mechanism of religious pilgrimage is displacement, which includes the experience of movement through a foreign terrain. Physical displacement is temporary, since the journey has a beginning and an end. But the displacement is also related to the goal of enduring transformation. Religious pilgrimage is often described as a liminal experience, insofar as it crosses the threshold from one state of existence to another.[5] Pilgrimage takes the practitioners out of their ordinary life and allows time for reflection, contemplation, and prayer, which is how they become more aware, gain religious wisdom, and perhaps encounter the divine.

Finally, pilgrimage involves a community.[6] Burton's hajj depended on a caravan for safe passage, and the rituals he performed in Mecca were done in the company of others. My students experience the Camino as a group, which sets the pace of their journey as well as provides them with peers to enjoy and reflect on the experience. Even the pilgrim who travels alone travels in the footsteps of someone who came before and is often working within a system of precepts and rules constructed by others.

Institutions can infuse more specific meanings into a pilgrimage. The popularity of medieval Christian pilgrimage, for instance, increased when the Church began offering a plenary indulgence for completing specific journeys. Indulgences are part of the penitential system of the Church. They are based on the theological idea that some sins are so offensive to God that asking and receiving forgiveness is not enough; the faithful must also complete some sort of penance. This can happen through suffering in purgatory, a place in the afterlife where one works off past sins to get to heaven. But in the eleventh century, the Church began granting indulgences, a "remission of sins," for extraordinary acts of faith as a way to do penance in this life. A plenary indulgence canceled all debts, and a partial indulgence canceled a portion.

In 1122, Pope Calixtus declared pilgrimage to Santiago eligible for a plenary indulgence. This meant that if a medieval pilgrim could make it to Santiago and perform some basic tasks, such as giving confession, attending Mass, and making a donation, they eliminated their time in purgatory for past sins. It is still possible to earn plenary indulgences for visiting Santiago in a Holy Year (such as 2004, 2010, 2021, or 2027) or by arriving in Santiago on one of the St. James feast dates (May 23, July 25, and December 30).

Understanding the different ways pilgrimage is theologically conceptualized by Catholics and Protestants is helpful, especially since this tension came up in my student groups. Pilgrimage was a popular Christian endeavor, especially in the medieval period. But during the

Reformation, it became one of the ways leading Protestant Reformers challenged the authority of the Catholic Church, which controlled many of the popular pilgrimage sites. Martin Luther, for instance, explicitly condemned pilgrimages. "There is no good in them," he declared in 1520; "no commandment enjoins them, no obedience attaches to them. Rather do these pilgrimages give countless occasions to commit sin and to despise God's commandments."[7] Luther warned that pilgrimage led to neglecting Christian duties at home and even to extramarital affairs.[8]

Conventional wisdom is that Catholics go on pilgrimage, whereas Protestants do not. But pilgrimage is increasingly popular among American Protestants. One of the findings of a 2008 pilgrimage study was that Protestants approach pilgrimage with a specific motivation: "Protestants tend to search for authenticity in an existential sense, with regard to the emotional experience of their personal relationship with Jesus, rather than focusing on the quest to witness sites that are considered by religious authorities to be authentic, in an objective sense."[9] This makes the Camino an unlikely destination for Protestant pilgrimage. It is based not on a strongly developed biblical narrative but rather on extrabiblical legends, and the destination and route are located in a predominantly Catholic region and controlled by the Roman Catholic Church. This all has the effect of making Protestants to some extent "outsiders" on this Christian pilgrimage, which we will see has implications for the experience as a learning opportunity, particularly for my Protestant students.

That said, American Protestants do walk the Camino as part of the increased popularity of pilgrimage among American Christians in general, and this trend coincides with the rise of religious liberalism I described in the Introduction. As Hillary Kaell argued, pilgrimage began to be conceptualized as a "tailored, personal experience" where "pilgrims pay for a short-term experience that enhances their spiritual lives, supplementing their regular church services and activities."[10] The new Protestant motivation to embark on pilgrimage looks very similar to the motivation of a "none" or SBNR (spiritual but not religious) person: an experience appropriated to facilitate self-actualization, but without submitting to local religious institutional authority.

Today, Santiago is considered, along with Jerusalem and Rome, one of three major Catholic pilgrimage destinations. But this status is puzzling. Rome is the home of the pope and the location of St. Peter's Basilica, the burial site of St. Peter the Apostle. Jerusalem is where many important biblical events took place, making it an obvious destination for pilgrimage. In contrast, the Bible says very little about the Iberian Peninsula. The Camino's prominence is best explained as a result of power struggles in the region—both political and religious— as well as the broader military expeditions of the Church, such as the Crusades.

Since the Christian Bible tells us that much of Jesus's ministry occurred in Jerusalem, a fair question is, How did St. James the Apostle come to be buried in Galician Spain? Legend has it that when the apostles divided the world into missionary zones, the Iberian Peninsula was assigned to James. There is textual evidence—although it is thin— that he spent a few years preaching in Spain before returning to Jerusalem, where he was executed by decapitation in 44 CE by King Herod. Upon his death, the followers of St. James are said to have carried his body to the coast and placed it in a stone boat that miraculously sailed until it reached the northwest coast of Spain. From there, a local queen named Lupa ordered a team of oxen to transport St. James's body to an inland marble tomb. Then, despite this astonishing voyage, the apostle's tomb was forgotten for centuries.

The story of St. James's entombment picks up again around 813, when a curious Christian hermit named Pelayo followed music and twinkling stars to a remote hillside in Galicia, Spain. There, he discovered bones at Campus Stella (Compostela), the remains of St. James the Apostle, or Santiago as he is known by Spanish Christians. By the end of the ninth century, Christian authorities had declared St. James the patron saint of Spain, and a shrine was built inside the cathedral of the city eventually named after him: Santiago de Compostela.

The timing of the rediscovery of Santiago's tomb is significant, given the religious politics of the region. From 711 to 1492, Muslim Moors from North Africa ruled the Iberian Peninsula. It is hard not to speculate that the miraculous discovery of St. James's bones by Pelayo in 813 was somehow inspired by Christian anxieties over the arrival of these foreigners. One consequence of promoting pilgrimage to Santiago was that more Christians entered northern Spain from other parts of Europe at the very time when the Church was trying to encourage such migration as a way to support the Christian kings who were trying to reclaim Spain from the "invasion" of the Moors.

Legend has it that St. James himself got involved in mounting tensions between Christians and Muslims in the region. He is said to have magically appeared in 844 in Clavijo, in northeast Spain, to help King Ramiro I defeat the Moors. And for the next six centuries, the late apostle showed up in the Iberian Peninsula at crucial moments to help Christian forces defeat Moorish ones. At these moments, he was no longer a humble disciple but a fierce medieval knight, atop a white steed, brandishing a large sword and often carrying a white banner. Santiago's reinvented image as a warrior shows up in paintings and sculptures from the period, and those representations and the stories behind them earned him a new Spanish nickname: Matamoros, "Moor slayer." The iconography of Matamoros was eventually exported to Latin America as part of the conquistadors' subjugation of local populations.

So far, we have seen two narratives associated with St. James: the apostle who spread Christianity to Iberia, and a military leader who helped with the Christian reconquest of Islamic Spain. Other "versions" of St. James emerged in response to contestations over who controlled Christianity in the region. For instance, the French-based monastic order known as the Cluny leveraged St. James in its attempts to offset the power of Rome. The Cluny promoted a version of St. James that it called Sanctus Jacobus, a gentle pilgrim who traveled through the French Pyrenees to anoint northern Spain as a second Holy Land and who appeared in a dream to Charlemagne, promising him possession of Galicia.[11] The Cluny used Sanctus Jacobus to shore up its power in the region, building much of the network that comprises today's most popular route to Santiago, known as the French Way, which strategically passes by major Cluniac shrines.

Despite the dueling versions of St. James as Matamoros and as Sanctus Jacobus—or perhaps because each attracted different sorts of travelers—the Camino became a popular medieval pilgrimage route. However, by the sixteenth century, several factors contributed to a sharp decline of pilgrims on the Camino. Well-used pilgrimage routes helped spread the bubonic plague, and high infection rates on the Camino convinced some pilgrims to stay home. The Protestant Reformation also decreased the popularity of pilgrimage, since early Protestant leaders preached that relics and indulgences were anti-Christian because they depended on an intermediary (whether an object or institution) between the believer and God.

This decline continued until the twentieth century, when Spanish and European governing bodies tried to recuperate the Camino as a symbol of protonationalism and European ecumenism, respectively. Francisco Franco, the Spanish general who led Spain from 1939 to 1975, promoted the Camino as part of his attempt to use political

Catholicism to shore up his power. But during Franco's rule, the number of pilgrims continued to decline. The Pilgrim Office of Santiago maintains statistics on Compostelas, the official certificates of completion awarded by the Church. In 1987, fewer than 3,000 pilgrims earned a Compostela, an indication that this route was nearly lost to history.

A more successful reinvention took place after Franco, as Spain began to seek membership in the European Union in the late 1980s and the Camino became promoted as an example of European exchange and ecumenism. The Council of Europe declared the Camino the first European Cultural Route in October 1987, and that same year, it was named one of UNESCO's World Heritage Sites, putting it on the tourism map. When the logo for the Camino was designed in 1988, it mimicked the nascent European flag: a stylized yellow abstraction of a conch shell on a blue background.[12] By 2004, Spain's main cultural foundation was promoting the Camino as "a true axis for the first common European consciousness."[13]

Instead of a sectarian devotional journey, the Camino was recast as an example of European integration, a modern version of religious pluralism and tolerance that was reminiscent of the period of Spanish history when Muslims, Jews, and Christians coexisted. For this to work, certain features of the Camino and its associated historical narratives had to be emphasized over others. For example, Matamoros was not part of this reinvention, and the focus became the route to Santiago—the Camino—as opposed to the destination—the tomb of St. James.

As a result, something almost as miraculous as Pelayo's ninth-century discovery occurred: the Camino again became a popular and heavily traveled pilgrimage route. In the Holy Year of 2010, the number of Compostelas passed a quarter of a million for the first time in modern history. In 2015, the number rose to 262,516—and that wasn't even a Holy Year. In 2019, the number of Compostelas broke all previous records—347,578. Americans earned over 20,000 of these certificates of completion.[14] These numbers do not even capture travelers who did not end their journey in Santiago or those who did not register at the Pilgrim Office.

Christian revivalism might be one reason for this sudden increase in the popularity of the Camino, since part of its modern reinvention has entailed emphasizing the Camino's role in pre-Reformation Christian unity. And yet, although tens of thousands of Christian pilgrims set out each year from their doorsteps or from popular starting points across Europe, they are not alone. The Camino attracts plenty of non-Christians. This is even encouraged by the modern Catholic Church, which promotes the route as an opportunity for personal spiritual reflection for those of any faith. Statistics collected by the Pilgrim Office of Santiago give some indication of the number of non-Christians on the Camino, at least those who apply for a Compostela. At the time of application, a pilgrim must declare one of three possible official motivations. Those of the year 2019 reflect a typical distribution: 40 percent religious, 49 percent religious and others (a category that used to be called "spiritual"), and 11 percent nonreligious (a category that used to be called "cultural").[15] The Pilgrim Office assumes Christians will declare religious motivations. The second category, "religious and others," is to capture pilgrims motivated by non-Christian religious commitments. From these statistics, it appears that Christian pilgrims were in the minority in 2019 and that as many as 60 percent of pilgrims seeking a Compostela were not Christian. Even more non-Christian pilgrims were not captured by this data, since an individual who doesn't care about a certification from the Catholic Church wouldn't necessary apply for a Compostela in the first place.

Some scholars have argued that the Camino's new fame is linked to a growing body of popular literature and media about this pilgrimage. Over the years, I've met several American pilgrims who mentioned the 2010 movie *The Way*—directed, produced, and written by Emilio Estevez and starring his father, Martin Sheen—as inspiration for their Camino. I have also seen pilgrims carrying a copy of Paulo Coelho's 1987 novel *The Pilgrimage* (or *O Diário de um Mago* in Portuguese). The timing of increased traffic on the Camino may also be explained by a series of demographic factors, such as the first wave of boomer retirees. Or it could correspond to economic turning points, such as the world economic crisis of 2008, which increased unemployment and created a class of people with time to contemplate their next steps in life.

But these factors alone do not explain why more and more individuals continue to devote up to a month of their lives to a pilgrimage across northern Spain. The Camino's growing popularity is based in part on the cultural fact that we increasingly see religion as something to be experienced for a variety of nonreligious goals. All pilgrims, even non-Christian ones, are hoping that the Camino will be a transformative experience. They have chosen the Camino, and not the Appalachian Trail, based on the same assumption that motivated Richard Burton's hajj: there is something to be learned from experiencing a religious pilgrimage, even without religious affiliation or fidelity.

Converting the Camino into a Classroom

The purpose of study abroad programs is most often articulated as the acquisition of intercultural competency, which education scholar Darla Deardorff defines as "the ability to communicate effectively and appropriately in intercultural situations based on one's intercultural knowledge, skills, and attitudes."[16] But educators differ on how they think this acquisition occurs based on their epistemological assumptions. The "positivist model" assumes that understanding another culture can occur without challenging one's existing worldview and ethos. This was Burton's approach to his hajj. He assumed he would gain insight into the Muslim world without any significant disruption to his European way of life. In contrast, many contemporary study abroad programs are based on the "relativism model," which holds that cultural perspectives differ based in part on context, but does not rest on the idea of a hierarchy among cultures.

I would say my Camino program was grounded on a third option, the "experiential model." Study abroad programs that try to operationalize this model do not rely solely on immersion to facilitate learning, but instead build in instructor interventions that encourage students to identify and challenge their own cultural assumptions. This sort of learning creates discomfort and encourages students to reflect critically on how their own cultural contexts shape what they see as ontologically true and morally good.

Experiential learning has always been part of the pedagogical identity of my current employer—Northeastern University. Northeastern is best known for our robust Co-op program, which lets students apply classroom learning in a work environment. According to a university poll, 76 percent of our students agree that work outside the classroom increases retention of important course concepts.[17] We also offer global experiential opportunities that allow 3,000 of our students to go abroad each year.[18] In addition to traditional immersion models, where students live and learn at foreign institutions of higher education, Northeastern offers intensive, month-long programs, called "Dialogues of Civilization," during the summer terms, which are led by our own faculty. Based on the experiential paradigm, the Dialogues of Civilization are designed to combine faculty interventions (through coursework, reflections, curated experiences, etc.) with cross-cultural experience to facilitate student learning. My Camino program was one of these Dialogues. But, as I will show, when it comes to the subject matter of religion, such experiential offerings raise distinct ethical concerns.

From 2014 through 2018, I led a Dialogue of Civilization to Spain for Northeastern Honors students, and I may start it up again. This program included two courses: one was usually focused on religious diversity in Andalusia, and the second was always about pilgrimage. I draw on my experience with the second course, which centered on the experience of walking the last 150 miles of the Camino, during which we both studied and performed the act of pilgrimage. I developed and then offered a program that asked students to "play" at being pilgrims, much as Burton had done, promising that by doing so, they could have a particular sort of insider experience.

Spain was an unlikely choice of destination for me to lead a Dialogue. Before I developed my program, I knew very little about the Camino and had never been to Spain, despite having conducted research overseas in many other locations. I spoke only beginner's Spanish. I did not study pilgrimage in my own research. I was not particularly interested in medieval religious history or architecture. But for a scholar of comparative religion, the Camino had substantial draw. Given the religious history of Spain, it offered a way to make religious diversity and interaction central to the program of study. And I could teach about religious practice—in this case, pilgrimage—by having students engage in that practice. They could experience the emotional and physical hardships of a long journey by foot, visit towns with vivid ecclesial art and other material evidence of this tradition, and meet fellow pilgrims, many of whom would be traveling to Santiago as a religious rite of passage.

In any given year, Northeastern offers up to one hundred various Dialogue programs. Mine always had a deep waitlist and stellar evaluations. My former students have described the pilgrimage as one of the most important experiences of their college career, discussed their Camino in their applications to graduate school, and highlighted it in their commencement speeches years later.

It was also a very special teaching experience for me. I got to know my students better than is possible in a traditional on-campus course, and I found this intimacy fostered trust that facilitated both their learning and mine. But I agree with historian of American religion Elijah Siegler's statement that a "thoughtful teacher will realize there are ethical and philosophical problems underlying the whole study abroad enterprise."[19] Siegler has in mind the ways programs in Asia and the Middle East tap into Western college students' desire to have orientalist adventures to exoticized lands, much like Burton's infamous journey to Mecca.

My program did not offer an orientalist encounter. But, like any study abroad in Europe, it did appeal to my mostly American students as a sort of grand tour to sites associated with the rise of Western civilization. This is the flip side of orientalism, privileging Europe as the most important region of "classic" cultural and historical production. But Spain as a destination cannot alone explain the popularity of my Camino program, since other Northeastern Dialogues in Spain often had trouble enrolling enough students to run.

After the first year of my program, I started assigning a motivations paper to my students, asking them to reflect on why they were interested in walking the Camino and what they hoped to get out of it. I also followed up with interviews of twenty students in the fall of 2017 and winter 2019 who I knew identified as either "nones" or SBNR.

Several of my students said that their motivation for completing the Camino was to learn more about religion. But buried in their answers were assumptions about what religion is in terms of an object of study, assumptions that disclosed how they were repelled and attracted to specific sorts of religious beliefs and practices. It was not the study of religion per se that was the draw, but rather the chance to experience religion as a technique. Put differently, I would say most of my students didn't begin the program thinking of religion as a topic of serious academic study or as relevant to their professional track. They were interested in what religion could do for them personally.

Energetic, upbeat Kristy expressed an interest in religion as a way to understand people different from herself.[20] "I have always been interested in religion," she told me. "Why do you think that is?" I asked. "I don't really know. I guess I am interested in talking to people. I have tended to be the outsider when people talk about religion. And I thought those conversations would be more in depth on the Camino." Still not sure what "religion" meant to Kristy, I asked her to say more. "Well," she said, "the Camino is the better parts of religion, such as taking time to think." Here we see the core of religion that spiritual seekers are most interested in. The safe and benevolent parts. The rituals of introspection. The modes of thinking about the meaning of life. And Kristy's hope was that on the Camino she would experience these aspects while avoiding the mess of dogma. To her, the attraction of my program was the opportunity to enjoy a religious rite of passage without having to commit to a religious tradition.

Successfully completing the physical and mental challenge of the Camino was another common motivation of my Honors students. For most of their lives, they had earned good grades, collected trophies, and won awards. These achievements created conservatism: they tackled only those tasks they knew they would excel at. The Camino was the first thing many of them had signed up to do that they were not sure they could complete. Since it was for a grade, it was the ultimate risk to their perfect records. And yet likely enjoyable, as a group outdoor adventure akin to a summer camp nature experience.

When I think about students motivated by the physical challenge of the Camino, Paige immediately comes to mind. Paige was a neuroscience major and talented photographer. She had a habit of looking off into the distance, as if posing for a photograph herself, emoting angst or deep thought. Paige had reason for some of her intensity. She had broken her back in high school, and for a few scary hours in the hospital, she wasn't sure she was going to walk again. When I met her, she talked a lot about pushing herself harder than she should. She would say things like, "I think I'm so strong, but I don't know my limits," but it was clear that part of her hope for the Camino was learning to believe those words.

When we spoke in Boston three years after her trip, she had a much clearer idea of why she had signed up to walk the Camino. "To be honest," she said over a chocolate croissant, "I wanted to do it because it frightened me. It seemed impossible, unreasonable, and hard." She looked down, and then out the window. "I needed to know that I wasn't broken, and the only way I knew how to do that was to get far away from everything. I needed to know my own strength."

It probably sounds clichéd to say that time to reflect was a motivation for my students' pilgrimage, but it certainly was. Part of this was unplugging from life's responsibilities—work, class—and distractions, such as social media. Lara was a funny girl who raised the mood of others with camp songs about mushrooms despite struggling with a chronic foot injury that made our daily walks painful for her. Thinking back on her Camino experience almost four years later, she told me, "The idea of pilgrimage is to cleanse yourself, arrive better than you left. No one does the Camino because they are perfect."

My students hoped pilgrimage would be an opportunity to become more self-aware. Lucas, a soccer player with a lovely singing voice, explained, "I wanted to walk the Camino to see what I could learn about myself and my connection with anything that may be greater than me." A large number of my students began the journey with a "secret" they were hoping to share with others, once they felt safe enough to do so. They believed that the Camino would allow them to be vulnerable in ways they were not in their everyday normal life. And this became a self-fulfilling prophecy.

Martin Sheen walks to mourn the loss of his son in the film *The Way*, and some of my students hoped the Camino would help them process the recent loss of a loved one. More than one of them walked the Camino within eighteen months of losing a parent. They wrote about this in their journals or shared this detail of their personal life with me in late-night conversations. Learning of these losses was the hardest part of the Camino for me and made me wish I had something more helpful to offer than the space to talk.

Matt was a quiet freshman. A very quiet one. I'm not sure he had talked much to girls before he was suddenly on a month-long study abroad program with fifteen of them. A couple of the loudest girls adopted him, at first like a pet, and then as their undisputed favorite. I noticed about a week into our trip that he was writing prose he had memorized on the back of the field sketches I assigned to get students to slow down and look at things in a new way. Matt didn't need class assignments to do that.

Matt never spoke to me about his mother during our walk. But he told me the day before we arrived in Santiago that he didn't want to get a Compostela because he didn't think his mother would approve. That was when I guessed she had passed. His final reflection confirmed my suspicions; it was a letter to his mother in which he described with excruciating honesty how lonely he was without her.

Kurt told me "religion is all weird superstition," and that what drew him to my program was a chance to visit Spain, a place where his mother had spent significant time when she was younger. When I pointed out that Northeastern offered lots of programs in Spain, and he had managed to pick the only one that dealt with what he called superstition, he replied, "Well, I think religion is interesting in sort of a social scientist perspective." For Kurt, like Burton, religion was the stuff of "other people," to be studied much as an anthropologist would study a primitive culture.

But Kurt was not just a student. He was also someone who had just lost his mother to cancer. I knew this before we departed, although he hid this fact from every student on the trip by creative use of tenses when he discussed her. Years later, he confessed to me that he had signed up for my program because he was searching for a way to process his anger and sadness over her death. He wanted the religious experience, even if he did not want the religion.

If the students came into the program with their own expectations, so did I. And my expectations affected (and perhaps infected) each student's experience, given that I designed the program with certain learning objectives in mind. According to the syllabus, the program had several specific goals:

> Upon successful completion of the course, students will be able to *describe* the role of ritual practice in religion and the continued significance of physical ritual in the contemporary world; to *identify* major ecclesial art and architecture along the pilgrimage route; to *interpret* religious art objects, relics, and church in light of their historical contexts; and to *display* habits of critical and appreciative understanding of people different from themselves.

These are standard religious studies learning objectives that did not necessarily require an immersive study abroad experience.

In hindsight, I can now see what was missing from this articulation: the specific forms of learning I assumed engaging in a religious practice might foster. I had organized the course around physical experiences, readings, tours of historic sites, opportunities to meet "the locals," and reflections. These activities were based on my assumption that the Camino, like Burton's hajj, might function as a unique learning experience in which playing at being a pilgrim could be the central learning activity. We will see that in the program, however, religion was idealized, only partially historicized, and frankly flattened to make it suitable for an immersive experience. But before engaging in that critical work, let's start with a description of what my Camino program entailed. Put simply, it incorporated the dimensions of religious pilgrimage I discussed earlier: performance, spectacle, displacement, and community.

In terms of performance, the most consistent part of my Camino program was walking. Every day, rain or shine, we walked. Through hamlets and big towns, mountains, forests, and pastures, on pavement, dirt, and through cow shit, we walked. Sometimes the route was pleasant, such as the sections on old Roman roads. But for long sections, we were forced to walk alongside the national road. My program required the students to spend eleven days walking. Many of them sustained physical injuries. I saw panic attacks. The majority cried in front of me at some point. This was part of the course design.

Manuel, a large Galician man with a shaven head, was the local guide I hired each year. As a guide certified by the Spanish authorities, he was an encyclopedia of historical facts. But from my point of view, his primary job was to set our route each day.

The students often complained that Manuel provided terrible directions. There was some truth to that. His directions followed a formula: "Today, the first meeting point is at a bar, called . . . ," then something superfast in Galego, the local dialect that to my ear sounded like a mash-up of German and Portuguese. "What?" someone would ask. He would repeat the name of the hamlet quickly again, and then proceed with something like, "You are going to walk through a small hamlet. There will be a church on our left, a bar on your right. Then, there is a bridge. A rock. Another bar. Pass by all of that and stop at the bar on our right. You can't miss it." We missed it every time.

But their complaints and mine were really about a lack of control. We did not know where we were going, what the weather would be, or when we would eat lunch. We did not know whether our knees would feel better or worse that day, how long the walk would take, or whether the hotel would have hot water or Wi-Fi. The Camino was in control. High-achieving students, many with diagnosed anxiety issues, didn't like that. I didn't like that. But at some point, we gave in and just walked.

We measured our days on the Camino in kilometers, completing twenty to thirty km a day (thirteen to eighteen miles). We began the day at 7:30 a.m. with a Spanish breakfast of pastries, toast, cheese, and ham. By 8:30, Manuel gathered us to explain the topography for the day with one of his signature descriptors, such as "Today it is a false flat," by which he meant it would be uphill all day. Then, by 9:00, we were on our way, following the yellow arrows that mark the route. We reached our next inn by 4:00 p.m., where we took showers and did sink laundry. Class was at 6:30, followed by "family dinner" at 8:00—my favorite time of the day. Then, I headed straight to bed while students streamed Netflix in their rooms. And the next day, we repeated. And the next. The daily routine was both enjoyable for its simplicity and incredibly monotonous. My students identified the repetition as part of what allowed for self-introspection. As Kristy put it, "When you walk, you think."

For almost every pilgrim—including my young students—walking the Camino involved some suffering. Physical problems ranged from something called the pilgrim flu—a nasty combination of food poisoning, exhaustion, and fever—to sore knees, inflamed tendons, and shin splints. Blisters were the most common affliction. Manuel attributed them to walking too fast. I got them every year, from the heat generated by walking for so many hours, no matter my speed. But I didn't mind since blisters came with status on the Camino. A legitimate pilgrim was one who had blistered and calloused feet once they arrived at Santiago.

My wilderness-savvy teaching assistant Sam was horrified to learn that the most common advice for dealing with blisters from locals was to sew them: take a needle and thread and sew an X onto a blister, leaving the thread to act as a wick. To Sam, this was a clear recipe for infection: a dirty piece of thread leading germs right into the blister. Yet I must admit it was my preferred method of treatment. I acknowledge that it sounds medieval, but that was the point. Sewing blisters was part of pilgrim performance. It was part of how those of us walking as secular pilgrims claimed to be doing it right.

The suffering was not just physical on the Camino, it was mental as well. To walk all day, knowing you must walk again all day tomorrow, is hard. There is always a day when the group hits a mental wall and starts complaining. I found it was often on our sixth day of walking. "I don't have time to read my novel." "When am I supposed to work on my music?" "I don't have enough downtime, me time." "This is pilgrimage!" I said one year, throwing my hands up in the air. "It's supposed to be hard." My reaction demonstrates that I thought the physical and mental challenges were part of what made the journey educational. It is true that the students who felt the most accomplished once we reached Santiago were the ones who at some point were not sure they would make it. But self-satisfaction is not necessarily a sign of successful learning.

Our pilgrimage involved accessories. Some were practical, such as a backpack, a sturdy pair of waterproof hiking boots, and a raincoat. Many pilgrims used walking sticks or a wooden staff. My students preferred the latter for their pilgrim authenticity. I opted for the former for their ergonomic correctness. Other props were symbolic. Medieval pilgrims wore a scallop shell—associated with various legends of St. James—and used it as a handy makeshift bowl. Today, many pilgrims attach a shell to their pack or around their neck as a marker of their status as pilgrim.

I provided every one of my students with a *credencial*, also known as a pilgrim passport. This document has been the official church accreditation since the Middle Ages. The credencial is printed on accordion-folded card stock. The pilgrim lists their personal data and starting location on the first page. The rest of the document has blank boxes to stamp, with a space for a final stamp administered at the Pilgrim Office of the Diocese of Santiago. Along the route, pilgrims collect stamps at churches, hostels, monasteries, cafés, and bars. Because the passport must be stamped and dated at least twice a day to earn a certificate of completion, it creates a visible record of progress through northern Spain.

The community that gave meaning to our journey included people we encountered during our walk, who shared with us their experiences with pilgrimage. Since Manuel has guided tours on the Camino for decades, he arranged conversations for my students with everyone from Father Javier, the Benedictine monk who leads the order in Rabanal; to Luis, an ambitious local hotelier in Ambasmestas who grew up on Camino; to Luis's mother, Pilar, who serves my favorite version of Galician broth on the Camino, and whose uncle was the local priest who first marked the Camino with yellow arrows.

Because we walked as a class, our social dynamics influenced everyone's experience of pilgrimage. Walking with a group, for instance, encouraged oversharing—almost a secular form of confession—by creating what was perceived as a safe space for messy emotional interactions. Students reported telling one another, and sometimes me, things even their best friends at home didn't know. As Jane, one of my former students, wrote to me in an email, "On the Way, I could exchange life stories (often extremely personal ones) with complete strangers but be comforted by our shared connection as pilgrims." Sometimes, the listening was what mattered. As Lucas processed some tough feelings about his dad, he told me that "most meaningful were the conversations in which I was merely a privileged guest, hearing about the horrors, fears, and struggles that in many ways define the people I was with." He credited the Camino for these interactions. "Those conversations and insights *could* happen anywhere, but they simply *wouldn't*, and especially not to the great frequency that they did on the Camino."

In addition, I tried to create opportunities for self-reflection during the program. For example, for one leg of the journey, I had students walk in silence; for another portion, they took a twenty-four-hour tech-free pledge. Every day, they were required to journal. These are parts of my course design that now give me pause because they reinforced the idea that the Camino experience was primarily valuable as a form of self-discovery. While I don't want students to think the only purpose of walking the Camino is intercultural competency, I also don't want them to consider religious ritual merely something to instrumentalize for personal growth.

So far, I have described the performance of pilgrimage in my Camino program, the physical things we did—walk, suffer, dress the part, collect stamps, and overshare—as well as the role of community. The Camino was also meaningful because of things we saw: the spectacle aspect of our pilgrimage.

The Iron Cross (Cruz de Ferro) was one of our first stops. In most years, on our first day of walking, we arrived at the highest point on the French Way (nearly a mile above sea level), where we found a simple iron cross atop a thirty-foot, weathered wooden mast, surrounded by an enormous pile of stones and other mementos. No one is sure of its origins, but one theory is that it was a marker of a border between territories during Roman times. By the eleventh century, pilgrims would carry a stone from the start of their journey to leave at the Iron Cross as part of their penance. Today non-Catholic pilgrims carry and deposit rocks and other tokens of emotional burdens that they hope to relieve themselves of. In this way, a religious penitential system has been reimagined as personalized therapy, authorized by the historical significance of a particular location.

Some of my students carried a stone from home to add to the enormous pile of mementos at the cross. Those who didn't felt a touch of regret. Lucas, for example, told me in an email about feeling anxious as we were approaching the Iron Cross:

> I wanted to follow the rules of the land, granting my pain to a stone, and leaving it behind at the base of the cross. But I could not think of anything. I kept trying to force my thoughts to work on assessing what traumas I had experienced to find the important ones, but they kept wandering off. That continued until we were probably minutes away, and suddenly, I found myself thinking of my dad, a delicate topic, but one which I had never thought actually bothered me. Evidently, I was very wrong, as shown by the pain I have discovered, made familiar, addressed, and finally, learned from.

In Lucas's case, encountering the Iron Cross was enough to force him, as he said, to lift a burden from deep within himself. The relationship with his dad that he alluded to here became the focus of most of his journal entries on the Camino after the Iron Cross. Once we reached Santiago, his final reflection was a gut-wrenching letter to his dad that was angry, poetic, raw, and entirely unexpected. And he credits the Iron Cross for beginning that process of reflection.

For those of us who didn't bring a stone, the Iron Cross was still a spectacle. We watched as pilgrims walked up slowly and left a stone, a note, or a stuffed animal. I never realized how odd it was to sit under a tree and observe this pilgrim ritual until the year we saw a drone flying over the cross, filming the scene. Our group was outraged at this voyeurism, even though we were engaged in something similar: viewing other pilgrims emote at the Iron Cross, hoping it would make us feel something as well.

Visiting sacred objects along the Camino, such as the physical remains of a saint or their personal effects, would have been one of the motivations for a medieval pilgrim. Many Catholics believe these relics make a deeper religious experience possible, because they confront us with the presence of God, and are thus an opportunity to know God in a deeper way. For my non-Catholic students, these items were significant to their experience, but differently so. They were historical artifacts that connected us to a tradition of pilgrimage, and created opportunities, if not for prayer, at least for deep introspection and reflection. Over the course of the journey, we saw dozens of relics, including two purported holy grails, and of course, the remains of St. James.

Relics were also an opportunity to observe the religious practice of others. For instance, some years we took a longer route to pass by a monastery in Samos to see what is claimed to be a thorn from Christ's crown. The monastery is impressive, nestled in a valley, with a spectacular courtyard filled with fruit trees and fresco paintings. Still inhabited by monks, it was an important Clunaic monastery during the height of the Camino's popularity. Today it houses several significant copies of the Codex Calixtinus, the twelfth-century text about the pilgrim routes through France and Spain. But a thorn purportedly from Christ's crown is the relic that draws hundreds of Christian pilgrims each day. I was unimpressed with the "stick" in the glass case, but nonetheless moved by the large group of bused-in pilgrims who filed solemnly past it and took many photographs. To them, this thorn was being closer to God. For me, observing them was being closer to the human experience of religion, and that was powerful.

Perhaps the most obvious sacred places pilgrims visit along the Camino are parish churches and cathedrals, whether to get a stamp, attend a Mass, or merely take a peek. Paige remembers the humble small old churches on the Camino. "They weren't glamorous or richly decorated, but they were sincere. They felt real." Kurt, a musician who carried a guitar for the entire Camino, was struck by the acoustics of the simple church in Portomarín. As we were leaving a Mass, he leaned over and told me, "I wish I could stand in front and sing something." Other churches we saw were grander, such as cathedrals. Kurt was struck by the aesthetic of these sacred spaces as well. "The architecture of these places was meant to inspire . . . it hopes to evoke a certain state of mind." The Cathedral of Santiago made him feel "like the Lord is bearing down on you." Note that Kurt, my self-declared atheist who considered religion the weird superstition of other people, was nonetheless able to feel something when confronted with the religious aesthetics of sacred spaces. He made this experience more comfortable by disconnecting the "state of mind" the religious aesthetics put him into, from the devotional worldviews they were informed by and meant to inspire.

Masses addressing the specific challenges of being a pilgrim are offered in churches along the Camino. All are welcome at them, regardless of their religious affiliation. My students were required to attend at least two. The first was in a small parish church in Rabanal, the night before we started walking. The plaster of this twelfth-century church is crumbling, the pews are small and uncomfortable, but the space is intimate and charming. It is packed every night for a pilgrim Mass offered by the three-monk Benedictine community that lives in that hamlet. A brief spoken sermon is offered, but the sung version of the liturgy called Vespers is what gives me goose bumps every year. There is no organ, only a repeated melody, with Latin words, a communal liturgy led by the monks in which the entire congregation participates. Every year I find the Vespers haunting, solemn, and intimate.

The climactic act of our pilgrimage is arriving in Santiago, even if the last day is arguably the least aesthetically pleasing stage. It requires walking by an airport, and then through the unattractive modern city outskirts of Santiago before finally reaching the old city. Then, we pass by the cathedral's north entrance, through a short tunnel where bagpipe players perform traditional Galician music. Finally, we reach the Praza do Obradoiro in front of the west facade of the cathedral, the official end of the Camino.

Walking as a group has many advantages, some of which I have already discussed, but facilitating a meaningful arrival is one of the most important. After the daily routine of pilgrimage, to finish can be somewhat of a letdown. During the walk, my students relied on one another to get through the journey, and the closeness that created made it much easier for them to have an experience of completion that they were looking for. Take the first year. That was the year we had a day of unexpected snow and we walked almost every day in rain. Manuel and I bickered for a large portion of the trip. There was an internal faction between two groups of girls. I wasn't sure we would make it to Santiago, so the students weren't sure either. Despite all this, or maybe because of it, when we arrived in Santiago, we hugged. We sat down in the square and cried. We were proud, not just of ourselves, but of the group. "The Camino was meaningful to me because by the end, I felt like I found a sense of belonging," Jackie, a pharmacy major, told me. "I really cared about everyone in the group and somehow felt that everyone cared about me."

Even after arriving, there are additional pilgrim rituals to perform, such as visiting St. James's relics resting in a silver chest under the Cathedral of Santiago. Entering the crypt can be an awkward experience for my non-Christian students, especially since they don't believe the chamber holds the bones of anyone of particular significance. Many students prefer the ritual of hugging the jewel-encrusted bust of St. James that sits high behind the altar. Lucas mentioned this as a particularly significant moment for him: "Standing on the steps before hugging the statue of St. James and looking back at the altar on the way out is probably the closest I have ever been to a definable sensation of a Christian God."

Most of my students obtain a Compostela, the official certificate of completion. All summer, long lines of pilgrims snake through the Pilgrim Office's courtyard in Santiago, and some years, we waited over two hours to receive our Compostelas. The requirements were simple: completing the last hundred kilometers (roughly 62 miles) of the Camino on foot, collecting at least two stamps a day on our credencial, and having religious or spiritual motivations. The reward was a stylized certificate, complete with a hand calligraphy–rendered Latinized version of our name and the date of our arrival.

As a certification authorized by the Catholic Church, the Compostela is an odd document for a non-Catholic pilgrim to want. Nevertheless, most of my students were determined to get one, and spent a lot of time concerned that injury would prevent them from completing every stage of the walk. Manuel poked them about this, asking, "Why do you care about a piece of paper from the Church if you are not a believer?" Part of the reason was that my Honors students collected achievements: awards, minors, and lines on their résumés. Kristy said she wanted a Compostela as "proof, or something physical I could keep to remember that I did it. . . . it was like winning a medal at the end of a race, even if it is just a participant's medal." A Compostela was the certification of experiential religion done well.

Obtaining a Compostela requires a declaration of what kind of pilgrim you are. The official categories have shifted slightly, but the first year we walked, the options were religious, spiritual, or cultural. Most of my non-Christian students chose spiritual. Paige told me, "Religious didn't feel right for what we had done and neither did cultural" because "it was more than just a painful physical journey; it was a soulful one too." She explained why in an email to me in her usual dramatically poetic language. "It wrung out of us all the nonsense, all the noise, all of the everything that wasn't us and left behind a stinging awareness of our own strength and messiness. We wrestled with our own demons, our boredom, ourselves, and came out feeling cleaner and more whole on the other side."

Initially, Lara had reservations about declaring spiritual motives in Santiago. "By the end it didn't feel strange at all putting down spiritual. I think there was definitely a sense of having earned it—mine was a hard-fought Camino." That was true, as her foot injury made her walk physically painful. "I thought of the Compostela as a way of legitimizing the pain I went through to get there, I guess," she said. "I wanted something to show that I had done it."

Lucas also selected spiritual. "It would have been false of me to select the religious purpose, but I still felt a deep affinity for the entirety of the experience. The emotional turmoil, the deep introspection, and the regular interpersonal connection that arose from shared experiences all built an undeniably spiritual experience for me." "What does 'spiritual' mean to you?" I asked. "I do not think I know," he said. "But just because I cannot say what caused it does not mean it was any less real." For Lucas, spiritual helped explain the part of the Camino his rational mind could not.

Kurt, the student who insisted he did not care about religion at all, selected the cultural category and was quite vocal to the group about this decision. But he did stand in line at the Pilgrim Office to get a Compostela. "I was torn on wanting the Compostela, since that had some kind of authority to it—like it would help to legitimize the experience," he said. "On the other hand," he admitted, "I also didn't want to receive it. I didn't want to falsely represent myself, nor cheapen the value of this experience and this symbol for people who sincerely believe in this stuff." Technically as a cultural pilgrim, he shouldn't have received a Compostela, but he did. He felt this authorized his experience in some way. "It was a bit of external validation, but it also feels like a fluke that I got it at all."

Over the years, a few students have decided not to apply for a Compostela. Jackie told me, "I did not get the Compostela because I didn't feel like I needed one. To me it was just a piece of paper. My credencial, the pictures we have, and just the knowledge that I walked are most important to me." For Matt, the reason was slightly more personal: he had walked for his mother, who had passed in the previous year of breast cancer. And she wasn't Catholic, so he didn't think she would have wanted a Compostela. But it was because he believed the Compostela meant something—Catholic authorization of his journey—that he didn't want one, not because he thought it was just a piece of paper.

Our last act as pilgrims is to attend the pilgrim Mass in the impressive Cathedral of Santiago the day after we arrive. In summer, it is standing room only, where dirty pilgrims and tourists fresh off cruise ships crowd into the nave and transept. The pilgrim Mass is long, with very little in English. If we are lucky, the Botafumeiro makes an appearance, an enormous incense burner that weighs 180 pounds. Suspended from the barrel-vaulted ceiling by a series of pulleys, the Botafumeiro requires eight men to swing it and reaches speeds up to fifty mph as it swings through the transept, almost to the ceiling at each end. The first year, it covered me with ash that made my skin tingle.

When I use the analytical lens of appropriation to look back at the course design of my Camino program, I can see that I had inadvertently helped authorize interpretations of pilgrimage that made my students feel that they were indeed "doing it right." Take the readings I assigned. We began with Nancy Frey's classic ethnography of Camino pilgrims, *Pilgrim Stories: On and off the Road to Santiago*, because it emphasizes the diversity of pilgrim experience, which prepared my students for the sort of judgments they would face as pilgrims who did not walk "the entire Camino" and utilized a luggage transfer service.[21] Put another way, this text gave my students ways to frame their pilgrimage as just as "authentic" as someone who walked 500 miles, carried all their possessions on their back, or was motivated by religious devotion.

But reflecting on my choice to assign Frey, I now realize I used her work to help construct a liberal idea of pilgrimage in which any form of transportation was permissible, spending money was encouraged to support the local economy, and nonreligious motivations were as legitimate as religious ones. The downside was that this framing allowed all my students to believe they were defining pilgrimage for themselves, and this hid how their experience was constructed by me, the local tourism industry, the Spanish government, and the Roman Catholic Church, among others.

Since my students were very committed to the idea that some authentic Camino experience exists, it is not surprising that one of the most intense exchanges of my program occurred during a discussion when I trying to challenge this notion. For class that day, I had assigned anthropologist Alexander Moore's article "Walt Disney World:

Bounded Ritual Space and the Playful Pilgrimage Center."[22] Moore argues that Walt Disney World was constructed much like a pilgrimage center, insofar as it features a bounded space, shared activities for visitors, and the presentation of symbols. Moore refers to a visit to the Magic Kingdom as "playful pilgrimage," a rite of passage he thinks is particularly well suited for secular society. "At a time when some proclaim God is dead," Moore writes, "North Americans may take comfort in the truth that Mickey Mouse reigns at the baroque capital of the Magic Kingdom and that Walt Disney is his prophet."[23]

I assigned this article to challenge the idea that there is a clear distinction between tourists and pilgrims as well as between secular and religious ritual spaces. The first year of my program, the reading worked as planned. My students argued with such conviction that visiting Walt Disney World was an important American rite of passage that I booked a visit for my then seven-year-old daughter, despite having previously vowed never to give into this cultural pressure.

But the reading worked differently in 2017. That year, the students doubled down and were adamant that since the Disney corporation constructed and controlled the experience of the Magic Kingdom, it was fake. One student in that cohort had spent a summer interning at the Magic Kingdom, and shared stories about secret tunnels that allowed trash collection to take place without visitors noticing, because apparently sanitation detracts from the Disney experience. And we were all fascinated to learn that no redheads were hired to play the princess Ariel for fear that they would be mistaken for the mermaid when outside Disney World. These details all confirmed for my students what they thought they already knew: the experience of visiting the Magic Kingdom might be organized like a pilgrimage, but it was an artificial experience, created to make money. Its inauthenticity made it "morally tainted."[24]

In contrast, they defended their Camino experience, steeped in hundreds of years of tradition, as an authentic pilgrimage and thus completely positive.[25] The reasons the students gave for this determination are the same characteristics that make pilgrimage religiously transformative: the performance of pilgrimage, including walking and suffering; the spectacles of pilgrimage, including relics and Masses; the displacement of pilgrimage, expressed as annoyance at Manuel's directions; and the community the pilgrim becomes part of. It was not despite the religious dimensions, but because of them, that my non-Christian students found meaning on the Camino. Put differently, the religious character of the Camino was part of how they knew it was authentic, and that authenticity is what allowed them to justify the religious appropriation.

I caused quite a ruckus in 2017 when I pushed back against my students' categorization of the Camino as real and Disney World as artificial. I insisted that there was nothing "natural" about how their pilgrimage had occurred. When pressed, they conceded that the Catholic Church still has an interest in promoting pilgrimage to Santiago, that Manuel was trained by the Spanish state to tell a specific version of Camino history, and that local business owners had an economic stake in promoting an ecumenical version of the Camino. But they were shocked when I mentioned that I, too, had curated their experience; for instance, by assigning specific texts to intellectually frame the experience or requiring daily journal entries to encourage personal reflection. I had "scripted" their experience, I told them, with silent walks timed for certain remote sections of the path, and a variety of team-building activities to foster intimacy. In fact, I pointed out, I had scheduled their entire day, including where and what they ate, when they took breaks, and who would be their roommate. They had believed themselves to be genuine pilgrims, and realizing that was the result of an intentional pedagogical design was a letdown.

The presumption that something authentic can be experienced is part of what justifies study abroad programs as well as many religious appropriations, but authenticity can be defined in various ways. Sociologist Ning Wang, for instance, describes three models for authenticity: objectivist, constructionist, and existentialist. The objectivist model assumes authenticity emanates from the site. In the case of the Camino, that might be the tomb of St. James. Few of my students believed the bones of an apostle were really housed in the Cathedral of Santiago. They did, however, think it was important that the route we walked, marked today by yellow arrows, was traveled by pilgrims for centuries before us. This model of authenticity fits with what Wang calls the constructionist model. In this model, the authenticity of a pilgrimage is created by the socio-public discourse about it. My students were convinced they were having an authentic pilgrim experience because others—including me—had told them they were.

But most of my students insisted that their Camino was authentic because they had internalized what Wang calls an existentialist model of authenticity. In this model, the authenticity of a pilgrimage resides not in an object or destination, or even the discourse about it, but in the subject engaged in the practice. According to Wang, existential authenticity "denotes a special state of Being in which one is true to oneself, and acts as a counter dose to the loss of the 'true self' in public roles and public spheres."[26] It is a customer satisfaction conception of authenticity. If a student felt that the Camino pilgrimage was authentic, it was, and pointing out that I had constructed that experience for them was like lifting the curtain on the Wizard of Oz: upsetting because the illusion had felt so real. When I insisted their Camino was just as constructed as Disney World, I also challenged their right to define for themselves the meaningfulness of the experience, which for many relied on maintaining that the experience was unmediated by anyone, including the professor who had organized the entire trip and would be grading them.

Judging, Erasing, and Asserting Protestant Privilege

No matter how meaningful the students found the experience, no matter how much I enjoyed it, there is no denying that my Camino program required appropriation of religion for course credit. However, unlike the case of solidarity hijab, there is not a single group of religious insiders who have clearly articulated the exploitation caused by the Camino's popularity. Instead, we find that several actors experience harmful effects from programs like my Camino course: the students, the local population, and lay Catholics, among others.

Before embarking, my students often envision the experience as one in which they will enact their best selves. "I will walk every day, eat healthy, reflect deeply, and therefore become a better person," they think. In practice, I observed something less inspirational: hierarchies reinforced, vices encouraged, and rules relaxed in the pursuit of self-satisfaction. Overeating. Smoking. Loud, obnoxious behavior. Random hookups. The first year I ran my program, we met a "temporary Camino couple" in their sixties who spoke openly about their spouses back home. Manuel told me stories of local bus drivers who cater to pilgrims and have extramarital affairs all the time, and of his own experience of female pilgrims pressing up against him after too many drinks.

A shared system of norms does develop on the Camino, but as increasingly more non-Christians complete the journey to Santiago, these norms are shaped less by moral theology and more by consumption and hedonism. For many pilgrims, the Camino is a space of fewer, not more, rules.

The most common bad behavior I saw on the Camino was judging other pilgrims. For instance, we heard over and over that walking the

500 miles from St. Jean Pied de Port was required for doing "the entire Camino." From a historical point of view, this is ridiculous. Traditionally, pilgrimage started from the pilgrim's home. "The entire Camino" is a modern invention and St. Jean as a starting point is arbitrary. But as an idea, it is powerful. My students felt their pilgrimage was deficient because we walked only 150 miles.

Other forms of judgment contribute to a pilgrim hierarchy: those carrying packs, superior to those paying for a luggage shuttle service; those staying in the bare-bones hostels called *albergues*, superior to those staying in three-star inns; and those who were walking, superior to those on a bus tour. It was hard not to feel superior when a bus full of clean, smartly dressed pilgrims pulled up to the Samos monastery to view the thorn from Christ's crown, when we had been walking for days to reach the same destination.

We judge others because of our own insecurity—it is easier to say someone else is doing the Camino wrong than to feel confident we are doing it right. But the practice of judging others on the Camino creates a competitive atmosphere that rarely contributes positively to anyone's experience. I would argue it is also decisively against the religious ethos of pilgrimage as a great equalizer.

One hierarchy my students internalized was the belief that religious travelers were doing pilgrimage right, or at least much better, than were leisure tourists. Scholarship about a decade ago was concerned with defining tourists and pilgrims as distinct groups, but more recent work in both tourism and pilgrimage studies has accepted that the boundary is blurred. I am not interested in defending the idea that tourists and pilgrims are distinct categories, but I do think the categories remain analytically interesting because they are both used to justify various experiences of travel to sites of religious interest.

On the Camino, for instance, self-described pilgrims and tourists to some extent depend on one another to give meaning to their experience. We felt particularly proud of our long day of walking to the Samos monastery, when that bus full of visitors arrived shortly after us. To them, we were pilgrims because we traveled by foot, and were therefore part of the spectacle those people were there to see. But as devoted Christians from Korea, they arguably had more of a claim to the title of pilgrim than we did. Their presence authorized the relic the monastery housed, and thus justified our detour to see it.

Although, for the most part, various types of pilgrims and tourists coexist on the Camino without a problem, conflict can occur when the two groups might be confused for each other. For instance, the Cathedral of Santiago is visited not only by pilgrims at the end of their journey but also by hundreds of cruise line tourists who visit Santiago only for the day. Catholic theologian Keith Egan described this uncomfortable scene. "Both groups of visitors shift uneasily in each other's company, the pilgrims unhappy to have to wait in line with adulterating tourists and the day-trippers somewhat disconcerted by the odor emanating from such scruffy visitors."[27] The discomfort occurs not because the two groups are so different, but because in that space, "they are not different enough."[28]

For my students, the internalization of a pilgrim-tourist hierarchy created a conundrum. They desperately wanted to be "legit pilgrims," as they put it, but most of them also wanted to avoid being perceived as religious. Much like the non-Muslim woman who wears a hijab as a sign of solidarity only because she feels confident no one will mistake her for an actual Muslim woman, my students were only comfortable with a pilgrim identity if they could conceptualize it as something other than devotional. Some adopted the label "spiritual pilgrim" to communicate that they thought they were successfully walking the line. "Spiritual" used in this manner did not mean "irreligious," but rather religious in a way that the students found acceptable because it was disconnected from religious identity, institutions, values, and doctrines. Kurt insisted that his pilgrimage was purely educational, and that as a student he was neither pilgrim nor tourist, and yet able to participate fully in activities associated with both. For my students, claiming to be a spiritual or educational pilgrim was based on a hierarchy in which these types of pilgrims were superior to religious ones because they remained unaffected by the aspects of religion considered less compatible with secular modern life.

Pilgrimage is northern Spain's main tourist product, and its growing popularity has been a boost to the local economy. The Camino allowed for the development of less explored areas whose valuable cultural resources, appealing to pilgrim tourists, enticed them to stay longer and spend more there to pursue their interests.[29] Entire towns along the routes have been built or revitalized by people looking to make their living off pilgrimage, and a variety of businesses in northern Spain—such as restaurants, cafés, bars, hotels, hostels, and stores—depend on the Camino for their success. And this has caused new economic pressures on the area. During my 2018 program, several inn owners told me the Camino was at capacity, and that while they appreciated being busy, the current level was not sustainable to them personally. They also feared it would fundamentally alter the Camino experience, which is marketed in part as a journey that allows for isolation and solitude.

Others have specific complaints about the effect of pilgrims on the local economy. In July 2017, protesters in Logroño, located in the northern Spanish region of La Rioja, launched a campaign called STOP Gentrificación Logroño. They stood outside two pilgrim hostels with signs that read "Pilgrims go home" and "Less walking and more working." In interviews with the local press, the protesters pointed out that pilgrims spend very little money in their city during their stay. Hostels are free or very inexpensive, and many pilgrims eat as cheaply as possible. Despite La Rioja being an illustrious wine-making region, protesters claimed pilgrims are dragging down the quality of food and wine available because they prefer their food cheap and basic. Protesters also blamed pilgrims for the rent hikes in the city as more and more housing is converted into short-term tourist apartments.[30]

An alumna of my 2016 Camino Dialogue, Sara Scott, was an international business major who became interested in pilgrims' spending habits during their time in Spain. She won research funding from Northeastern to return to the Camino in the summer of 2017 for a month to study the impact of pilgrimage on the local Spanish economy. Scott asked one hundred English-speaking pilgrims to complete a survey once they reached Praza do Obradoiro in Santiago. She found that her respondents spent an average of fifteen euros a day on food and less than ten euros on nightly lodging, proving the Logroño's protesters' claim that pilgrims were paying only for cheap housing and meals.

But Scott's most significant finding, which surprised both of us, was that the religious pilgrims spent far more during their Camino than did ones who self-identified as tourists. She found that, on average, religious pilgrims spent 652 euros during their journey, whereas the tourists spent only 352. This difference is explained mostly by the fact that the trips of religious pilgrims are, on average, nine days longer than are visits by those who consider themselves tourists. But Scott also found that tourists and pilgrims reported different spending habits: tourists were more willing to spend money on products or luxury services, but pilgrims tended to limit their spending to items—such as food and housing—necessary to make it to Santiago.[31] Scott's findings suggest that as increasing numbers of tourists walk the Camino each year, they will contribute to the local economy in ways that support further gentrification.

What is missing from the marketing of the Camino to potential tourists and pilgrims alike is Spain's complicated and often violent history of religious pluralism. Historically, the Iberian Peninsula, where the Camino is located, was home to a wide range of religious traditions, including Celtic, Greek, and Roman animist and polytheist practices. Christians didn't obtain a stronghold until the Visigoth occupation in the fifth century, and that ended in 711, when Visigoth decline allowed Muslim Moors from North Africa to claim this territory. Islamic rule of the area known today as Spain lasted seven centuries.

Under Islamic rule, Christian, Jews, and Muslims interacted culturally in new ways in the region, leading experts to call this period La Convivencia ("The Coexistence"). It is worth noting that many historians consider this period of Islamic rule the golden age of Spanish intellectual and artistic production, even as the rest of Europe was stuck in the Dark Ages.[32] In 1492, Muslim control of the region ended with the fall of the city of Granada to Christian forces. The Muslim population, over 500,000, was forced to choose between conversion to Christianity, expulsion from the region, or death.

However, there is another way to describe the period of Moorish rule of Spain: as the invasion and occupation of Iberia by foreign forces whom Christians fought to expel for over 700 years. In this version, from 711 to 1492, rather than being a golden age of cultural production, Spain was occupied by outsiders, and the Reconquista was an effort to reclaim Spain as Christian. This is the narrative that is most common in Spain today.

Consider now the role of the Camino within the context of these competing narratives of Spanish history. Suddenly, the timing of the discovery of St. James's tomb, at around 813, is significant. This was during Islamic rule and provided Christian authorities with a pilgrimage destination that could help bring more Christians into the region. Then, legends circulated that St. James had inserted himself into mounting tensions between Christians and Muslims by miraculously returning as Matamoros, a knight helping defeat the Muslim Moors. Proudly displayed all over Spain, there are still visual representations of Matamoros murdering Moors, crushing their heads and bodies under the hoofs of his white steed. I have seen them in the cathedrals of Burgos, Granada, Toledo, and Cordoba. Once you know to look for him, he is everywhere.

I find the statue of Matamoros in the Cathedral of Santiago the most egregious. It is a medium-size statue, placed behind a metal grate in the north side of the transept. Over concerns that this, an explicit depiction of violence against Muslims, would make the cathedral a target of Al-Qaeda, white daisies were added to the base, partially covering the Moors that St. James is crushing. The daisies literally cover up the truth of religious history in Spain.

The Camino's part in Spanish history provides an opportunity to understand a local history of religious conflict and violence. And although most of the pilgrims we met were aware of only a sanitized version of that history, my Camino program used readings and discussions to expose students to the ways the Camino has contributed to and benefited from Christian domination of the area. When my students arrived at the cathedral in Santiago, for instance, I marched them right over to the Matamoros statue whose victims had been prettied up. I asked them to think about what it meant that we had just walked not only to Sanctus Jacobus but also to this more gruesome version of St. James. Sometimes, the culture we borrow, I told them, is guilty of violence. Othering Muslims allowed for the expulsion and forced conversion of Muslims in Spain and continues to fuel hate crimes and hate speech against Muslims in Spain today. I likened ignoring this history to walking—literally, in this case—past the scene of a crime.

Statue of St. James as Matamoros, slayer of the Moors, in the Cathedral of Saint Mary, Burgos, Spain. (iStock/mahroch)

Even if I avoided the erasure of the religious violence in the Camino's history, my Camino program inadvertently perpetuated another form of exploitation involving the assertion of what I call "Protestant privilege"—claiming that Protestantism is the correct or normative expression of Christianity as well as assuming that all forms of religion should follow a Protestant model in form and structure. This form of exploitation was dramatically enacted during my 2016 program, which included four Evangelical students. These students were part of a campus religious organization, knew one another well, and thus were emboldened to express criticisms of Catholicism throughout the program. They were convinced that their interpretations of Christianity were the only right ones. The other students dubbed them the "God Squad." They didn't seem to mind.

The God Squad began their Camino journey hostile to the Catholic nature of the pilgrimage route. They were suspicious of relics. Distrustful of anything that had to do with Catholic institutions. Concerned about hierarchies that mediated their access to religious knowledge. To embrace the Camino as their own, the first step in any form of religious appropriation, they reconceptualized this journey as Protestant instead of Catholic. I noticed a couple of tactics they used: framing their participation on the Camino as a personal, unmediated experience; using it as a form of reconciliation of Catholicism and Protestantism; and trying to convert the nonreligious students in the program, effectively co-opting a study abroad program into an Evangelical missionary trip.

A particularly vivid example of this dynamic occurred on day six of the walk that year, the day we stopped in Portomarín for the night. As I mentioned earlier, something dramatic always happens on day six, when the group seems to hit an emotional wall. That year was no exception.

The topic of class discussion that day was sacraments in the Catholic Church, including how different the Catholic Eucharist is from what most Protestants call Communion. For both, this ritual commemorates the Last Supper of Jesus with his disciples before his crucifixion. It involves the eating of bread or a wafer and the drinking of wine. For Catholics, the wafer and wine, once consecrated by a priest, become the body and blood of Christ. This is called the doctrine of transubstantiation. In Protestant Communion, bread and wine are merely symbolic of Christ.

Protestants welcome the baptized to participate in Communion. In some Protestant churches, this means baptism in a particular tradition; for others, all Christian baptisms count. In the Catholic Church, however, you must believe in the doctrine of transubstantiation to participate in the Eucharist. It is also preferable that you have been baptized in the Catholic Church and have been to confession so that you are in a "state of grace." Putting it more simply, we can say that in most Protestant churches, Communion is allowable for all Christians, but in most Catholic churches, it is limited to Catholics in good standing. For instance, I was baptized as Catholic, but since I have never been to confession, and I don't believe in transubstantiation, I have never taken Communion in a Catholic Mass.

During our class discussion about Catholic Eucharist, the God Squad, true to form, shared their opinion that Communion was the same for all Christians, and that it shouldn't matter what church it took place in. I pushed back. "To you, it might be, but what would it mean to take the beliefs of your Catholic hosts seriously?" One of the God Squad, whom I'll call Chris, raised his hand and said slowly, "For me, as a faithful Christian, my Camino has been about coming to peace with Catholicism. I now see how much in common all Christians have." "That is great, Chris," I said as patiently as I could, quite used to his attempt to shut down conversation by claiming expertise in all matters Christian based on his being a faithful Evangelical. "But I wonder how you might respond to the question I'm raising. If 'Communion is for everyone' is a Protestant idea, could asserting it here, on a Catholic pilgrimage, be a form of privilege?"

Chris shot a look to Abigail, another member of the God Squad. She shifted in her chair. There were a few moments of uncomfortable silence and then a quiet, red-headed Catholic student named Emily offered, "It is true that Communion is something pretty serious in the Catholic Church. I mean, my parents won't even take it if they haven't been to confession." I saw another Catholic student nod his head. Emily went on, "It does seem different than how I am hearing some of you talk about it."

I had thought naively that conversation went well, that we had raised some interesting, if uncomfortable, effects of taking the diversity of Christianity seriously. I thought that Chris had begun to see that claiming to speak on behalf of all Christian faithful was a form of erasure. But I was wrong.

After class, a small group of us headed to evening Mass at the local church. The group included the God Squad, who attended every optional church service possible, two Catholic students, and me. Because it was a small church, we were able to sit as a group: the God Squad together and the two Catholic students and I directly behind them.

The moment for the Eucharist came. The God Squad stood up. I didn't think, just reacted, and bent forward into the pew in front of me and whispered very slowly, "Sit back down." They did, reluctantly.

For the rest of the Mass, I was really upset because I knew I had messed up. My reaction was inappropriate. Encouraging them to think critically about religious differences within Christianity was one thing. Preventing them from a religious ritual they thought they were entitled to was another. In my attempt to teach them to see Communion through a Catholic lens, I had overstepped, becoming a scolding parent who put them in time-out.

Even worse, my shushing showed I was a bit of a hypocrite. I was frustrated at the God Squad for trying to own Christianity, and yet I was policing its borders as well by insisting that a Catholic Communion was only for Catholics.

I stopped everyone as we were leaving the church and asked them to huddle up. I took a breath. "I apologize for stopping you. It is not my job to tell you how to be a good Christian." Another breath. "I am sorry." The God Squad seemed pleased. When we got back to the inn for dinner, I overheard Abigail tell her end of the table, "Liz really messed up at Mass just now," and then saw her grin smugly.

As I sit and write about that day, I can see that I had overreacted. Who would have known those students were planning to participate in the Eucharist to colonize Christianity? Not the priest, not the other pilgrims. But I would have known. To me, the God Squad's attempt to take Communion felt especially disrespectful to the Catholic students sitting next to me, given that they knew these students would understand their actions as a transgression. But that was not enough to justify my whispered command.

Even if I had messed up that day, it was also a moment that helped me identify two additional forms of exploitation that occurred within my Camino program: decentering Catholics from the Christian experience and creating a crisis of faith.

Pilgrimage to Santiago started before the distinction between Catholic and Protestant existed. But given the critique of pilgrimage by leading Protestant Reformers, after the Reformation, the Camino lost most of its British, Dutch, and German Protestant pilgrims, while it remained an important destination for Catholics. Today, the Camino is institutionally maintained, supported, and promoted by the Catholic Church. A Catholic cathedral houses the remains of St. James. Catholic churches dot the route to Santiago. The Pilgrim Office, which issues Compostelas as certificates of completion, is run by the Metropolitan Archdiocese of Compostela.

Yet, despite the importance of Catholicism to this pilgrimage route, the God Squad made me aware of how Protestantism has become dominant in pilgrim culture. I saw up close how the God Squad domesticated the Camino's Christianity for their Protestant goals. Their reimagined Camino was no longer part of a penitentiary system but an experience of Protestant devotion. It was unmediated by the Catholic Church. They explicitly resisted any course material I introduced that was meant to highlight the diversity of global Christianity. Their experience of Camino did little more than reinforce their existing understanding of religion.

But the dominance of Protestantism was not something the God Squad introduced to the Camino; rather, it was a dynamic that we can observe on many levels. Catholic Masses in towns we passed through were empty, whereas pilgrim Masses, intentionally developed to appeal to a wide range of Christian and non-Christian pilgrims, were packed. This created a context in which the God Squad felt justified to participate in the Eucharist. The Catholicism of the pilgrimage has been diluted sometimes by the Catholic Church itself—such as granting Compostelas to non-Catholic and even non-Christian pilgrims—to make the experience universally accessible.

There is one more lesson I learned from the God Squad that year: If part of the goal of experiential study abroad is for students to become self-critical about their own cultural values, programs that focus on religion can lead to a crisis of faith, and that would be a profoundly offensive result. This seems a particular risk when students enroll in a study abroad program that focuses on what they consider to be their own religious tradition.

The God Squad were all white Evangelicals. In the United States, they had grown up as part of the religious majority and had enjoyed a support system that affirmed their Christian practice, including an active Christian student group on Northeastern's campus. However, as Protestants in Spain, they were a religious minority and had been confronted for the first time with the possibility that they did not have exclusive ownership of Christianity. Given how much course time I spent on the role of Islam in Spanish history, they also faced unsettling narratives of violence and oppression carried out in the name of Christianity. The God Squad dealt with what they perceived as challenges to their faith by doubling down on their belief that their version of Christianity was not only correct but also universalizable.

I was at a bit of a loss of what to do when the God Squad shifted class discussion to topics of a more personal devotional nature. I was confident that I knew quite a bit about the interaction of multiple religious traditions in Spain, the power dynamics that have created the modern Camino, and various forms of ethical thinking that can help us describe the pilgrim experience. But when it came to Christian faith, the God Squad were quite right: they were the experts. I did not have any insight to offer into a journey to become a better Christian.

This leads me to ask, What is the proper role, if any, for a religious studies instructor in guiding personal religious experiences that can occur in study abroad programs? I think the answer "none" is too glib. Like it or not, at least in intensive faculty-led study abroad programs like mine, instructors are often asked to take on the role of not only teacher but also mentor and even surrogate parent. When the topic of study is religion, some students will look to their instructor for religious guidance. My tactic has been to use scholarly readings to guide our class discussions of religion, and to encourage the working out of personal beliefs in informal group conversations that happen organically while we walk—in which, instead of me, their peers give advice and serve as sounding boards—or in daily journal entries. Sometimes Manuel steps into the role of religious guide. His personality, which I'd describe as Galician macho caveman meets poetic teddy bear, and his role as a judo coach, means he feels comfortable giving advice to young people about just about everything. He also identifies as Catholic and had spent a few years working in the Pilgrim Office of the Cathedral of Santiago, so he has his own devotional and work experience to draw on.

All my tactics to remain out of students' personal religious journeys, however, failed the year of the God Squad. That failure was seen in my scolding them in the Portomarín Catholic chapel but also in how uncomfortable the God Squad made some students in the group. What I intended to foster was an environment where students could confront discomfort and sit in it, not feel attacked or judged by their peers or me. And certainly, I had not intended to create an environment that encouraged a crisis of faith. But my failure shows that the stakes of study abroad programs that focus on religion can be quite different from those that concern other subject matters, and especially for students who identify with the religion they have signed up to have an immersive experience with.

Explicit theological reflection often occurs when a student engages in an experiential program that focuses on their own religion, independent of the instructor's intention.[33] As a religious studies professor, for instance, I am uncomfortable and frankly unqualified to guide personal theological learning for confessional insiders, and this is not the purpose of a liberal arts approach to religion. Put differently, I don't see my job as to assist with my student's religious formation—it is to provide context and analytical tools to understand and think critically about the role of religion in human life. And yet, to reiterate what has become a theme in this book, religion is not so easily controlled, especially in a real-world setting. Despite my intentions, I could not guarantee that the experience of the Camino for a Christian student would only be a case of humanistic learning.

Economic Inequality, Christian Hegemony, and the Hierarchy of Higher Education

My students hope that pilgrimage will be an experience in which they leave behind the expectations put on them in their normal life, so as to become the best version of themselves. The exploitations I enumerated tell a different story. As with other case studies in this book, existing structural injustices are not avoided during a pilgrimage; instead, they are illuminated and even intensified. In my Camino program, these include economic disparities, Christian hegemony, and a hierarchical theory of learning.

Medieval pilgrimage was meant to be a great equalizer. Kings and peasants walked the same path to Santiago in the hope of earning an indulgence for their sins. But today, the Camino exacerbates existing economic inequalities.

If walking the Camino is justified as a form of experiential learning, access to this form of learning depends in part on socioeconomic status. For US-based pilgrims, the cost of completing the Camino includes, at the very least, pricey airfare, often well over $1,000 during the prime tourist months of the summer. As my former student Sara Scott found, pilgrims can spend over 600 euros in Spain during their journey, making the cost of completing a pilgrimage to Santiago easily over $2,000 for an American. Pilgrims who complete the 500-mile route from St. Jean Pied de Port, France, to Santiago de Compostela, Spain, need to be able to afford a month without work, a reason that the journey is so popular among retirees or others with disposable income.

To enroll in my Camino Dialogue program, students must pay a fee on top of tuition for two courses. I keep this fee as low as possible, usually around $1,500, and the program covers their airfare, housing, and some meals. Northeastern has some scholarships for Dialogue fees. But studies have shown that the extra costs of study abroad make it less accessible to lower-income students. Ninety percent of US undergraduate students never go overseas, and cost is consistently ranked as the top reason for this.[34]

I agree with scholars of religion who insist consumption is part of the modern manifestation of religion.[35] But that doesn't mean that the forms of consumption entailed in religious appropriation don't cause harm. In the case of the Camino, its increasing popularity contributes to gentrification along the route in ways that worsen the unequal distribution of wealth. For instance, since pilgrim tourism is such a large part of the economy in northwest Spain, catering to pilgrims has changed everything from housing—increasing the number of short-term rentals—to dining options, now dominated by cheap pilgrim menus. As the STOP Gentrificación Logroño protesters pointed out, this exacerbates the challenges locals face in trying to access affordable housing and quality food.

While the success of Camino tourism has brought development along popular routes, it has also left the region vulnerable to fluctuations in the number of visitors to Spain. Worldwide COVID-19 travel restrictions, for instance, put a damper on foreign tourism to Spain, which was the country's leading economic sector. As a result, Spain lost one million jobs from April to June 2020, its biggest ever recorded quarterly decline. In July 2020, only 9,700 Compostelas were issued, compared to 53,000 in July 2019, suggesting that tourism on the Camino might have been down as much as 80 percent six months into the pandemic.[36]

Economic disparities are not the only forms of injustice created by religious appropriation on the Camino. Perhaps ironically, Christian hegemony is also part of the problem. The domination of Christian values and beliefs in Anglo-American and Anglo-European societies operates in many ways, and two are highlighted by the Camino. The first is the naturalization of Christian nationalist narratives. The second is the internalization and manifestation of what I have called Protestant privilege.

Even though the Iberian Peninsula has always been religiously heterogeneous, the narrative that Spain is and always was Christian dominates current political and cultural discourse. This narrative is at the root of the Christian-centric historiography that recounts the Muslim rule of Spain as traumatic and celebrates their expulsion in 1492 as a return to the "true" Christian way of life.[37]

Protecting Christian hegemony in the region is likely part of why the medieval Church promoted pilgrimage to Santiago: it brought more Christians physically into the region. It is behind St. James's depiction as Matamoros, in which the patron saint of Spain is reinvented as a medieval knight ousting the infidel invaders. Christian hegemony is also at the root of anti-Muslim racism in Spain today. If Spain has always been a Christian nation, and the 700 years of Islamic rule an occupation, then contemporary Muslim converts and immigrants are framed as a threat: invaders who have come to conquer Spain once again. The modern popularity of the Camino pilgrimage helps to authorize the version of history that insists Spain is rightly understood as a Christian nation.

While Christian hegemony benefits all Christians, it does not benefit all Christians equally. We saw this when the God Squad attempted to define and own normative Christianity. They reframed the Camino as a Protestant missionary trip and even claimed Catholic Communion as their own, rejecting its theological meaning and recasting it as an expression of ecumenicalism. The God Squad made my Catholic students feel like outsiders in their own tradition.

I should have anticipated this expression of Christian hegemony, given the dominance of white Protestantism in America. My colleagues who study American religion have documented how white Protestantism is assumed to define not only "normal Christianity" but also normal religion.[38] Protestant hegemony is so powerful in the United States that when my American Protestant students went on a Catholic pilgrimage in Spain, rather than defer to local norms, values, and stakeholders, they doubled down on the centrality of Protestantism. The God Squad is an excellent illustration of this phenomenon.

But even my non-Christian students' definition of what makes a Camino pilgrimage authentic rested on Protestant rather than Catholic ideas. Let me explain. American Catholic priest and sociologist Andrew Greeley has described the tendency in Catholicism to emphasize an individual relating to God as a member of a community while Protestantism emphasizes the direct relationship of the individual with God.[39] This latter, unmediated experience of pilgrimage is what my nonreligious students were pursuing: one that focused on their personal experience and self-actualization and that was not controlled by the Church, the Spanish state, or even me. Framing the religious experience of pilgrimage as personal spiritual growth was the first step to domestication and universalization of the experience of others. It was what made us all feel entitled to engage in pilgrimage even as religious outsiders, but it was also the expression of the internalization of Protestant logic. Put simply, Protestantism eased the way for the appropriation of pilgrimage.

The pursuit of Burton's hajj and my Camino program share the assumption that there is some educational benefit to borrowing the religion of others. And while I remain committed to the idea of experiential learning, I have come to understand that the stakes are high when a course incorporates "trying on" a religious practice. The last set of structural injustices I want to highlight is found in higher education, and specifically in the justification for study abroad programs. As with the other cases of power asymmetries discussed in this book, my Camino program does not cause these injustices, but it does operationalize them in ways that lead to forms of exploitation.

The first power asymmetry worth our attention is endemic to higher education: the hierarchy of teacher over student. In this model, information flows from institutions of learning to professors to students. In the context of the Camino program, this model means any form of religious appropriation is my responsibility.

I have come to see that the aspects that are meaning-making for my students—performance, spectacle, displacement, and community—are the same things that make pilgrimage meaningful for the faithful. And that means I created and led a program that encouraged students not just to observe religion, but in a very real way, to do religion. Perhaps more dangerous, during the course some students see me as a religious expert, instead of just an expert of religion, and look to me for guidance for how to be a religious pilgrim. I'm not sure where the humanistic teaching of religion ends and a devotional trip begins, but I do know I have no interest or competency in leading the latter.

A second issue related to the hierarchical model of higher education is more conceptual but also more insidious: it implies that knowledge is something we can obtain or master. Philosopher Shannon Sullivan's idea of "ontological expansiveness" that I introduced while discussing solidarity hijab in Chapter 1 is exacerbated in the study abroad setting.[40] As education scholar Anthony Ogden wrote, our "students have a sense of entitlement, as if the world is theirs for discovery if not for the taking."[41]

But a further layer of complication is added when a course entails a firsthand religious experience. Playing pilgrim is only pedagogically valuable within the context of secular education if we believe that the religious meaning of pilgrimage is available to us without any danger of, as Malory Nye would say, "religioning." This reinforces a "them versus us" distinction for the students by allowing them to believe they can safely remain religious outsiders even while claiming to master a religious practice. To put it another way, when engaging the religion of others, the idea of knowledge mastery is how students both avoid being unsettled by the diversity they encounter and maintain their position of superiority to the culture, community, or belief system of the other.

There are some things we can't know about religious pilgrimage because we don't understand, share, or even respect the metaphysical, cosmological, or ethical commitments of faithful practitioners. My Camino experience is not the same as a devoted Catholic's Camino. The God Squad's is not either. To insist otherwise is to assert we should have access to all religious knowledge even as we are invested in remaining outsiders to religious communities and traditions.

Rethinking Study Abroad

Applying the lens of cultural appropriation to my Camino program has convinced me that religion as a topic of experiential global learning comes with specific ethical challenges. Elijah Siegler has written about best practices the academic study of religion can offer study abroad in general, and I intuitively integrated some of his suggestions into my Camino program from the beginning, such as centering how religious belief and practice change over time and the role of embodied experience in religion. But I could integrate others more fully.

One of Siegler's suggestions is to make methodological awareness a goal for both instructor and student. Many courses in religious studies include a module that problematizes the colonial history of the academic study of religion, but not all allow ample reflection on the conceptual framework of the specific course content. In the other course I regularly teach as part of this program, focused on religious history in Andalusia, I have been more successful at problematizing dominant religious narratives. In that course, by the time we get to Seville, my students are often correcting the Christian-centric Reconquista version of history the local tour guides try to feed us. I need to foster a similar critical engagement with the myths and expectations for transformation that surround the Camino.

For my Camino program, for instance, I wish I had made the idea of religious appropriation an explicit methodological approach of the course, instead of fearing it would undermine the students' satisfaction with the experience. For instance, I focused on historical narratives and ethnographies of the Camino, which fed into student pursuit of an "authentic" pilgrim experience. If, instead, I had used appropriation as an analytical framework, I would have complicated both the desire "to do the Camino right" and the possibility of achieving this goal. I could have started the course with attention to what differentiates a pilgrim, a tourist, and a student, and then asked the class to consider what justification each provides to appropriate the religion of others. This would have primed the class to be on the lookout for instances of exploitation that our journey would entail, and underlying forms of structural inequities that made those exploitations possible.

Siegler also suggests that the goal of study abroad as obtaining cultural competency needs to be rethought in the case of religious studies. Engaging temporarily in a religious practice does not make a student competent in that practice or the tradition from which it comes. And yet, it was clear my students thought that, even as religious outsiders, they would gain some competency of pilgrimage by the end of the course. And, in some ways, I encouraged this.

One way to avoid the cultural competency model of study abroad is to ground the program on an epistemology of productive anxiety instead of the more common epistemology of mastery. Siegler describes anxiety as a positive sign that students are "having an experience [of the other] of depth and richness that the analyzing, calculating, categorizing mind cannot contain."[42] To me, a student's anxiety shows not only that deep contact is taking place, but also that they are not trying to erase or domesticate difference, or merely tolerate it, but instead are allowing the difference to challenge their assumptions about what is true and right.

The challenge becomes how to create a learning environment that encourages anxiety but also allows students to feel safe and supported so that the anxiety is productive. In the past, I have tried two things that have helped. One was fostering a sense of "radical collegiality" in the group so that students respect and care for one another in ways beyond a normal campus classroom interaction.[43] I articulate from the outset the importance of supporting one another in our journey to Santiago, which I promise will be hard for everyone in different ways. I also try to encourage a sense of intimacy among all students by mixing up roommates and organizing nightly "family dinners." Radical collegiality certainly helped with the physical journey of the Camino: it is why my strongest hikers sometimes stayed in the back of the pack to distract a student who was struggling with an injury, and it is why, in most years, our journey ended with tears and hugs in the Praza do Obradoiro. But radical collegiality also allowed for more vulnerable engagement of the material we studied, because our group became a safe place to try out new ideas.

The second tactic I have used to support a learning environment of productive anxiety is to encourage what philosopher of religion Wendy Weisman calls an aporetic ethic approach to learning. This approach is based on a theory of knowledge that makes not only intimacy, but also disorientation and disturbance, the goal of learning.[44] A study abroad program that uses this approach encourages students to discover contradictions in their engagement with others and to allow these contradictions to endure as a way we respect the distance between ourselves and the people and cultures we are studying.[45] Adopting an aporetic approach to religious borrowing would help us stay out of intercommunity debates about authenticity, accept that we will remain outsiders, and make sense of the insecurity the experience creates.

A third tactic I'd like to use more explicitly in the future to foster productive anxiety is democratizing the classroom. Much of higher education functions with the presumption that knowledge is created by the university, mastered by the professor, and then communicated to the student. This creates a hierarchy of professor and student, in which the professor disseminates knowledge through specific readings, lectures, and assignments and the students acquire it through memorization and synthesis. Learning becomes predictable—what the professor tells us will be on the test—and at times it can be passive. The study abroad setting provides an opportunity to rethink this one-directional flow of knowledge because it has a different learning environment. During my Camino program, my students see me as dirty, tired, and sometimes literally lost. It is hard under those conditions to maintain the same sort of authority I do in a campus classroom.

Of course, a professor presumably knows a great deal about the subject they are teaching. Why else would the student take a course from them? But my expertise does not need to reinforce a hierarchy. Students can collaborate about content and learning objectives in a more reciprocal teaching and learning environment.[46] When learning is a two-way street, it proceeds like a conversation in which knowledge is produced through the interaction. It can be unsettling for both instructor and student, but it also opens, as education scholar Alison Cook-Sather and her student Zanny Alter have said, "possibilities for change that dwelling in the assumed certainty of established structures and states cannot."[47]

Finally, I agree with Siegler that "the real pedagogical reason to teach religious studies abroad is not because it gives students a more authentic picture of a religious tradition, but rather because it calls into question such preconceived notions of authenticity."[48] If I am honest, my Camino program fell short in this area. I used the idea of authenticity implicitly to encourage students to do hard things and move outside their comfort zones, but I never problematized the presumption that there was some "right way" to complete the pilgrimage. My course would have been improved if I had more explicitly insisted that religious practices are themselves constantly in flux, that religious communities have internal debates over authenticity, and finally that the students' particular pilgrim experience was curated by several stakeholders, such as the Roman Catholic Church, the Spanish government, the local tourism industry, and, of course, me. I should have encouraged the students to consider the way authenticity was constructed and conveyed and how tensions over who determines what defines an authentic or inauthentic Camino were rooted into power dynamics. This would have made the goal of my Camino program witnessing authenticity as a process of constructing meaning, versus a goal to achieve.[49]

The last time I offered my Camino course was in 2018. Since it was popular and revenue generating, my university would be delighted for me to offer this program again. And every time I have led the program, it was clear to me it was meaningful to the students. But just because I can teach this way, and students like it, doesn't mean I should. Asking students who are not necessarily practicing Catholics to perform a pilgrimage along the Camino comes with serious physical, emotional, and existential risks, which is lot of responsibility to shoulder as an educator. But more importantly, it can undermine the goal of learning by reinforcing the students' existing worldviews and presumptions about religious practices.

When I started this book, I had stopped leading my Camino program. And when I first drafted this chapter, I planned to never do so again. But as I was revising it, I came to a different conclusion: my Camino program still has tremendous potential for learning, even if not in the ways my students and I thought it did in those first years. Does the program raise complicated issues about religious tourists, authenticity, and Christian nationalism? Yes, but if those questions are made central to the learning, a study abroad program on the Camino can be a learning opportunity more robust than mere self-actualization. I can redesign my Camino program in a way that puts acknowledging exploitation at the center of the experience, so that the goal becomes not consuming the religious other, but identifying what structural injustices are hidden by the assumption that such consumption is desirable in the first place.

3

Respite Yoga

It is 7:00 on a Monday morning. I'm in a 90°F room along with twenty other early risers. We've just completed an hour-long heated yoga class. I'm curled up on my side on a latex mat soaked with my own sweat, but everyone else is sitting upright, palms pressed together in Anjali Mudra, prayer position. The teacher leads a few sun breaths. "Inhale arms over head." I close my eyes tighter. "Exhale prayer hands down the center line." I move my left arm to cover my left ear. The teacher lowers her head and says, "The light in me bows to the light in you. Namaste." And the entire class in unison bows and answers, "Namaste." Still lying on my mat, I grimace.

"Namaste" is a Sanskrit word deriving from the verb *namaha*, meaning "to bend." The *te* at the end means "to you." According to Madhav Deshpande, professor emeritus of Sanskrit, the meaning of namaste has changed over time. In the Vedas, a collection of ancient South Asian texts, namaste was used to show respect to a divinity. In everyday use, however, it evolved to mean simply "salutations to you" or "greetings to you," a sign of respect, often for elders, but without necessarily referencing divinity.[1] This is how namaste, and its other regional forms, such *namaskar* and *namaskaram*, are commonly used in South Asia today. To close a yoga class with namaste is like ending with "hello."

Scholars are not sure exactly when namaste began to be used in yoga instruction, but today it is a common part of American yoga practice. Solemnly, reverently, hands pressed together at the heart's center, often with a bow of gratitude, yoga teachers tell us "namaste" can be translated as "the light in me bows to the light in you." Rather than the everyday South Asian namaste as a greeting, this yoga namaste recuperates and redeploys the more religious meaning found in the Vedic texts, yet without any specific religious content. Namaste becomes a spiritual shortcut, one that can be assigned any meaning the practitioner desires. It adds acoustic gravitas, but only through the reinvention of a foreign word.[2]

Of the three examples of religious appropriation explored in this book, claiming a connection of yoga to religion is the most controversial. A hijab might not be seen as obligatory by all Muslims, but its wearing is generally accepted as something rooted in the early Muslim community as well as subsequent communities of practice. In fact, the adoption of hijab as a symbol of progressive politics depends on hijab's readability as Islamic. Likewise, the Camino is widely acknowledged as a Christian pilgrimage route that the Catholic Church takes a strong role in promoting and maintaining. But yoga is not one discrete thing, nor are today's popular yoga postures linked to one "world religion."

US court cases have been fought over whether yoga is religious or not, with judgments on both sides.[3] Polling the thirty-six million American yoga practitioners wouldn't resolve the issue either. Yoga is religious for some who practice it; for others, it is not. Some people begin yoga merely to deal with back pain (as I did), to increase flexibility, or to enhance performance in sports. Others describe benefits that sound more religious, such as connecting to an energetic source. Nor is a comprehensive list of things about yoga that "look religious" helpful. Such a list would likely include sacred places (such as Rishikesh,

India), sacred texts (such as the Bhagavad Gita), prayer (such as *surya namaskara*), rituals (such as chanting mantras), and ethical systems (such as *yamas* and *niyamas*). But such a list discloses more about the list maker's assumptions about what counts as religion—the list I just provided is clearly drawing from Abrahamic religions—and would fail to provide a comprehensive description of the religious aspects of yogic traditions.

Instead of trying to convince you that yoga has religious roots, a distinction is helpful. When I look at yoga as a religious studies scholar, I see two types: devotional and respite.[4] More than just a series of postures, devotional yoga requires fidelity to beliefs, such as cosmologies and metaphysics. It can also involve adherence to rules and norms, such as to the ethical guidance of the yamas and niyamas. In some forms, it requires a monastic lifestyle. Devotional yoga is work. It can be hard and upsetting, just as likely to churn things up as to settle them down. Excruciating holds of postures, dizzying breath retentions, and forms of meditation that require trigger warnings—these are some of the physical markers of devotional yoga. This type of yoga is unapologetically religious.

The yoga of my 7:00 a.m. heated flow is qualitatively different. It is feel-good yoga for self-care. Gentle postures, supported holds, breath work to calm the nervous system, and affirming meditations to quiet the mind are all forms of what I call respite yoga, as are the athletic sequences of my morning heated flow meant to get the endorphins pumping. Respite yoga, so popular in the West today, is a practice to reduce stress and achieve well-being. It is marketed as vaguely spiritual and yet requires no religious commitments, making it accessible to everyone.

Respite yoga relies on practices, including physical postures, borrowed from devotional yoga, as a way to present itself as ancient, mystical, and powerful, but often without the larger systems of thought and belief they developed from, such as ethics and cosmologies. But modern respite yoga also adds new things to the mix to make the practice seem more "authentic," including the opening and closing of a class with namaste as a form of pseudo-liturgy. In other words, respite yoga depends on the appropriation of devotional yoga. It is just as much an invention of something new as the practice of something old.

The question before us is, How does religious appropriation in the pursuit of health raise specific ethical concerns? I show up for my respite heated yoga class almost every Monday because it reduces my stress. And yet I find some aspects of that practice exploitative. Namaste is one. Respite yoga has been in my life for a long time, but this uncomfortable awareness is new. And it makes me question whether the pursuit of personal health is as innocuous as I thought.

My family's appropriation of yoga is multigenerational. My mother began practicing yoga shortly after I was born, learning postures and simple meditation techniques, like so many white women in the 1970s, from Lilias Folan's PBS show *Lilias, Yoga and You*. Yoga was partly how she dealt with the isolation of being a corporate trailing spouse and a stay-at-home mom. She describes it as countercultural at the time, which was part of its appeal. But it was also on PBS, so not too out there. She enjoyed yoga, and as a former public-school teacher she had pedagogical chops, so after my sister was born, she began to teach yoga, decades before it was cool to do so.

My first memory of her teaching is from 1979. I was in first grade, and she offered a weekly yoga class at our church, wearing a Jane Fonda–inspired leotard and leg warmers. She went on to teach inexpensive or donation-based classes at churches, community centers, and for a time, as part of the University of New Hampshire's continuing education program. Now in her seventies, she still begins every day with yoga. Because of my mom, the idea of respite yoga as a daily ritual is something I grew up with, but I didn't begin to practice yoga in earnest until after a rowing injury in college.

My mother has been a devoted Christian for most of her life. She does not consider her yoga religious, but instead a self-care practice for her health. And yet, I will build the case that yoga's association with wellness is only possible because of religious appropriation. Forms of popularized mainstream yoga borrow practices from devotional traditions within a framework of modern biomedical and psychological systems of health. The attraction of respite yoga depends on its association with ancient forms of spiritual wisdom and practice, but it requires no adherence to these Eastern devotional systems. Devotion becomes respite, salvation becomes health. The success of the appropriation is how hidden the religion is.

In general, this topic should come with a warning: if you are devoted to your yoga practice, taking seriously the ethical implications of yoga might change the way you feel about your practice. It has for me. The critiques of respite yoga as orientalist, racist, and classist have all hit very close to home. I'm realizing that there are monsters hiding under my yoga mat, monsters that I need to confront.[5] When my Monday hot yoga class chants "Namaste," I now hear ignorance, entitlement, imperialism, and capitalism. By the end of this book, you might too.

For some readers, my insistence that yoga has connections to religion will create unease. I saw this firsthand in fall 2019, when I taught a seminar titled "Selling Spirituality" to a group of seven undergraduates. Our focus during the semester was on the commodification of Eastern religious practices in the West. Our case studies were meditation and yoga.

From an informal poll at our first meeting, I knew most of my students hadn't started the semester associating yoga with religion. But then we read historical accounts that argued yoga arose in Indian communities that practiced what we now call Hinduism, Buddhism, Jainism, and Sikhism, and that yoga in those contexts was part of a devotional practice. We engaged scholars who described how yoga was scrubbed of some of its more "difficult" religious dimensions to market it to Western consumers. We learned that K. Pattabhi Jois, who popularized Ashtanga yoga, had said anyone who practiced yoga postures would come to "experience God inside. . . . whether they want it or not."[6]

For our last meeting, I arranged for us to attend a slow flow yoga class at a local studio. As we were setting up our mats for our session, I realized my students were worried that their own participation in the yoga class was going to be religious in some way. During the semester, their opinion on the role of religion in yoga had changed and now there were concerned they would be, to again use Malory Nye's term, "religioning."

Trying to summarize the religious meanings of yoga, as I did with hijab and pilgrimage, is tricky because I must be careful not to valorize the myth that today's yoga is a replica of an ancient Indic practice. Modern yoga is best understood as the result of the interaction of multiple South Asian traditions, nationalism, imperialism, capitalism, and globalization. To say, for instance, that yoga is a Hindu practice is inaccurate. But it is also inaccurate to say yoga has no connection to Hindu and other Eastern devotional practices.

Andrea Jain argues in *Peace Love Yoga* that the scholarly pursuit of yoga's origins is itself a colonial practice that often proceeds "without critical reflection on [the researcher's] own scholarly, gendered, racial positionalities and how those might shape a particular story of yoga's roots."[7] For example, one way scholars have tried to argue that yoga has religious meanings is to trace them back to premodern South Asian texts.[8] However, the idea that texts are somehow the best repository of yogic ideas and practices rests on orientalist conceptions of knowledge. When scholars try to articulate the origins of yoga, they make decisions about which Eastern and Indic forms of knowledge and practice are worthy of our attention.

"This posture has been around for thousands of years; it must be powerful" is something we often hear in respite yoga classes, so it is impossible to avoid engaging the idea of the roots of yoga entirely. Instead of providing my own summary of yoga's roots, I will explore how the wellness community uses the concept of origins to explain why its practices are powerful and meaningful. This history of yoga is a story of inventing authenticity, rather than excavating an original source. But it is still an important history for us to learn. It includes moments when various stakeholders promoted specific yoga practices, often as strategies to preserve asymmetrical power dynamics, by disconnecting them from larger cultural and religious contexts to make them more valuable to British colonialism, Indian nationalism, and, finally, American wellness culture.

Since I will later give an account of my experience getting certified as a Kripalu yoga teacher, let's begin by discussing some of the oldest traditions Kripalu claims in its lineage. Specifically, I want to briefly describe Vedanta and Tantra, because Kripalu references Vedanta's notion of the sacred and Tantra's understanding of the physical body as a vehicle for enlightenment to explain why yoga is good for one's health.

In Vedanta, we have an example of sacred metaphysics assumed by yogic systems. Vedanta is a system of thought and practice based on a collection of more than one hundred texts called the Upanishads (800 BCE–300 CE). A central idea of Vedanta's metaphysics is that the highest reality, called Brahman, is the unchanging, permanent, and collective consciousness. According to Vedanta, the source of human suffering is Maya, the illusionary nature of the material world that our fears and desires make us think is real. Vedanta teaches that within us there is an unchanging self, Atman, and if we can identify with that self, we can be free of pain and suffering because we are identifying with Brahman, the unchanging reality. During my teacher training at Kripalu, these ideas were explained to me with an aquatic metaphor: Brahman is the ocean of collective consciousness; Atman, our soul, is a drop of Brahman caught in the illusion of Maya. If we think we are separate from Brahman, we suffer. If we could reunite our drop with that ocean, we would suffer no more.

Vedanta metaphysics were adopted by many premodern communities that practiced what we now call yoga. Any devotional practice within this worldview—such as meditation, prayer, or movement—was to help the practitioner reunite with Brahman. This means yoga traditions have their roots in a worldview that understands a sacred consciousness that is beyond our human experience. To put the point more directly, I would label the Vedanta worldview as religious. When yoga teachers tell you to "connect with your energetic source" or "practice nonreaction," they are making vague references to Vedanta metaphysics, whether they know it or not.

The Vedanta teaching of Maya as illusion could lead to doubts about our physical experience, which would make an emphasis on yoga postures difficult. That is why respite yoga also depends on nondualist premodern systems of thought that emphasize a positive role of the body in spiritual growth. The most influential, according to Kripalu, was the nondualism of Tantra.

When Tantra arose in 500 CE, it offered a departure from early systems of thought that saw the material world as separate from the sacred world. According to Tantric philosophy, by experiencing the things of this finite world fully, rather than avoiding them, we access infinite reality.[9] The nondualism of Tantra allowed a positive role for the body in premodern devotional practice, but it is also referenced in modern respite yoga to support the claim that spiritual health can be obtained through body work. Scholar of religion Hugh Urban, who studies both religions of South Asia and American new religious movements, goes as far as to claim that Tantra is at the heart of all New Age spirituality, "a spirituality that would no longer repress the human body, sexuality, and the desire for material prosperity but integrate them with the need for spiritual nourishment."[10]

One Tantric-inspired way to lead a yoga class that Kripalu suggests in its training manual is a body scan: the teacher instructs the students to focus on every part of their body, from toes to head, to affirm that everything is functioning as it should.[11] These simple instructions, offered with no context or background, are an example of how diluted forms of ancient Eastern traditions are invoked in respite yoga without requiring fidelity to devotional systems. My Kripalu yoga training, for instance, drew on Vedanta and Tantra to justify the power of respite yoga and to explain its efficacy, but I was encouraged to merely adopt the prompts that worked for my students and told that the philosophy behind them was too difficult for most.

In addition to drawing on ancient systems of thought, respite yoga presents itself as part of a continuous history of yoga practice. In truth, modern respite yoga is the result of a process that started about 150 years ago, in which some aspects of heterogeneous devotional systems were promoted as part of a healthy lifestyle, while others were left behind. In his book *Yoga Body*, Mark Singleton describes how first Indian elites and later US-based yoga advocates made decisions about what elements of premodern yoga to emphasize in response to pressures from the dominant culture. Those decisions were politically and economically strategic, and understanding them helps make clear why it is correct to say that modern yoga is something new and something ancient, and that it wouldn't exist without the West, but that it is also inherently South Asian.

Singleton begins the story of modern yoga in nineteenth-century Europe, when a new ethos of athleticism encouraged strengthening the bodies of individuals to strengthen the body politic of the nation. Fitness at that time began to be seen as not just about acquiring physical strength or flexibility. It was also associated with a series of character traits that would be required for engagement in the modern world, such as manliness and patriotism.[12]

Within the context of British colonialization, South Asian elites began to accept the idea that physical fitness was important for creating modern citizens and looked for ways to develop a local version of a physical training regimen. The physical postural yoga practice called asana was an obvious choice, and the Indian government began to promote it in a new way. But asana (postures) is only one practice associated with yogic traditions. For instance, Patañjali's *Yoga Sutras* (circa 400 CE) describes eight "limbs," or practices, of yoga.[13] In this text, asana was neither the first nor most important, even if it is the primary way yoga is consumed today. This means the element of yoga that was brought forward by Indians themselves was the one that British imperialists deemed valuable, and thus, from its beginning, the idea of using yoga postures delinked from devotional practice was the result of an interaction between the East and West.

The association of yoga with health, masculinity, and political power was not limited to the Indic national context. British military officers formerly stationed in India promoted yoga back home as a way to teach men to be strong leaders. For instance, in the 1930s Francis Yeats-Brown went as far as to reclaim yoga as part of the Aryan race inheritance, which allowed him to promote his vision of white supremacy and the British Empire at a time when the latter's global dominance was waning.[14]

When yoga moved west to the United States, its proponents began to redefine it for a new context. There, metaphysical systems associated with yoga found early fans in such mid-nineteenth-century thinkers as Henry David Thoreau and Ralph Waldo Emerson. However, yoga's physical practice was initially met with suspicion and often associated with occult magic.[15] Yoga scholar Andrea Jain suggests a helpful distinction: "neck-up yoga" was associated with philosophies and rules, and "neck-down yoga" with physical postures. At the end of the nineteenth century, most Americans considered "neck-down yoga" too weird for adoption.

By the 1930s, there was an increased visibility of neck-down postural yoga in the United States. But it was still considered too countercultural for mass consumption because it continued to be closely associated with Eastern philosophical and metaphysical commitments as well as a guru, an advanced yogi with whom to learn from directly.[16] Neck-up and neck-down yoga were still linked, and most Americans were not interested in either.

This began to slowly change for several reasons—some demographic, others related to the shifting landscape of US religion. For instance, in the early twentieth century, state and federal laws restricted Indian immigration to the United States. After World War II the nation reopened its doors to legal Indian immigration with the Luce-Celler Act of 1946, but it set a quota of only one hundred Indian immigrants a year. The Immigration and Nationality Act of 1965 made entry significantly easier. From 1965 until the mid-1990s, about 40,000 people immigrated to the United States from India.[17] This exposed more Americans to Asian cultural and religious practices. It also allowed more Indian gurus to travel to the United States to spread their teachings.[18] Although racism had prevented Indian immigration for decades, white Americans were nevertheless eager to adopt all sorts of Asian practices as part of the spiritual revivalism of the 1960s.

Hugh Urban describes two specific forms of alternative spirituality that became popular in the 1960s and 1970s: new religious movements and New Age spirituality. Both drew inspiration from Eastern religions, but in different ways. New religious movements emerged around a charismatic figure and created an often countercultural community. Urban defines New Age spirituality as a looser, decentralized network of beliefs and practices including everything from crystals to aromatherapy. This alternative spirituality tended to be quite individualistic, "focused on the optimum physical, psychological, and spiritual development of the individual practitioner, who is free to pick and choose from a wide array of spiritual options."[19] Although there were high profile figures within New Age spirituality, according to Urban, this form of spirituality did not depend on a charismatic leader in the same way. I want to suggest that while yoga started off associated with new religious movements, its popularization only happened after yoga was recast as New Age spirituality, and this required another moment of appropriation. Let's take a closer look at how that happened.

One example of a new religious movement with Indian origins is the International Society for Krishna Consciousness (ISKCON), popularly known as the Hare Krishna movement. The American story of ISKCON begins in 1966 when A. C. Bhaktivedanta Swami Prabhupada (1896–1977) came to New York and established a countercultural community. As Urban writes, Swami Prabhupada was in the right place at the right time: "The message of a peaceful Indian Guru speaking about love and joyous worship was exactly what many people wanted to hear."[20] One of the first places Swami Prabhupada operated out of was a yoga studio, and the Bhagavad Gita is ISKCON's core text, the same text studied by many modern yoga teachers. The early ISKCON community practiced a form of devotional yoga that integrated "neck-up" and "neck-down" elements of yoga. Praphupada's teachings appealed to a 1960s generation of mostly white hippies who were interested in world-rejecting teachings. That fact that ISKCON was not mainstream, not American, was the point.

But ISKCON was not without controversy.[21] It was implicated in several scandals about abuse and accused of brainwashing its members. More generally, ISKCON was seen as disrupting mainstream society, with its vegetarian diet, dress codes, and monastic lifestyle.[22] Frankly, it was considered too Eastern, in ways that made white Protestant parents especially concerned. ISKCON became even more dangerous in the "cult scares" of the 1980s when the media convinced a lot of parents that new religious movements were trying to steal the youth.[23] If yoga had stayed only in counter-cultural religious communities, such as ISKCON, it would never have achieved mass appeal.

Yoga advocates began to present yoga as a form of New Age spirituality in successful mass marketing campaigns in the late 1960s. They did so, Jain tells us, by emphasizing the physical practice of asana and giving up "all or many of the [yoga] rules such as those dealing with alms, celibacy, scriptural study, and retreat from society or social norms that traditionally functioned to separate the yoga practitioner from society."[24] This was the point at which respite yoga was born. This form of yoga offered direct access to the benefits of "neck-down yoga" by downplaying "neck-up yoga," allowing Anglo-Americans to access the benefits of Eastern wisdom without the perceived danger of joining a countercultural community, such as ISKCON. And thus, when my mom encountered yoga for the first time in the 1970s, she didn't see it as conflicting with her Christian identity or values.

Yoga was further popularized in the 1980s and 1990s by celebrity yoga teachers, including B. K. S. Iyengar, K. Pattabhi Jois, and Bikram Choudhury. They were successful in reaching broad audiences by describing yoga as a wellness practice that did not require fidelity or conversion to Eastern philosophies or ways of life.

Today over thirty-six million Americans practice yoga. Most consider it an ancient Eastern practice that is valuable for their personal health and well-being. Most have little interest in the more radical counterculture aspects of devotional yoga that would require asceticism or allegiance to complicated cosmologies and metaphysics. In other words, the popularity of yoga depends on the successful reinvention of yoga from a devotional practice to one aimed at self-care. It is not a coincidence that the yogic traditions left behind are the ones most legible as religious. Americans had to be convinced that yoga was not religious, or at least not religious in an Eastern way, to believe it could be as American as apple pie.

Becoming a Certified Yoga Teacher

There are several popular types of yoga in the United States. Hatha, Ashtanga, Iyengar, Bikram, Vinyasa, Yin Yoga, and restorative are a few of the most popular, but the list goes on from there. Each is marketed as a "lineage," often claiming roots in an Indian devotional community led by an Indian-born guru. Yoga teachers are certified to teach by an accrediting body called Yoga Alliance after completing at least 200 hours taught by a registered individual, studio, or yoga center. This creates a lot of diversity in yoga offerings nationwide.

I decided the best way to learn how respite yoga relied on religious appropriation was to enroll in a yoga teacher training program. My first task was to identify a lineage that claimed devotional roots to establish itself as authentic and spiritually sincere, but that also marketed itself as accessible to all Americans regardless of religious affiliation. I wanted a training program that required me to live and study with other students. As someone who has conducted fieldwork for much of my scholarly career, I knew a residential program would mean more time with a group of people I could potentially interview as well as a physical location and local community to immerse myself in.

At first, I considered a school called Shoshoni, located outside Boulder. One of three residential ashrams founded by Sri Shambhavananda, a spiritual leader raised on a dairy farm in Pennsylvania, Shoshoni is in Rollinsville, Colorado. I made a site visit to the mountain compound in September 2018. There, I ate vegan meals, attended yoga and meditation classes, and participated in additional mindfulness programming, such as art therapy. I met briefly with one of the current spiritual leaders, a petite white woman the community calls Swami Omkari Devananda, who studied with Sri Shambhavananda for almost thirty years.

The form of yoga at Shoshoni, Hatha yoga in the ShambhavAnanda Yoga tradition, has a distinctly American lineage, so it checked that box. And I really liked Swami Devananda, whose adopted name means "daughter of the gods." She was smart and warm, welcoming but not pushy or overly intense.

But there were a couple of drawbacks to Shoshoni as a research site for respite yoga. First, although the yoga classes I attended were excellent, they were populated only by guests. The residential community is focused on meditation as its central ritual practice. Plus, Shoshoni is explicitly devotional. The full-time community functions like a cooperative commune, with an active swami leader, vegetarian diet, chanting, and meditation. It is more like the countercultural versions of yoga popular in the 1960s and 1970s (such as the yoga of ISKCON) than the respite versions of yoga that have gone mainstream. Or to use Urban's classification, Shoshoni is a new religious movement, not merely a form of New Age spirituality. Certainly, there is a story of religious appropriation to explore here—a community that models itself on a South Asian ashram, led by white US-born people who adopt Sanskrit names and eat a mostly vegan diet—but it was not one that would allow me to explore how most Americans encounter yoga.

In the end, I found a teacher training program closer to home that would provide access to a successful American yoga brand: Kripalu Center for Yoga & Health, in Stockbridge, Massachusetts.

Swami Kripalu was an Indian-born guru who practiced Kundalini yoga, a form of yoga based on awakening energy to connect with Brahman, the divine consciousness. In 1960, Swami Kripalu sent one his favorite pupils, Amrit Desai, to America to establish a community that would eventually become the educational nonprofit known as Kripalu.

In the early days, the US Kripalu community tried to replicate Indian devotional yoga, including establishing an ashram. Traditionally, ashrams in South Asia are residential places of intense religious study. Ashram residents pledge to live an ascetic life and are known as renunciates within the system of dharmic stations. When yoga was taken up in the Western world, some residential communities, such as Kripalu and Shoshoni, called themselves ashrams as they built counter-culture utopias of spiritual practice.

When I started the research for this book, I had never been to Kripalu, but my mother had attended a retreat there in 1984, the year after Kripalu opened its Stockbridge location. At that time, Kripalu was still an ashram and the community's yoga was devotional. I was eleven, and I still remember her stories of the visit. She got a bowl of boiled spinach for each meal. No coffee was allowed. There were shrines everywhere. Residents dressed in white. At that point, my mother had been teaching yoga for over a decade, but Kripalu was her first experience with formal yoga instruction, Indian philosophy, and vegetarian food. When we talked recently about her experience at Kripalu, she told me, "I couldn't really relax that weekend because it was all so different." It turns out that a lot had changed at Kripalu since 1984. Rather than "so different," Kripalu felt extremely normal to me when I visited—well designed, and organized for my New England sensibilities, with a vibe that was more spa than ashram.

Today, Kripalu bills itself as a center of study, practice, and retreat, open to not only renunciates but also householders, those of us who continue to have jobs, families, and other social obligations. It requires of its visitors no understanding of Indian philosophy or fidelity to Indic metaphysical or ethical systems. In other words, although the early Kripalu community was focused on devotional yoga, today Kripalu yoga is marketed as respite care. I had been attracted to the idea of Kripalu as a former ashram, but the fact that I would be able to attend a 200-hour yoga teacher training at Kripalu's retreat center meant that the community had evolved to something institutionally much different. It never occurred to me that the reason Kripalu was no longer an ashram was important, and it should have.

Kripalu has been training teachers for more than forty years, and it claims to be the oldest school of yoga in the United States. One of the students in my training referred to Kripalu as the Harvard of yoga schools. It was certainly priced like an Ivy League. Tuition and a shared room for the training set me back $5,200. But I liked that Kripalu had a brand and standards. If I was going to spend time and resources doing this, why not do it right?

Located in the heart of the Berkshires, Kripalu Center for Yoga & Health is a little over two hours west of Boston. I reserved a tiny shared room, with a shared bath, in the main building. The walls were painted cinder blocks. The only furnishings were one bureau and two twin beds pressed against the walls, with just enough room to walk between them. A small sink jutted out over one of the beds. It was sparse, very sparse, but that felt right.

When I arrived, I had a couple of hours before our opening session, so I explored Kripalu's property, which contains 350 acres and several buildings. The main building, Shadow Brook, was originally built to house a Jesuit order. The midcentury chapel remains and is now used for large events. Whereas the sleeping quarters of Shadow Brook feel monastic, the public areas are more like a hotel. There is a café, as well as a gift shop, healing arts center, and dining hall. Kripalu is known for its food, and its executive chefs have published popular cookbooks. Despite my mom's warning of boiled spinach, I found the food varied and delicious. You can eat the healthy gruel and steamed vegetables for every meal from the "Buddha bar." But there is also an impressive hot buffet and salad bar of rotating items. Meat and coffee are available.

Before my training program began, I made an appointment for an assessment at Kripalu's wellness center. When my consultant, Tina, learned I was a scholar of religion, she assumed this meant I was personally religious, and went off script. She told me that most of her clients weren't interested in yoga as a religion. "They aren't ready for it," she said. "They are only interested in the body-care aspects. Only about how to bring balance to the body." But "you can't be a real yogi," she said, "unless you believe in God. It all starts with God." Then, she told me that Hare Krishna is the purest form of yoga. I nodded slowly in agreement.

That helped convince her I was on her team, and she began to dish a little more. "Yoga in the US is full of hypocrisy," she confided. "Even here," she added, "at this famous yoga center. I mean, we never used to have meat. We had to add it because people demanded it." With these comments, Tina made clear that she thought authentic yoga was the devotional type. For her, meat in the dining hall was offensive, and a blatant marketing ploy to make yoga more accessible and attractive to more American consumers.

Instagram posts tagged #yogis are dominated by thin, able-bodied young white women, modeling challenging poses in postcard-perfect beach and mountain locations. That was who I thought I'd meet in my Kripalu training. But the first woman I saw when I checked in was older than me. The next one I met when I picked up my binder was much larger. At our first session I counted only four women in their twenties; everyone else was middle aged, and the majority were fifty or older. Twenty-eight women, five men. Three people of color and only one South Asian woman. Everyone else was white.

The group included an appellate court judge, an ex-military medic, and an aspiring actress. A number, like myself, worked in the field of education. Almost a third were interested in using yoga to work with special populations, such as cancer or trauma survivors. Most were retired or financially supported by spouses or extended family. Even with the availability of scholarships, only a handful of the participants were working class.

The training began with an evening session where we met our two lead teachers, Julia and Huey. As we entered the classroom, they greeted us one by one, clasping our hands, looking into our eyes.

Julia was tall and in her thirties. She wore tie-dyed pants and had rainbow tinsel in her hair. She had just returned from three months in India, which she just happened to mention in our first session. Direct experience in India is part of how American yoga teachers often establish their expertise. Huey was about sixty, balding, with thin gray hair and a small ponytail at the base of his neck, skinny legs, and a round belly. He spoke so slowly that I was often concerned he had lost his train of thought entirely. When he led us in a short series of postures that night, he closed his eyes, circling his hands on his knees. Huey had lived at Kripalu when it was an ashram. At one point in his life, yoga had been devotional for him, even if he would later insist over a meal we shared that the yoga he was teaching us was not.

Huey and Julia told us we were forming a *sangha*, Sanskrit for "community." Jains and Sikhs use this term to refer to religious associations. A sangha is a monastic community within Theravada and Mahayana Buddhism, but it can also refer to any Buddhist community of belonging. In India, however, all political parties are called sanghas. The fact that "sangha" is both a religious and secular word is part of why Kripalu used it: it aesthetically coded our experience as both Eastern and religious, while allowing participants not interested in the devotional associations of yoga to ignore them.

Over the next few days, we fell into a rhythm. Every day began at 6:30 a.m. with a ninety-minute yoga posture training class, followed by breakfast eaten in silence. We met again from 9:00 a.m. to 6:00 p.m. with a break for lunch. We journaled in response to prompts. We attended lectures on teaching methodology, yoga and science, anatomy and physiology, Ayurveda, and Indian philosophy. We learned techniques for teaching asana in ways that were safe and accessible for all bodies, using modifications or props such as blocks and straps.

A large part of my homework every night was memorizing the Sanskrit name for each posture. I made flash cards to help—*tadasana* (mountain), *utkatasana* (chair), *virabhadrasana* (warrior), and set some longer names, such as *janu sirshasana* (head to knee pose) to the melody of an aria. I fumbled through longer names, even for common postures like *adho mukha shvanasana* (downward facing dog).

It is common to hear Sanskrit—but not one of the other twenty-two official languages of India, such as Bengali, Hindi, Nepali, or Urdu— spoken in American yoga classes. In addition to Sanskrit names of postures, some teachers quote from Sanskrit texts, including *Yoga Sutras* and the Bhagavad Gita. For many devotees of Indian religions, Sanskrit is a sacred language, one that allows access to knowledge through an aesthetic effect. Sanskrit is used in some Buddhist and Jain sacred texts and is a liturgical language of many Hindu traditions. The use of Sanskrit in a respite yoga class is an attempt to invoke the feeling of devotional yoga, but without necessarily referring to any of its content.

But privileging Sanskrit as the language of Indian knowledge turns out to have a complicated history. From its beginning, this was an orientalist move made by European philologists such as F. Max Müller, who is credited with establishing the Anglo-European academic field of Indian studies. Müller argued that Sanskrit was even older than

Semitic languages such as Hebrew. In the scholarly quest to discover ancient Eastern wisdom, if Sanskrit was the oldest, Sanskrit texts were the best.[25] This privileging of Sanskrit had political consequences as well: it allowed for the telling of India's linguistic history as a story of the infection of pure Sanskrit by Persian, Arabic, and Turkish—in other words, infection by the languages of Muslim invaders.[26] And since Sanskrit is associated with Indian Hindus, the presumption became that true Indic culture is something only Hindus have access to.

Since I was aware of these linguistic politics, the emphasis on Sanskrit in our training felt to me like an orientalist acoustic tactic. This was only confirmed by things the instructors said. As many of us struggled to learn the new terms, for instance, Julia shared her own challenges. "My Sanskrit pronunciation isn't great, but it is important for you to know and use these names. It gives you credibility in front of a class." Her comment signaled to me that at Kripalu, we were learning Sanskrit so that our future students would experience our class as authentic. As a bunch of Americans, at least we could sound Indian.

The most consistent ritual at the beginning and ending of each Kripalu training session was the calling out of "om." Om is a sacred mantra in Hinduism and Tibetan Buddhism, appearing at the beginning and end of most Sanskrit recitations. Although a single syllable, it consists of three letters, *a*, *u*, and *m*, and thus three sounds, "ah," "ooh," and "m." Each sound has a different metaphysical association, which serves as a meditative focus: "ah" represents our consciousness of the outer world, "ooh" is our consciousness of our inner world, and "m" is our experience of ultimate unity. Said together, om represents the primordial sound of the Universe.

According to Kripalu staff, when we chant "om," the sound vibrates in our body, calming our central nervous system and connecting us to the universal energy. Kripalu's use of om is an example of deploying religious language to create a visceral experience that is both vaguely spiritual and decisively devoid of religious content. As sociologist of religion Véronique Altglas puts it, in yoga, "Hindu liturgy is not appropriated for the symbolic world it embodies," which frankly few practitioners take the time to understand, but instead "it is 'diverted' for practical aims."[27] In respite yoga, chanting om is presented as a technique to calm and connect us. It is adopted not for conversion, but to help achieve self-actualization. In fact, insisting that the technique is not religious is what enables its widespread adoption. The yoga student can overcome any initial discomfort at borrowing a mantra because they are told it is possible to do so without attaching any religious meaning to it.

Kripalu is explicit that yoga is not religious, but understanding what Kripalu means by religion is hard to pin down. The only thing the training manual says directly about religion is that it is "adopted as ultimate truth." From a religious studies point of view, this claim is not controversial. Ultimate concern, as I mention in the Introduction, is a common way to describe a central characteristic of religion.[28] But the Kripalu manual goes on to say that yoga is a way to refine knowledge, as opposed to a fixed mindset.[29] The implication is that religion promotes a fixed mindset, and that is a statement most scholars of religion would disagree with. Even when describing religions as traditions, historian of religion Marilyn Robinson Waldman argued, those traditions are modalities of change. They provide resources for us to cope with new political, technological, and social realities, allowing these new realities to make sense, and to become accepted and normalized.[30]

I went looking on the Kripalu website for more clarity about its definition of religion and found a section titled "Nondogmatic and Nondenominational" that reads in part:

> The Kripalu tradition is decidedly not a fundamentalist mindset.
> It is a nondogmatic and nonsectarian approach to life that cele-

brates diversity and recognizes that all approaches are valuable and venerable . . . and that truth is freely available to members of every nationality, race, and religion.[31]

This statement sets up a religious straw man against which Kripalu yoga is being defined: religion is bad; it is a fundamentalist, dogmatic, and sectarian approach to life, a definition most religiously affiliated individuals would reject. In contrast, Kripalu claims that its yoga is good. It is inclusive, nondogmatic, and nonsectarian.

Instead of a religion, the Kripalu manual defines yoga as "an ancient wisdom tradition" comprising three building blocks: a direct experience, a practice, and a philosophical view. Let's look closely at each.

The manual explains that yoga is a "direct experience" insofar as it is "the firsthand knowledge that comes from an unmediated contact with reality." The use of "unmediated" signals that Kripalu leadership wants to define yoga as outside the institutional forms of hierarchy that we usually associate with religion, such as the guru-disciple relationship; instead, it offers personal and direct access. The choice of the word "reality" in the Kripalu training manual is important as well: this secular term is accessible to a broad American audience.

The second building block of yoga, according to the Kripalu manual, is a practice, "a method to inquire deeply into the nature of reality" that "activates the life force, heightens self-awareness, awakens intuition, and grants access to deeper states of consciousness." The reference to "life force" could imply a religious cosmology, and certainly it did for Swami Kripalu. But leaving it undefined allows a student to adopt the practice without any commitment to larger systems of belief attached to it.

Kripalu's manual defines the third building block of yoga as a philosophical view, that yoga has "a particular way of seeing yourself and the world around you." To me, it seems that this might be equivalent to a religious "worldview," but the manual insists it is not. Instead, it describes a philosophical view as having "a working hypothesis," whereas religion requires "a fixed mindset." Notice again how this presumes a narrow and negative perception of religion. But there is something else going on. The authors of the Kripalu training manual do not deny the devotional qualities of their lineage, but they also insist that Kripalu yoga requires no religious commitments. This lets folks who already have a religious affiliation, and also those who are suspicious of all religion, feel welcome and safe. Insisting that yoga is not religious is a tactic used to ease the way for widespread adoption in the American context, including of those elements that are rooted in Kripalu's more devotional past.

Finally, even as the Kripalu manual tries to strongly differentiate yoga from religion, it does so with what can only be described as religiously coded language. "Revelation" is mentioned explicitly in the section from which I have quoted, and throughout the manual. Yoga is described as connecting us to our energetic source and the heart of creation. References to Brahman, Shiva, Krishna, and "divinity" are all used during the training to help explain yoga's cosmology. The Kripalu teacher training occurs in a room with an altar, in a building that used to house an ashram. The program is named after a guru. Every session opens and closes with the chanting of "om" and a centering to honor the divine within each of us. And none of this is religious, or so we are told.

To me, the simultaneous insistence that yoga isn't religious and the abundance of religious content in our training seemed a contradiction. I didn't understand why there was such a strong emphasis on Kripalu yoga not being religious, especially given the lineage's devotional roots. That is, until I learned about an incident in Kripalu's past that made the reason for this clear.

The author practicing *navasana*, also known as boat pose, in a training room at Kripalu, Stockbridge, MA. (Liz Bucar)

In addition to the two lead instructors and additional guest lecturers, my Kripalu sangha was supported by teaching assistants, volunteers who received room and board in exchange for assisting with the training. They took turns sitting in on class, carrying a mic around for Q&A portions of the program, and hosting study halls. There were four assistants for my program. The youngest, I'll call Will.

Will very much looked the part of a yogi, with his man bun and unselfconscious sartorial choices that included a pair of orange pea-cock feather–patterned leggings. Since neither of us could sit still, we'd often find ourselves together in the back of the room, twisting out our backs, doing dolphin dives, or rolling our hips on foam rollers. We chatted a fair amount during breaks.

On day four, when I had settled into the training routine, Will asked how things were going as we were breaking for the day. With a big smile, I said, "Great." And then I tossed out, "You know, I sort of wish it was still an ashram here." "Unlikely that will ever happen again," Will said, with a bit of a smirk. "You know, because of the scandal."

The what?

I didn't ask him what he meant because I instinctively switched into researcher mode, saying to myself, "He thinks I know what he is talking about, so I should just go along with it." I went to dinner directly from class, took a shower, and fell asleep before my roommate at 8:30. But at midnight, I woke up, sat straight up in bed, grabbed my phone, and Googled "Kripalu scandal."

It turns out that Kripalu, like almost every major yoga lineage in the United States, has had a sex abuse scandal. One that I had never heard of. At the center of the scandal was Amrit Desai, the attractive and charismatic Indian guru—someone who hadn't been mentioned at that point in my training. Swami Kripalu was the namesake of Kripalu yoga. His teachings were peppered throughout our training manual, and a shrine to him was on the fourth floor of Shadow Brook. But it was his disciple, Amrit Desai, who had founded the US community.

Sent by Swami Kripalu to the United States in 1960, Desai was his favorite pupil, who became a popular yoga teacher in the Philadelphia area. In 1972, he established a small residential ashram in Sumneytown, Pennsylvania, that focused on Swami Kripalu's Kundalini yoga teachings and practices. In 1975, the community purchased a larger residential facility in Summit Station, Pennsylvania. Residents gave up their jobs, adopted Sanskrit names, and devoted themselves to yoga study and practice while immersed in a monastic-like community.

The community outgrew its Pennsylvania facilities, and in 1983, purchased the Shadow Brook property in Stockbridge, Massachusetts.

Desai moved north to become the new ashram's spiritual leader. At its peak, the Stockbridge community included over 300 residents, many attracted to Desai's countercultural vision. But cracks formed in this utopian experiment as some in the community became dissatisfied with Desai's leadership.[32]

Part of the breakdown can be attributed to Desai's failure to follow the moral teachings he preached. According to Desai, yoga's ethical guidelines are laid out in the first two limbs of Patañjali's eightfold path: yamas (restraints) and niyamas (observances). Desai emphasized the importance of all the yamas and niyamas and presented himself as a model of virtue. But it turns out that he was violating one key yama: *brahmacharya* (sexual celibacy).

Desai was married, but in 1968, after the birth of his third child, he declared he would practice celibacy. And he had strict rules about sex for ashram residents. He required all unmarried residents to take a vow of celibacy. In the early years, marriages among residents were forbidden. Huey, who met his wife at the ashram, told me that even when marriages eventually were allowed, they were strictly regulated: the couple had to be residents of the ashram for four years, go through a supervised courting period, and gain the approval of the community before they could marry. Having children was discouraged.[33]

But Desai couldn't live up to the ideal of sexual moderation he required of others. In 1986, a female resident accused him of having an ongoing affair with Sandra Healy, the administrative head of the ashram. He denied the allegation and denounced his accuser as mentally ill. She left the community.

In 1994, a respected senior member of the permanent staff disclosed that Desai had pressured her to have sexual relations when she was in her twenties. Given her position in the community, and her lack of consent, this time the accusation was not ignored. Senior residents called a community meeting to confront Desai. He admitted to the ongoing affair with Healy he had earlier denied, as well as having sex with two other women in the community.

Nowadays, it seems as if every high-profile yoga guru has been accused of abuse. But the Kripalu scandal was one of the first, and it involved a large residential community. That community had to figure out what to do. And once I knew about the scandal, I had to figure out what to do as well.

The morning after I had stayed up Googling the scandal, I considered leaving the training. I didn't like that I was placing my body into postures associated with a sexual predator. I was mad at myself for not knowing about the scandal before I had started the training, but I also felt that I had been lied to through omission by Kripalu's marketing materials.

Instead of packing my bags, I told the Kripalu staff what I had learned and how I was having trouble processing it. I asked whether they could arrange for me to speak to someone who had lived through the transition and who still "believed" in Kripalu. Five people spoke with me over the next two days. At the Kripalu gift shop, I purchased four memoirs, written by former ashram residents, that discussed the scandal, and I read them all over the next two nights. The following is what I learned from those conversations and books.[34]

Former residents explained that the scandal was traumatic in part because many residents were rape or incest survivors and had been drawn to the community precisely because of its vow of celibacy. To have the guru break what they understood to be one of the central ethical tenets of the ashram was a form of violence and undid the safety and comfort they felt in that community. There could be no forgiveness for this transgression. Once Desai admitted to what he had done, the board of trustees asked him to resign immediately.

Desai and other gurus, as well as many celebrities today in the wellness industry, can be understood as charismatic leaders insofar as they are recognized by their followers as having extraordinary qualities or knowledge.[35] But a leader's authority depends on their followers' recognition of them as leader. And once the community no longer sees them as having special status, they functionally have none. Desai went from guru to exile overnight.

Today, there is no formal relationship between Kripalu and Desai. His inspirational quotes are nowhere in my training manual, nor are they posted around Kripalu. Huey, who had lived in the Stockbridge ashram while Desai was a guru, quoted Desai once during the training that I noticed, and he only attributed the quote to Desai when someone asked the source. Kripalu has successfully redacted Desai from the American yoga lineage he helped create.

More than just breaking ties with Desai, the Kripalu community has changed how they define leadership. Before 1994, Kripalu emphasized the role of the guru in conveying yogic knowledge to disciples. After the scandal, the community adopted a new model of leadership, one that attempts to be more democratic. "I discovered that my real spiritual teachers and gurus were all around me," former ashram resident Stephen Cope said while describing this transition. "It was the community that played the role of mother for me, not the guru."[36] This new model of leadership is reflected in a new organizational structure. Today, Kripalu is an educational nonprofit led by a CEO and run by paid employees, no longer an ashram led by a guru and staffed by unpaid residents.

Kripalu explains this transition as a necessary break from its Indic lineage to make its yoga more suitable for Americans. "Rather than relying exclusively on ancient texts and Sanskrit terminology," its website states, "the teachings of Kripalu Yoga were increasingly voiced by Western teachers in language that meshed with the contemporary world."[37] Making yoga more American, it seems, required distancing it from its Eastern roots.

The transition in the 1990s was a process of jettisoning aspects of devotional yoga that residents thought were not working in the US setting: a guru, an ashram, and a community of renunciates. Put another way, the Desai scandal is why today Kripalu insists yoga is not religious, despite a lineage that is undeniably devotional. Selective promotion and redaction of its own tradition is how Kripalu survives. It allows Kripalu to keep the aspects of yoga it likes—postures, breath work, meditation—and discard anything that it thinks doesn't work in an American context.

Injury, Bypassing, Alt-Right Politics, and Whitewashing

Respite yoga entails a constellation of unintended exploitations. One form involves injury to the agent of appropriation, given the physical and mental risks that accompany respite yoga. Another is experienced by yoga teachers, whose labor is undercompensated. Exploitation is also seen in the way yoga is packaged as secular, which erases the religious context of its development and its metaphysical implications while fetishizing Eastern spirituality. The opposite happens as well: yoga's religious roots are overemphasized and then weaponized, such as in manifestations of Hindu nationalism. We will even see that respite yoga creates the conditions conducive for alt-right conspiracy theories to take hold in the United States. And finally, there is a way in which yoga's social media presence and studio culture create spaces of whiteness, profiting off brown cultures even as brown bodies are excluded.

We normally think of cultural appropriation as exploiting the community from which an idea, practice, or object is borrowed. But there can also be harm to the person doing the appropriating. We saw this a bit on the Camino, where playing a pilgrim encouraged self-destructive behavior, such as overeating and excessive alcohol consumption. For Christian students, my Camino program risked producing a crisis of faith. Respite yoga is marketed as safe, based on the ideas that yoga has been around for centuries, people all over the world do it, and so it must be good for us. But the facts tell a different story.

On a very basic level, yoga can cause bodily injury. According to a study published in the *Orthopaedic Journal of Sports Medicine*, between 2001 and 2014, almost 30,000 people in the United States experienced yoga-related injuries requiring a visit to a hospital emergency room.[38] A 2008 study of Ashtanga—a type of athletic yoga that follows a set sequence—found an average of 1.45 injuries per 1,000 hours of practice.[39] *Yoga Anatomy* published a 2017 survey of yoga practitioners in which 54 percent reported physical problems from their asana practice.[40] And yet, the risk of physical injury is rarely mentioned by doctors who suggest yoga for back care or stress, nor by instructors, who cue postures that might not work in all bodies. Even though I originally began to practice yoga to deal with a back injury, I have pulled lower back muscles in forward folds. And I had to ice my knees every night by the end of my Kripalu training because of overuse.

Yoga is also marketed as a method to deal with mental stress. Stephen Cope, a trained psychologist, yoga teacher, and current scholar-in-residence at the Kripalu Center, explained why he thought yoga is effective at supporting mental health. The human condition, he wrote, is "a painful sense of separation" from the body, from the mystery of life, from our source.[41] Resolving this alienation is the point of yoga, according to Cope, one that predates Freud, Jung, and New Age spirituality. Yoga is "a psychological language not yet rendered impotent by cliché or commercialism, and, even more refreshingly, one that is . . . free of the Western obsession with guilt and shame."[42]

Instructors present postures linked with breath to control our thoughts. Perhaps we set an intention at the beginning of practice, such as gratitude or self-acceptance, which then allows the practice to reinforce positive thoughts or feelings. A difficult asana becomes an opportunity to think about how to cultivate resilience, akin to cognitive behavior therapy, retraining our response to difficult situations. My favorite studio instructor turns up the heat and puts us into challenging postures, asking us to hold them for a minute or more, and then talks to us about how "this is the opposite of suffering" and reassures us "we can do hard things" while we sweat, breathe hard, and shake. She tells us that learning to not react to discomfort on our mat is a skill we can take into the rest of our life. When yoga practice becomes the treatment plan, a $25 yoga class suddenly seems like a bargain.

Yoga as therapy didn't occur to me as a potential harm until one of my students shared with me a bad experience she had with a form of meditation, one that required her to focus on negative feelings. It was a powerful self-guided exercise, she told me, but not one that was good for her mental health. She felt it was even dangerous. That started me thinking about how sometimes the most intense yoga classes I've taken, led by an instructor untrained in psychology or psychiatry, have encouraged a churning up of negative feelings, with little guidance on how to find resolution.

In the early 1980s, John Welwood, a Buddhist and psychotherapist, introduced the term "spiritual bypass" to describe "spiritual ideas and practices to sidestep personal, emotional 'unfinished business,' to shore up a shaky sense of self, or to belittle basic needs, feelings, and developmental tasks."[43] Forms of respite yoga fit this description, such as when teachers encourage us to use our time on the mat to "empty our mind" and "let everything go." Bypassing is part of how respite yoga makes us feel good.

Clinicians don't necessarily regard spiritual bypassing as an unhealthy technique for dealing with difficult emotions, although some have warned that it is a defense mechanism; "it is more about checking *out* than checking *in*."[44] But beyond the ambivalent effect of our spiritual bypassing on our own mental health, it is a technique that can lead us to ignore forms of injustice in the world by encouraging avoidance when it comes to uncomfortable things. Melissa Shah, a yoga teacher and antiracism activist, points out that "chasing the light without sitting in the shadow" allows us to avoid acknowledging our privilege. This means there are consequences for others when we use respite yoga as spiritual bypassing, especially when painful systems of violence are ignored.

Tracey Anne Duncan, a journalist who writes about the intersection of wellness and social justice, described an upsetting case of spiritual bypassing during a Zoom yoga class she attended in the aftermath of George Floyd's murder in 2020. A student in the class said she was really stressed out about the state of the world, and the teacher responded, "That's why this practice is so important right now. Fold your hands at your heart and let's chant."[45] For Duncan, the teacher's response "denies the material and political realities we exist in and prevents otherwise goodhearted people from becoming warriors in the fight against injustice."[46] Spiritual bypassing in this case led to complacency toward forms of injustice and violence that affected others. Or, as Duncan puts it, "we are one" is just the yoga version of "all lives matter."[47]

Education scholar Funie Hsu argues that spiritual bypassing becomes particularly fraught as a justification for mindfulness programs in at-risk schools. Hsu points out that often the explicit purpose of yoga programs in urban, low-income, predominantly Black schools is to offer these students techniques for dealing with stress and anxiety. Since these programs focus on tools of self-regulation, not changing existing systems that lead to the stress and anxiety in the first place, they reinforce the idea that individuals have a responsibility to "react less" to their lived experiences of discrimination. That makes yoga programs in these settings a form of behavioral management for marginalized populations, a way to placate, prevent revolution, and maintain the status quo.

In her work on transformational festivals like Burning Man and Wanderlust, religious studies scholar Amanda Lucia comes at this issue from a different perspective. She argues that the relief offered by spiritual bypassing might be appealing to groups that are only minimally unfree to begin with. "Disenfranchised populations subordinated under oppressive structures of inequity may not find similar solace in the temporary relief of an affective experience of freedom," she writes. "For those populations, 'freedom work' is focused less on creating a spiritual experience of freedom that occurs *outside* of conventional reality and more on achieving freedom from racialized and economic structures of bondage *within* society."[48]

The form of harm to individual yoga practitioners most often covered by the media is sexual abuse. It seems like almost every lineage has its own scandal. Bikram Choudhury, founder of "hot" or Bikram yoga, was sued for sexual misconduct. John Friend, the founder of Anusara yoga, admitted to sleeping with several students. Videos of B. K. S. Iyengar show he slapped and kicked students while teaching. Stories of genital touching and rubbing have begun to surface since the death of Ashtanga yoga founder K. Pattabhi Jois.

A former resident of Kripalu, whom I spoke to after learning of the scandal during my teacher training, blamed the structure of the ashram on the sexual abuse that occurred within that community. She called the early Kripalu community "a failed utopian project" that attempted to re-create "an essentially Indian way of life that was not appropriate in the West." When the blame for abuse is placed on the "Indian ashram" in this way, it reinforces the idea that what is bad about these traditions is the elements perceived as foreign or religious. The problem isn't yoga, it is Indian devotional yoga. And that lets Americans off the hook.

Scholar of American religion Megan Goodwin has demonstrated in her recent book, *Abusing Religion*, that sexual abuse is an epidemic in the United States, and devotional communities are not exempt. However, Goodwin also argues that religion does not cause abuse, or in the case of yoga, gurudom does not cause abuse.[49] The person, not the position, is to blame. What the position can do, however, is create social conditions that make it harder to identify and speak out against abuse.[50] This is what happened at Kripalu: the community ignored the first reports that Desai was a sexual predator because of his position as their spiritual guide.

The respite yoga community has one form of abuse that devotional yoga does not: the exploitation of yoga teachers' labor. Revenue of the US yoga industry was projected to be $11 billion in 2020, with yoga classes making up much of that amount.[51] But most yoga instructors struggle to make a living wage. A 2019 *New York Times* article about CorePower, the largest yoga studio franchise, quoted one full-time CorePower employee who said she was paid $33.66 for each two-hour chunk of time she spent in the studio, making her salary so low that she qualified for food stamps.[52]

In my hometown of Boston, gyms pay a yoga teacher an average of $35 to $50 for an hour-long class. Yoga studios don't do much better. Some offer a flat fee per class (around $20) with an additional payment for each student who attends ($3 to $5). Almost all studios ask teachers to help market classes and recruit students into training programs. Teachers are expected to arrive early to greet students, and many must commute to multiple locations to cobble together enough classes to make a living.

To make matters worse, yoga teachers are encouraged to think about their labor conditions as created by the ethos of yoga itself, justified by the notion that teaching yoga is a spiritual calling, and that it is a privilege to share yoga with others. To complain about compensation would not be very yogalike. As one of the CorePower instructors interviewed in the *New York Times* piece put it, "You're being taught to be calm and breathe, but at the same time, being taken advantage of."[53]

In addition to low wages for teachers, yoga studios exploit the labor of their students by evoking the concept of *seva*, the idea of selfless service found in several Eastern religious traditions, to encourage members to act as volunteer janitorial and front desk staff. At one Boston-area studio, for instance, working four hours every week earns you the benefits of a full membership to the studio, which usually costs $1,200 for the year. That might seem like a good deal, but it works out to less than $6 an hour. Teachers are usually not paid for the seva students who show up in their class, so the expense of this benefit is shouldered by the teachers, not the studio owners.

After earning my teaching certification from Kripalu, I volunteered to lead a ten-week summer yoga class as part of existing Northeastern mindfulness programming. Volunteering to teach contributes to the underpaying of yoga teachers, but I want to discuss another form of exploitation I engaged in that summer: the secularization of yoga to make it more accessible.

My Kripalu teacher Julia specialized in teaching yoga in public schools, so I asked her for advice on how to develop my program for Northeastern. The first resource she pointed me to was *Best Practices for Yoga in Schools*, published by the Yoga Service Council and the Omega Institute in 2015. The takeaway from that short book is clear: in an educational setting, "yoga programs should be secular in their approach and content" to be "maximally inclusive of all cultures and beliefs."[54] Omega's suggestions on how to secularize a class include "avoid using practices that may cause confusion or misunderstanding," such as "Sanskrit, chanting, [or] placing hands in prayer position."[55]

For that summer yoga series, I followed this guidance and did what I could to make my class secular. I used English names for postures. I did not utter a single om. I did not mention Brahman or the divine, or any other explicitly religious terminology. I didn't quote the Bhagavad Gita or *Yoga Sutras*. I didn't share the teachings of Swami Kripalu. I didn't mention the yamas or niyamas. I left my mala beads—used for prayer and meditation—at home.

Figuring out how to end a secular yoga class proved challenging. Prayer hands to heart, a bow, and a namaste to "seal the practice" was how almost every class I had taken ended. It was the final punctuation, yoga code for "class over, time to roll up your mats." But it didn't feel right in a secular class. Instead, I adopted the closing of one of my favorite Kripalu teachers. With hands in prayer position—not exactly secular—I said the following: "Place your hands to your forehead for kind thoughts, lips for kind words, and heart for kind actions." And then, I thanked everyone for coming and told them to have a great evening. Recently it occurred to me that this ending is a rendition of the central tenets of Zoroastrianism. So, even while attempting to remain secular, I had let religion creep in.

When I think back on the choices I made in that ten-week series, I can now see that as I tried to avoid one type of appropriation, I committed another. When I scrubbed my class of what felt like appropriated Eastern words, gestures, and beliefs, my intention was to avoid using the acoustic and visual borrowings from Indian culture to establish my authority as an "authentic" yoga teacher. But by erasing the devotional aspects of yoga, I offered yoga that was diluted to make myself and my students more comfortable. I had presumed that "safe" yoga was de-religioned yoga, reinforcing the idea that religion, especially Eastern religion, is somehow too foreign for my Boston-based students at best, or too dangerous at worst. I had become the monster under the mat.

Erasure of devotional meanings of yoga is widespread in the United States, due in part to religious illiteracy. Take the common yoga pose *chaturanga dandasana*—in which the body is held parallel to the ground by the balls of feet and palms, elbows bent. I experience this pose as a challenging low plank useful for building core and shoulder strength or perhaps an opportunity to practice remaining calm under stressful conditions. But drawing on an interview with the famous yogi Bija Rivers, Amanda Lucia explains that this posture developed within a prostration culture. "Indians," Lucia writes, "if told to press the length of their bodies parallel to the earth with toes and palms touching the ground, would understand the movement as similar to, if not a signification of, prostration to the divine."[56] Rivers explained to Lucia that in Indic contexts, the prostration meaning of the pose is implied, almost like a grammar that all native speakers know.[57] The readability of chaturanga in the United States as merely a plank, Lucia explains, is based on "an erasure derived from the domestic lack of under-standing of the foreign cultural and religious context."[58]

I think this erasure is more nefarious than that. The US yoga in-dustry has intentionally distanced respite yoga from Eastern devotional systems, and specifically from Hinduism, to make yoga more comfort-able to the majority of Americans. The editors of the popular *Yoga Journal* have made public statements that they avoid acknowledging the connection of yoga to Hinduism.[59] I have heard teachers in yoga studios refer to aspects of yoga as Eastern, ancient, and Indian, but never as explicitly Hindu. My Kripalu training did not mention Hin-duism other than as part of Swami Kripalu's biography.

Over concerns about the severing of yoga's connection to Hinduism, in 2008 the Minneapolis-based organization Hindu American Foundation (HAF) launched its "Take Back Yoga" campaign. The campaign does not ask non-Hindus to give up yoga, but rather urges them to acknowledge that many of yoga's core ideas are grounded in the tradition we now call Hinduism. In a letter to the editors of *Yoga Journal*, Suhag A. Shukla, cofounder of HAF, wrote,

> I have become increasingly bewildered and disappointed by what seems to be an intentional and systematic disregard for Hinduism as a religious and spiritual tradition and its contributions to the world over the past 5000 years. As a practicing Hindu and second-generation Hindu American, I find the repeated references to the teachings and philosophy of Hinduism as "ancient Indian" or "ancient yogic" or "Eastern" to be, frankly speaking, disingenuous and disrespectful.[60]

HAF's website lists a number of reasons that yoga is "Hindu Thought in Practice," including the fact that it is discussed in ancient Hindu texts (for instance, the Bhagavad Gita); it relies on the Hindu tradition of gurus; and prominent Indian yoga teachers, such as B. K. S. Iyengar and K. Pattabhi Jois, were devout Hindus. In a blog forum for the *Washington Post*, and later published in *Newsweek*, Aseem Shukla, the other cofounder of HAF, blamed generations of Hindu yoga teachers for this situation. They had "offered up a religion's spiritual wealth at the altar of crass commercialism," Shukla wrote, and were guilty of "overt intellectual property theft."[61]

The Take Back Yoga campaign caused quite a stir in the yoga world, with many yoga practitioners insisting that yoga could not be owned. But these critiques missed the point. HAF made an origin, not ownership, claim about yoga. Their purpose was to point out the intentional erasure of religion that yoga teachers engage in, including myself in that first ten-week program I offered. They didn't want to prevent anyone from practicing yoga. If we read them generously, they wanted respite yoga to acknowledge its indebtedness to forms of devotional yoga.

However, as Andrea Jain has demonstrated in her work, HAF's claim that yoga has its origins in Hinduism is its own sort of erasure and exploitation. The problem with the Hindu origin position, Jain explains, is that its advocates "valorize what they perceive as a homogenous yoga system by reifying its association with what they deem authentic Hinduism and denounce those forms . . . that deviate."[62] In other words, the Hindu origins argument depends on deciding first what counts as true or authentic Hindu belief and practice, which by necessity values some aspects of a rich and varied tradition while erasing others.

The beliefs and practices that we today call Hinduism date back more than 4,000 years; however, they weren't understood as a single "religion" until the British colonial state and Christian missionaries identified them as such. "Hindu" was originally a geographic designation, referring to the Indus River Valley, which runs through what today is northwest India into Pakistan. To refer to the range of diverse worldviews, traditions, and practices as one world religion—Hinduism—was more for administrative reasons than theological ones, writes Philip Goldberg in *American Veda*. Goldberg points out that it is a bit like grouping together Judaism, Christianity, and Islam into one religion and then calling it Jordanism, after the river valley of their origin.[63]

Indian elites made their own arguments about what counted as authentic Hinduism within a Western model of "a world religion."[64] To make Hinduism legible as a world religion, for instance, they gave sacred texts (such as the Vedas) a new central role, as well as some theological teachings. In other words, Indian culture, philosophy, and religious practice are not appropriated in modern respite yoga, but rather a colonial imaginary of those things.

But there is another reason to be cautious of the HAF position: it ignores the fact that other forms of religion influenced yoga. As I have already mentioned, it is more accurate to say devotional yoga is grounded and informed by multiple traditions, such as Vedanta and Tantra. In terms of world religions, not only Hinduism, but also Buddhism, Jainism, and Sikhism could claim to be sources for yoga. A recent poll by the Pew Forum, for instance, found that today Jains, Sikhs, and Buddhists are all more likely than Hindus to practice yoga in India.[65] Making the claim that Hinduism is the only religion we should associate with yoga is more political than descriptive. And this becomes very clear when we notice how the Hindu origins of yoga are weaponized by the advocates of Hindutva.

Hindutva is a Hindu nationalist ideology that frames India as the homeland of Hindus. While it acknowledges that other religions exist in India, Hindutva is based on the idea that the state should cater first and foremost to Hindu concerns. Since the 1990s, it has become increasingly popular. Hindutva was the basis of recent electoral successes of the right-wing Bharatiya Janata Party and is promoted by current Indian prime minister Narendra Modi. For Modi, yoga is part of his political plan.

Although past Indian prime ministers have practiced yoga, none has done so as publicly and enthusiastically as Modi. As evidence of his dedication, he convinced the United Nations to endorse International Day of Yoga, which is now celebrated annually on June 21. Modi first suggested the idea in a 2014 speech to the UN General Assembly. "Yoga," Modi said, "is an invaluable gift of India's ancient tradition. . . . It is not about exercise but to discover the sense of oneness with yourself, the world and the nature. By changing our lifestyle and creating consciousness, it can help in well-being."[66]

Like Modi's remarks to the General Assembly that day, celebrations of the International Day of Yoga rarely mention Hinduism explicitly.

But the observance of this holiday is experienced by some religious minorities in India as profoundly offensive. As Andrea Jain sees it, this is a political ritual designed to appear inclusive, but its effect is to solidify the power of a select few.[67] Asaduddin Owaisi, a Muslim member of the Indian parliament, explained that, for him, "yoga is against the fundamental tenets of Islam—to pray to the sun, for example." When yoga becomes linked to national identity, it is a way to exclude Muslims. As Owaisi put it, "Just because I do not want to do yoga does not mean I am not a patriot."[68] Promoting yoga as the national pastime communicates that Muslim Indians are outsiders in their own country. And this means that when the world celebrates International Day of Yoga, it is valorizing and normalizing Hindutva.

Consider this image of a Western white woman, displaying a one-legged version of *urdhva dhanurasana*, also known as upward facing bow or wheel pose. This is an example of the conflation of ableism, whiteness, and health to promote spiritual tourism, but the location of the yoga photo shoot is also significant: in front of the Taj Mahal, arguably the most popular Muslim tourist site in India. Here, yoga is used to rebrand all things Indian as Hindu, even an iconic Muslim mausoleum, under the guise of attracting Western tourists. TripAdvisor and Expedia advertise opportunities to pay between $25 and $125 to take a yoga class facing the Taj Mahal to "learn about the real India."[69]

But lest you think the connection between yoga and right-wing politics is only an Indic problem, I want to point out that there is significant support for alt-right politics in the US yoga community as well, particularly around conspiracy theories. Over a decade ago, Charlotte Ward and David Voas coined the term "conspirituality" to signify how an alliance of spirituality and conspiracy theories had contributed to a growing movement "fueled by political disillusionment and the popularity of alternative worldviews."[70] In the last few years, yoga teachers and influencers used social media to claim Trump was a

A woman practicing *urdhva dhanurasana*, also known as upward facing bow or wheel pose, at Taj Mahal, India. (iStock/lkonya)

"lightworker," an individual who feels a pull toward helping others, and to circulate the viral documentary *Plandemic*, which promotes misinformation about COVID-19, vaccines, and mask-wearing.[71]

Support for QAnon, a far-right political conspiracy theory and movement centered on false claims that Satan-worshiping pedophiles control the United States, is particularly rampant in the wellness community. The *Conspirituality* podcast lists wellness influencers who have posted QAnon-related content. By the summer of 2021, forty-nine influencers were on the list.[72] Some yogis operationalized these commitments offline as well. Alan Hostetter, a well-known yoga teacher from Orange County, California, is facing charges for his role in the January 6, 2021, US Capitol insurrection.[73]

Months before the riot, in fall 2020, in response to what some saw as a worrisome targeting of their community, a group of 150 yoga influencers put out a public statement against QAnon. "QAnon is taking advantage of our conscious community with videos and social media steeped with bizarre theories, mind control, and misinformation–don't be swayed by these messages," the post reads. "QAnon does not represent the true values of the wellness community."[74]

Even as the signees of the fall 2020 statement insisted QAnon's values were at odds with those of the wellness community, they admitted that there were elements in their community that eased the way for the QAnon message. In an interview with the *New York Times*, Seane Corn, yoga celebrity, social justice activist, and anti-QAnon statement signee, said that she believed the emphasis on self-actualization through "truth-seeking" in her community makes members vulnerable to such groups as QAnon, who urge followers to #DoYourOwnResearch. Hala Khouri, a yoga teacher and author who also posted the anti-QAnon statement, explained in an interview with *Los Angeles Magazine* that members of the wellness community "want personal sovereignty over their health choices, so the idea that COVID is a hoax or a plot to get everyone vaccinated fits into their narrative."[75] Both Corn and Khouri are pointing out that health is conceptualized by the wellness community as the pursuit to find what works for an individual without deference to external expertise. This primes yoga practitioners for QAnon's message that we are being fed misinformation about, for instance, COVID-19, by the mainstream medical profession and the Centers for Disease Control (CDC). While it may be true that QAnon does not represent the values of devotional yoga, many values of respite yoga are consistent with QAnon's propaganda, which is likely why the conspiracy movement was able to gain such a stronghold in that community.

A therapeutic culture of self-optimization is part of the reason political conspiracy theories have taken hold within the yoga community, but I think the normalization of religious appropriation in this community also plays a role. Let me explain. As we have seen throughout the case studies in this book, appropriation of religious practices is based in part on what Leigh Schmidt calls religious liberalism, which includes the belief that we are entitled to the benefits of religion, even as we maintain an outsider status to avoid the demands of religious communities or institutions. Those engaged in religious appropriation tend to be distrustful of any source of knowledge or expertise outside their own experience or intuition. This is certainly the case for those who identify as SBNR (spiritual but not religious) and for many "nones."

As appropriation reinforces skepticism of authority, it prepares individuals to be receptive of antiestablishment conspiracy theories. As Sarah Wilson, an Australian-based veteran of the well-being industry writes,

> Contemporary spiritualism has tended to cherry-pick the "love and light" feel-good bits of the various traditions, the bits that

promote personal freedom and individuality, leaving out the responsibility, service and the sacrifice to the greater good. We connect to our yoga mats and go inward to connect to ourselves . . .
being told to isolate or wear a mask is seen as an affront to flowy
freedom—so must amount to a conspiracy, rather than a noble
act of civic engagement.[76]

Wilson argues that since spiritual borrowing is skepticism operationalized for the pursuit of personal health, anything that doesn't intuitively feel right—whether masking or vaccines—and curtails our
"flowy freedom" can easily be categorized as an external conspiracy to
control us.

For many, the wellness industry's insistence that "you know your
body best" builds on an existing medical mistrust rooted in experiences of trauma. Let's take my mother as an example. I would consider her part of the natural health and wellness community. That
community had offered her solutions for herniated disks, arthritis, low
energy, even depression—none of which required submitting to outside medical or scientific expertise. She prefers to self-treat any illness
with herbal remedies, such as echinacea for a cold, turmeric for in-
flammation, and Saint-John's-wort for depression. She doesn't get an
annual mammogram or take hormone replacement for menopause.
She rarely goes to the doctor. She thinks health-care professionals are
overly interventionist and prefers to trust her own body's ability to heal
"naturally." She has reasons for this mistrust, including my own birth
in 1973, when medical staff restrained her and tried to sedate her
against her will.

Although she is not a follower of QAnon, some of her reactions to
COVID-19 line up with its messages. She hates masks and, having
read online that they caused CO_2 poisoning, tried to convince me it
was dangerous to run in them. She insisted that she was strong and

healthy and that COVID-19 would likely only affect her like the flu. When she did get a mild case in the winter of 2021, her plan became to trust her own body's antibodies to guard against future infections and was only vaccinated when it became a condition of seeing her grandchildren. The wellness community had primed her to be more willing to trust theories that she could find online than the advice from the CDC.

The final category of oppression I want to highlight is how the rise of respite yoga in the United States makes desis—individuals from the Indian subcontinent—outsiders to their own culture. Yoga teacher and inclusivity advocate Susanna Barkataki describes this form of profound offense. "When I take a $25.00 yoga class by a well-known teacher who wants to 'expose us to the culture by chanting Om to start class,'" she writes, "and her studio hangs the Om symbol in the wrong direction, my culture is being stripped of its meaning and sold back to me." The entire process feels, Barkataki says, "humiliating at best and dehumanizing at worst."[77]

There was one Indian woman in my Kripalu training. I'll call her Nisha. In class, she never asked questions. Instead, she offered comments about "how we do this" or "why we do that"; for instance, "Perhaps some background about why we do that is helpful?" And she corrected the instructors. "Julia, if you rest your fingers on your temple for *nadi shona* like you just showed us, that is a different pose that we use if we have a sinus problem." "Huey, we actually pronounce that Sanskrit word differently." Nisha understood her experience growing up in India to make her the yoga expert in the room.

But Nisha was also the odd one out. We spent five hours a day moving through postures to learn them, and that was physically challenging for her. She couldn't touch her toes. Her knees and back bothered her. By the end of the program, she spent large portions of class in the back of the room, cocooned in a cotton blanket, asleep on her mat.

The challenge for Nisha was that we were not learning the devotional yoga of her childhood. We were learning Kripalu's version of respite yoga, an Anglo-American practice, an appropriated practice. And although this yoga supposedly came from her homeland, it was unfamiliar and uncomfortable.

Kripalu had no trouble teaching me. In many ways, I was an ideal student. I could afford the expensive tuition. I had access to a population of potential practitioners on my campus. I could teach as a volunteer since I already had a full-time job. Kripalu never made me question my choice to get certified to teach. But I know it made Nisha question hers.

When desis try to talk about the way American yoga culture excludes them, they are often accused of being the ones causing problems. Rumya Putcha, a South Asian scholar of performance studies, shares a story on her research blog, *Namaste Nation*, that illustrates this dynamic well. When Putcha lived in Texas, she was a member of a local yoga studio. Another member, a white woman I'll call Becky, used a pun, "Namastay together," that made Putcha uncomfortable. She decided to explain why to Becky. The conversation didn't go well.[78]

Becky initially reacted defensively, "I don't have to explain myself." Putcha responded with what she thought was a helpful analogy: the way Mexican Americans feel when Cinco de Mayo is turned into a pun, like "Cinco de Drinko." But the implication that her namaste joke was racist only put Becky on the offensive. She fired back several questions. What if she had lived in India for ten years? What if her husband was Indian? Both were hypothetical scenarios, but raising them made it clear Becky objected to the idea that Putcha had a right to critique her behavior in their yoga studio based on her embodied desi experience.

Despite the intensity of the exchange, Putcha had thought it ended semiamicably. The two women even hugged. But then, Becky tattled to the studio owner. And at that moment—when a white studio member complained to a white studio owner about a brown woman's critique of an insensitive use of South Asian culture—white privilege was triggered.

A few days later, the owner pulled Putcha aside, saying he wouldn't tolerate her "causing problems," and told her she was no longer welcome in the studio where she had practiced for three years. Putcha pleaded with the owner to reconsider, but to no avail. She had violated the unspoken rules of white civility in the studio, a place of unity, where white people came to feel good. Putcha had to go. The studio was happy to borrow from South Asian culture to make its members' yoga experience more "authentic," but actual South Asian members would be excluded if they questioned this appropriation.

Capitalism, Orientalism, and White Supremacy

Just like the students in my "Selling Spirituality" seminar, the more I learn about yoga, the more uncomfortable I become with my practice. I have come to see this discomfort as a good thing. It is a sign that I am becoming more aware of my role in larger systems of structural injustice, such as capitalism, orientalism, and white supremacy, that my consumption of yoga depends on.

Respite yoga is marketed, taught, and consumed within global market capitalism, the economic and political system in which trade, industry, and profits are controlled by private companies and individuals rather than the people whose labor creates those goods. The colonization of India, which exploited the capital of the colony for the benefit of the British Empire, was the catalyst for local elites to see asana as a valuable good that would be domestically promoted as well as globally exported. As yoga moved west, where capitalism gave rise

to a robust consumer culture, it became popular only after it was successfully marketed as a valuable wellness commodity. Underpaying
yoga instructors in studios is an example of capitalist injustice. Capitalist impulses are also why abuse within the yoga world has been tol-
erated for so long: To protect gurus turned yoga entrepreneurs and
their brand, abuse was swept under the rug.

According to a 2020 yoga market analysis published by Wellness
Creative Company, the yoga studio industry is worth over $88 billion
worldwide. If retreats, clothing, mats, blocks, and other accessories are
included, the global yoga market is worth well over $130 billion.[79] The
Ibis marketing firm found that the yoga industry in the United States
alone was worth $12 billion in 2018, and projected an almost 10 percent
annual growth before the COVID-19 disruption.[80]

The ethical problem is not that yoga is the commodification of
religion, but rather how this form of commodification emboldens
outsiders to appropriate religious forms for personal benefit in ways
that contribute to ongoing exploitations.[81] Here, I am arguing against
conventional wisdom that commodification is bad per se, so let me
explain. Using examples from popular culture, scholar of American
religion Kathryn Lofton shows that "much of consumer life is itself a
religious enterprise" insofar as it is "enshrining certain commitments
stronger than almost any other acts of social participation."[82] Similarly,
yoga studies scholar Andrea Jain argues that just because we pay for
yoga classes doesn't mean they aren't experienced as powerful rituals.
Both scholars understand that consumption does not disqualify something as religious. Jain characterizes spirituality, or what she spec-
ifies as "neoliberal spirituality," not as "a takeover or replacement of
religion or as an alternative to religion, but as a modern manifestation of religion."[83]

And yet, because conventional wisdom is that consumption is
somehow antithetical to religion, as yoga becomes increasingly com-

modified, people feel even more justified in erasing its connections to communities and traditions of devotion. Capitalism makes forms of appropriation involved in respite yoga possible by convincing us that yoga is just something we can buy, and thus available to any consumer to use as we wish.

Orientalism has an important role in the successful mass marketing of respite yoga. Internalized orientalism led Indian elites to mine traditions of devotional yoga for techniques they could promote as part of local physical fitness regimens, while simultaneously proving they were able to achieve European ideals of modernity, but in ways that were distinctly Eastern. And in a counterintuitive way, insisting that yoga was Eastern created the conditions by which it could be marketed in the West. A romantic fetishization of Asia made yoga attractive to countercultural and spiritual revival movements in the United States, as an ancient Eastern pathway to solve the problems of Western modern life. For yoga to become mainstream, the aspects that were considered too Eastern—metaphysical ideas, systems of leadership, and values—had to be placed aside. This made yoga appear accessible and safe to Western consumers, who in turn assumed they were entitled to use it in any way they saw fit.

Sophia Arjana's recent book *Buying Buddha* is helpful for identifying another effect of orientalism we can see in respite yoga, mainly "muddled Orientalism," the "careless mixing of images, terms, and tropes from the imagined Orient."[84] Muddled orientalism is how "namaste" gets infused with liturgical meaning in a US yoga studio when, in a South Asian context, the word is a simple greeting.

Orientalism is also why yoga's Hindu roots are overemphasized by such groups as HAF and Hindu nationalists, and erased entirely by others; for instance, secularized yoga programs in public schools. The HAF's Hindu origins of yoga claim only works if we accept that Hinduism has some ahistorical essence, and that is very much an orientalist construction. On the flip side, concern that Hindu ideas hidden in yoga are dangerous to US practitioners relies on an orientalist framing of Eastern religions as incompatible with Western ways of life. This is why Kripalu insists yoga is not religious and that a Western practitioner is not required to submit to the authority of any Eastern institutions, ethics, or metaphysical claims. Such submission would be inappropriate, given the positional superiority of an assumed Western "us" to an assumed Eastern "them."

Finally, it is important to highlight that in the United States, respite yoga exists within the system of white supremacy, but there are consequences for talking about that fact, especially if you aren't white. When Putcha raised concerns about the use of namaste in her yoga studio, she was asked to leave. Similarly, when religious studies scholar Shreena Gandhi and activist Lillie Wolff argued in a cowritten essay that yoga culture contributes to white supremacy, they faced hateful backlash.[85] To be more accurate, Gandhi, who is of South Asian descent, did. She was ridiculed by conservative news sites, such as *College Fix* and *Daily Stormer*, and was the subject of a Tucker Carlson segment on Fox News.[86]

This response from conservatives was to be expected. But white moderates and liberals reacted just as strongly to Gandhi and Wolff's claim that racism exists in yoga culture. Gandhi received one email, for instance, from a white yoga teacher, who accused her of inciting hate and suggested she "try to know true Americans a bit more." "The liberal white backlash," Gandhi told me, "was the most revealing about whiteness."[87] It also proved one of the points in Gandhi and Wolff's essay, "that white people are not taught to confront and examine the painful and uncomfortable realities of racism" and that "one of the goals of white supremacy is to buffer white people from the pain that comes from the process of exchanging cultural grounding for the unearned power and privilege of whiteness."[88]

If I'm honest, this is part of why I had difficulty with Nisha, the South Asian woman in my Kripalu training. To be sure, her insistence that she could speak on behalf of all Indians was problematic since she was part of the Brahmin caste in India, and yes, her constant interruptions were distracting. But I can now see that my annoyance was also about something else. When she pointed out things in the curriculum that made her uncomfortable, because she saw them as either inaccurate or at least not reflective of her experience, she was making everyone — instructors and students — uncomfortable too. She was forcing us to sit in discomfort with her, in much the same way I would later challenge my students to sit with discomfort in a studio yoga class. Nisha was a constant reminder of who we were: mostly white people, with little connection to South Asia, sitting in a room in the Berkshires, wearing expensive athleisure wear. And although many of us were devoted to our yoga practice, and would describe it as spiritual, she made us feel that we were stealing her religion.

Wellness without Negligence

While I was discussing this book with one of my colleagues, her initial response was that although it seemed clear that religious appropriation motivated by politics (solidarity hijab) or even education (playing pilgrim) might be problematic, she thought folks were entitled to appropriate anything they wanted in the pursuit of health. That makes sense, but only until we remember that health is not merely the reward for good genes or meritorious bodily habits. Health often depends on who we are and where we live. And sometimes our health comes at the expense of exploiting others.

Even for those of us who are not experts in public health, COVID-19 made health disparities impossible to ignore. The CDC reports Indigenous, Black, and Latinx Americans are over twice as likely to die from COVID-19 than are white Americans, and states that "race and ethnicity are risk markers for other underlying conditions that affect health, including socioeconomic status, access to health care, and exposure to the virus related to occupation, e.g., frontline, essential, and critical infrastructure workers."[89] I saw this play out in the Boston metro area during the first surge. While my hometown of Brookline maintained relatively low rates of infection, Chelsea, seven miles away, had the highest cumulative infection rate in the state. The median household income in Brookline is more than double that of Chelsea—$117,000 and $56,000 respectively, according to the US Census. And just under 80 percent of Chelsea's employed population work in occupations deemed essential compared to the statewide percentage of 61 percent.[90] As I worked remotely, Instacart workers whom I hired to do my grocery shopping—some of whom lived in Chelsea—were engaging in behavior I had decided was too risky for my health. I was increasing someone else's possibility of exposure to infection so as to lower my own.

Yoga creates a similar ethical dilemma for me. I believe yoga is conducive to my physical and mental health, and yet I am also aware of how yoga is implicated in our culture of capitalism, Western exceptionalism, and whiteness. I hoped to find some sort of resolution to the ethical ambivalence of yoga, but my concerns with yoga run deep. They begin with the observation that, to be accepted as an accessible healthy practice, yoga had to be redefined from a devotional practice to what amounts to respite self-care. That process involved commodifying, orientalizing, and whitewashing. At the same time, the allure of respite yoga still depends on its assumed ancient, brown, and religious roots. This makes respite yoga, especially for white Americans, a practice of constructing the other only to consume it in service of a healthy self. It is part of what I fear is a trend, described so eloquently by bell hooks, "that cultural, ethnic, and racial differences will be continually commodified and offered up as new dishes to enhance the white palate—that the Other will be eaten, consumed, and forgotten."[91]

Our wellness entails negligence when we instrumentalize the religion of others to optimize our personal health. Sanskrit as pseudo-liturgy, namaste and om as rituals, and following celebrity gurus—these are all appropriations that romanticize and exoticize South Asia without requiring any understanding of that region's cultures or communities. Much like my dependence on Instacart shoppers during COVID-19 lockdowns, in the pursuit of personal health, we are often failing to consider how our actions might injure or render invisible others.

There are political consequences to this negligence. The way respite yoga insists that health is self-directed is easily recruited by forms of fascism and ethno-religious nationalism, such as by proponents of British imperialism in the interwar period and advocates of Hindu supremacy in India today. The values of respite yoga also prime some practitioners to be more susceptible to conspiracy theories, which offer easily digestible suggestions for how to trust yourself on issues of health instead of believing in the validity of new scientific discoveries such as RNA technology.

To change this would require radical rethinking of health as self-optimization to a corporate ethos of flourishing for all. Our experience with COVID-19, including continual vaccine hesitancy, indicates this is likely not something Americans are ready for. But it may be possible to start at a micro level, changing our personal behavior to begin a social transformation. To continue to practice yoga, for instance, I decided my first step was to create criteria for what I will and will not do beyond "what feels good." My criteria aim at limiting profound offense to other communities and people, but also at doing what I can to disrupt systems of injustice that respite yoga can exacerbate, including problematic erasure of religion in ways that reinforce hierarchies between white Protestantism and Eastern forms of devotion.

Instead of accepting that respite yoga is universal and timeless, I have tried to sit in the discomfort that it has serious devotional roots that I do not subscribe to. Thus my practice involves an effort to educate myself.

As a white American with a Christian upbringing, understanding the devotional readability of my asana practice involves work. Chaturanga dandasana, we saw, assumes a culture of prostrations. In the US context, however, this posture is more commonly read as a bent arm plank to build strength. Namaste is another example I discussed that has different meaning in an American versus South Asian context. This is one result of appropriation: elements extracted from larger systems of meaning become readable in new ways. These new meanings are not necessarily exploitative, but they can be, especially given the ways existing hierarchies usually shape what elements are borrowed and how they are reinterpreted, as well as which elements are deemed too foreign or dangerous and so are left behind. Remember Kripalu's reinvention of itself after the sex scandal: the Indic elements — gurudom, ashram, devotion — were removed to make Kripalu yoga safer for American consumers. But this did three things. It disconnected Kripalu yoga from its religious roots, it whitewashed its practice, and it reinforced the presumption that Eastern religion is somehow dangerous.

Within the American context, I have concluded that where yoga is practiced matters for its ethical impact. For instance, the stakes of my home practice, my studio practice, and my campus teaching are very different. My home practice has evolved through the process of writing this book. I acknowledge that my time on my mat borrows from the religion of others, especially from South Asian communities, and I am constantly evaluating how orientalist stereotypes might shape my practice. I understand that while I first came to yoga to heal my back, my home practice at times dips into devotion.

When I move my practice to my Brookline studio, and thus make it public and communal in a different way, the stakes change. I grapple with the question of supporting the studio with my membership dues. Some things give me pause. For instance, it is a predominantly white space, both in terms of instructors and students. That began to change in 2020 with the hiring of several instructors of color and with the addition of a free community program called Accomplice Circle that examines "the impact of racial trauma on health, explores challenges to collaborative and healing discourse" and invites "moving beyond the comfort of allyship."[92]

At the studio, I do not chant "namaste." In that space, that gesture feels performative. A couple of years ago, I would say "namaste" in a respite yoga class out of habit, without understanding what I was saying. I now experience this ritual as a fetishization of Indian culture, finding it upsetting rather than soothing.

Things become more difficult when I step into the role of yoga teacher. I have come to see that this role requires leading others through religious appropriation, and my opinion about how best to do so is still evolving. As I mentioned earlier, the first time I taught yoga, I attempted to secularize my class. That is no longer true. Now, when I occasionally volunteer to teach on my campus, I add back the content that I initially scrubbed. Sometimes, I begin with a quote from the Bhagavad Gita or pick a yama as a theme. I explain and use concepts that I learned at Kripalu, such as *prana*, Buddhi, and Atman. I sometimes talk more in depth about yoga's history or philosophical systems associated with yoga. I call postures by their English and Sanskrit names. When I teach, I still focus on a respite experience, but try to provide an opportunity to learn about devotional yoga as well.

But I have made decisions to not include some elements, based on what I have learned from marginalized communities about harm. For instance, I never begin or end my class with namaste. For me, namaste crosses the line. I know too much about its history, and how it is experienced by some South Asians, to enjoy using this term. Occasionally, students approach me after class and ask me why I don't say "namaste." And then, in a conversation about the power dynamics involved in religious borrowing, my most important yoga teaching begins.

Conclusion

My goal in writing this book was to see whether cultural appropriation might be useful for investigating the ethical implications of harmful forms of religious borrowings. I was motivated by the fact that appropriation is increasingly used to call out cases of consumption that cause harm to marginalized communities, and yet from my vantage point, most instances of what look like religious appropriation are ignored in these discussions. When they are addressed, the religious actors who raise concerns are often labeled "fundamentalist" or "reactionary." Other times, the specific cases of appropriation are defended by calling them something else based on their liberal motivations—politics, education, therapy—all of which effectively hide their exploitative qualities.

If appropriation is a way the public thinks about the ethics of cultural exchange, as a religious ethicist, I want to be part of that conversation. But I also want to use appropriation in a different analytical way. "Appropriation" is usually used to express moral condemnation, which can prevent further ethical inquiry. Instead, I use it as a starting point to unpack the ethical issues at hand, such as why people appropriate from others, what exploitations these appropriations cause, and what existing forms of asymmetrical power dynamics they depend on and reinforce.

A couple of things make religious appropriation distinct from other forms of cultural appropriation. For one, religious communities have porous borders, and as a result, whoever counts as an insider is always ambiguous. This is not necessarily the case in nonreligious forms of appropriation; for instance, when white people appropriate practices associated with Black communities. In these cases, the public debate doesn't focus on who counts as Black, but rather on whether the borrowing is causing any harm or offense. In religious appropriation, the first challenge is figuring out who "owns" a religious practice in the first place.

Some religious communities are invested in evangelizing others; thus, they are motivated to make outsiders feel like insiders. Nevertheless, there is something very different about seeking potential converts who will accept doctrines, leadership models, systems of values, narratives, and institutions versus a self-proclaimed SBNR (spiritual but not religious) who appropriates a religious practice. The latter is simultaneously willing to criticize the very idea of "organized religion," to even belittle deeply held religious beliefs, while trying on religious practices for personal political, pedagogic, or therapeutic reasons.

Although the concept of cultural appropriation depends on an insider/outsider distinction, religious practices are often shaped by an interaction between these two groups. The hijab was elevated to the primary symbol of Islam only after Anglo-European colonizers identified it as the thing that distinguished Muslim women from European ones. The Camino doesn't exist without anxieties caused by the rise to power of Moors in Spain. Respite yoga has its roots in a colonial moment when European ideas about fitness and a modern citizenry encouraged India's elites to promote indigenous forms of physical fitness. In these cases, the "origins" of the practices cannot be easily credited to one group.

To make things even more complicated, knowing someone considers themselves to be a religious insider does not exempt them from scrutiny. In fact, one surprising feature of religious appropriation is that religious insiders can steal their own religion. In the case of the Camino, the God Squad's insistence on their right to participate in a Catholic Eucharist demonstrated a form of internal appropriation, one in which what counts as "true" Christianity was contested. It can't be said that the Hindu nationalists are religious outsiders, and yet Hindutva hijacks the association of yoga and Hinduism to exclude Muslims from a vision of the nation. In the United States, invoking evangelical values has been a defining feature of Republican politics since the Reagan era. Former president Donald Trump, for instance, promoted evangelical ideas, such as prosperity gospel, that helped consolidate his power, while ignoring others that would encourage him to change his political priorities, such as preferential treatment of the poor, or his personal behavior, for instance, chastity and monogamy. Trump identifies as Christian, but he is also a frequent appropriator of Christianity.

Appropriating one's own tradition is possible because religious communities are internally diverse and there are competing interpretations of what is considered right practice. For instance, some Muslims believe covering the head is necessary for women to cultivate the virtue of modesty. Other Muslims consider this practice a historical artifact, a sexist custom given that Muslim men's clothing is not regulated in the same way. Internal debates about the right way to practice a faith can find outward expressions that look like appropriation. This is why some Muslims are offended when non-Muslims promote hijab as a symbol of Islam, even as others welcome the gesture.

Despite these analytical challenges, I found it necessary to identify a religious outsider who steals the practices of others in each of the cases of appropriation discussed in this book. I used a couple of tactics to do this. First, instead of worrying about who counts as an insider, I focused on the self-reported outsider status of the borrower, who appropriated in part because they believed they could do so "safely" by remaining immune from religious entanglement. Second, when searching for exploitations, I focused on concerns raised by individuals already marginalized within a religious community. This allowed me to acknowledge the diversity within religious communities while also investigating claims of exploitation made by the most vulnerable.

Another characteristic of appropriation involving religion is that it has the potential to be profoundly offensive.[1] Religious practices are part of how religious group membership is formed and maintained, but they can also be the foundation to an individual's entire worldview. Forms of appropriation that disrupt those commitments can be traumatizing.

But I think the hardest thing about religious appropriation is that the solution to the forms of ethical harm it creates is not simple avoidance. Avoiding religious borrowing is impossible, given the way religion is consumed in the American context. It might also be undesirable because it could prevent forms of meaningful engagement. What we need instead is a way to understand when religious borrowing entails hidden exploitations that are grounded in broader forms of structural injustice, and what we might do to mitigate those harms.

Exploitations

Religious appropriation occurs when we reduce religion to culture by setting aside its associated institutions, communities, cosmologies, metaphysics, and systems of values. This separation is supposed to protect the borrower from being implicated in religion when they engage in religious practices, but it does not. We have seen that religious appropriation gets involved in intracommunity debates, reinforces existing religious hierarchies, erases histories of religious conflict, and even threatens to change the meaning of the practice for religious believers. And because these appropriations occur within existing systems of structural injustice, they can be experienced as exploitative by several actors.

The three cases in this book were all motivated by goals we would judge as "good" from a liberal point of view: demonstrating allyship with a religious minority (solidarity hijab), learning through firsthand experience about a religious rite of passage (playing pilgrim), or therapeutic treatment (respite yoga). And yet these motivations were not enough to prevent problematic consequences. Put simply, liberal intentions led to illiberal results.

By paying particular attention to the experiences of marginalized and vulnerable communities, I discovered a range of exploitations. Some appropriations erased or overemphasized aspects of rich devotional systems, such as in the case of respite yoga. Some redefined the religious meanings of the practices themselves, such as when a hijab was reimagined as a symbol of liberal wokeness. Some made invisible the connection of a practice to religious communities in order to sanitize it for potential consumers, such as in the reimagining of the Camino as a journey of self-transformation. And since religious meanings are socially constructed, religious appropriation can be a form of social reconstruction, thus interfering with a community's engagement with a practice.

Religious appropriation also has the potential for making religious insiders into outsiders. This happens when self-proclaimed outsiders present themselves as doing the practice more correctly, such as non-Muslim women's use of hijab for political protest, Protestants setting the norms for completing a Catholic pilgrimage, or Anglo-American yogis inventing pseudo-Sanskrit liturgy. In some of these cases, the appropriation becomes a form of virtue-signaling (as in Instagram posts of solidarity hijab); in others, it is a way to stake a claim on what counts as a correct interpretation of a religious tradition (such as asserting Protestant privilege on the Camino); and yet in others, it is the whitewashing of a practice associated with brown communities (as we saw with Putcha's Texas yoga studio).

We found exploitation that was financial. The adoption of solidarity hijab builds on, and contributes to, the mainstreaming of Muslim clothing by the for-profit apparel industry. The popularity of the Camino among non-Catholics contributes to gentrification of northern Spain and makes the region dependent on tourism. Sometimes the financial exploitation is even justified by the appropriation itself, such as when the American yoga industry promotes unpaid labor through the yogic ideal seva.

Appropriations have unintended political consequences as well. Even if solidarity hijab is meant to signal feminist Muslim allyship, it is experienced by some Muslim women as the expression of gendered Islamophobia. By building an educational program around a pilgrimage to St. James's tomb, I reinforce a particular version of Spanish history that privileges Christian nationalism. Respite yoga is implicated in both Hindu nationalism and alt-right conspiracy theories in the United States. It is common for religious liberals to insist that their brand of spirituality leads to an ethic of social compassion and progressive reform.[2] But the case studies of this book uncover ways in which liberal motivated forms of religious appropriation can have conservative outcomes.

We also discovered problematic effects for the stealer of religion. The Camino encourages self-destructive behavior. The popularity of respite yoga can incite intense emotional reactions and even create conditions that allow for physical abuse. These harms often go unnoticed because of the assumption that we can reduce religions to a set of cultural practices. But religious practices re-create and reinforce deeply held metaphysical, cosmological, and moral beliefs. No matter how safe we think dabbling in religion is, stealing our religion gets us involved in the serious business of religion.

Religion functions differently from other forms of culture because it involves not only human patterns of meaning and practice but also a longing for ultimate meaning often manifested as unconditional moral demands. This is why religious appropriation can cause a profound offense: it has the potential to destabilize entire worldviews, affront core values, and challenge a sense of self.

Given the diversity within religious communities, religious insiders rarely agree on exploitations that result from appropriation, much less profoundly offensive ones. And that means declaring something to be profoundly offensive can involve valorizing one religious member's experience over another. Nevertheless, I think we have seen incidents of profound offense in each case study. In the case of the #HeadscarfForHarmony campaign (Chapter 1), the combination of assumed kinship, virtue-signaling, and decentering Muslims was exploitation. But followed by attempts to publicly silence Black Muslim women, it became a form of profound offense, based on a religiously encoded form of misogynoir. I discussed Putcha's experience of the joke "Namastay together" as an example of how South Asian culture is exploited in white yoga spaces (Chapter 3). This incident changed from exploitation to profound offense when the white yoga studio owner kicked Putcha out of the yoga studio for expressing her concern, making it clear that maintaining the whiteness of the studio space was more important than Putcha's very sense of self and values. My reaction to the God Squad's attempt to participate in the Eucharist (Chapter 2) was caused by my perception of a profound offense.

My latent Catholic identity and pedagogical sensibilities were confronted in what I understood as an act that was disrespectful to Catholics. But in this case, my interference with what the God Squad understood as the sincere expression of its members' Protestant faith was also profoundly offensive. And if I had designed an academic program that produced a crisis of faith for my students, that would be profoundly offensive as well.

Structural Injustices

As I dived into the case studies of this book, I learned that religious borrowing becomes appropriation when it relies on and contributes to existing forms of structural injustice. These various forms of systemic oppression cause religious borrowings to be experienced as exploitative and sometimes profoundly offensive. They are also why the borrowing happens in the first place and the mechanism by which it is defended.

We have seen several specific forms of structural injustice at play in religious appropriation. Capitalism, and the economic disparities it exacerbates, was a structural injustice I expected to find, since the commodification of cultural products is the basis for much mainstream moral condemnation of appropriation. Respite yoga is perhaps the best example of how a religious practice is reinvented as a valuable commodity and then proliferates through systems of underpaid labor. But in the case of religious appropriation, not all exploitations related to commodification are about who financially benefits. For instance, the marketing of hijab as a fashion and political accessory is changing the readability of this head covering as a form of personal piety. And my study abroad program on the Camino highlights that access to such learning opportunities depends on socioeconomic status and that these sorts of programs can make local economies overly dependent on educational tourism.

Another structural injustice we saw was Christian hegemony, most easily observed in the case of the Camino in both the Protestant privilege displayed by my Evangelical students and a dominant Christian narrative of Spanish history. But more broadly, the dominance of Protestantism in the United States also affects how we culturally define what counts as religion—for the most part, beliefs that are familiar from a Protestant point of view—which makes practices associated with minority religions available for repurposing for our own aims.

Religious appropriation is also implicated in orientalism. Orientalism made non-Christian practices attractive for appropriation in the first place by framing them as exotic, ancient, and mystical. It is why hijab is adopted in solidarity politics as well as why so many Americans are drawn to respite yoga as a form of accessible ancient spiritual wisdom. Orientalism is also why these appropriations are framed as safe: if Eastern and Western people are fundamentally different, Westerners can consume Eastern religious practices without risking conversion.

In the Introduction, I mentioned that Americans tend not to call out cases of religious appropriation because they don't see them as racialized, but that just shows how insidious and hidden white supremacy and the ideology of whiteness are. Investigation of religious appropriation uncovers that religious practices of brown and Black communities are often the subject of appropriation, histories of racism are erased to make US consumers of religious practices more comfortable, and white Protestants are deferred to as the arbitrators of what counts as American religion.

I identified specific structural injustices caused by whiteness in all three cases of religious appropriation. The Camino depends on a racialized narrative, especially in the figure of Matamoros: an Anglo-European apostle turned medieval knight murdering nonwhite North African Muslims to "return" Spain to its imagined Christian, but also white, roots. We see the whitewashing of yoga for American consumers, as well as a backlash against the desi diaspora who point out the pervasiveness of white supremacy in the respite yoga industry. Anti-Black racism comes up in the case of solidarity hijab, both through representation of Muslim identity as brown instead of Black, and in the ways in which Black Muslims who spoke out again the #HeadscarfForHarmony campaign were ridiculed by non-Black Muslims. Religio-misogynoir, the intersection of anti-Black racism, sexism, and religious discrimination, produces specific forms of harm to Black Muslim women.

It might have surprised some readers that I have named feminism as one of the structural injustices involved in solidarity hijab. I had in mind a particular form of feminism, white feminism, which fails to cede space or power to women of color. Most women who adopted the solidarity hijab I discussed were white, and their actions reduced Muslim women to a token of diversity. Black Muslims found this particularly offensive. And non-Black Muslim women demonstrated an internalization of white feminism when they criticized Black Muslim women for expressing concerns. White feminism is also at play in the wellness community. We saw it expressed in the yoga studio owner's decision to bar Putcha from the studio after her argument with Becky: this act protected a white women's freedom at the expense of a brown woman's.

Often in cases of religious appropriation, the borrower considers themselves better—more autonomous, more free, and more rational—because of their outsider status. This status allows them to assume they can dabble in religious clothing, rites of passage, or rituals without the danger of succumbing to the doctrines, authorities, and strict moral codes that religious insiders are subject to. Appropriators are even sometimes convinced their form of a religious practice is "better" than the version embedded in community and tradition: solidarity hijab is presumed to be unencumbered by Islamic patriarchy, an educational Camino presumes to avoid submission to the power and doctrines of such powerful institutions as the Catholic Church, and yoga for health claims to sidestep adherence to Eastern gurus and metaphysical claims.

This points to a final form of structural injustice seen across the case studies that is epistemic in nature: a maldistribution of perceived expertise and asserted authority. As groups of outsiders—such as SBNR, Protestants, and Anglo-Americans—asserted competency or even mastery of religious practices, the credibility of religious insiders was diminished. Black Muslim women, Catholic students on Camino, desi women—these were all populations told that they were engaging in their own religious practices incorrectly by self-proclaimed outsiders.

A Way Forward

At the heart of religious appropriation is the misperception that if we avoid religious membership, we avoid involvement in negative things we associate with religion: institutions, rules, creeds, and hierarchies. We think we can avoid getting involved in the messiness of religion.

But when we appropriate religious practices, we are part of religion. We become involved in the internal power dynamics of religious traditions. We meddle in the religious meanings of practices. We further marginalize the already religiously minoritized. The more aware we are of the contexts and effects of our borrowings, the more likely we can mitigate our contribution to systemic forms of oppression. Even better, this awareness can help make engaging the religious practices of others more than an opportunity for self-enrichment.

Throughout this book, I have focused on political, educational, and therapeutic activities that are forms of religious appropriation, oppressive to others, but justified as "good" from a liberal point of view. This means I've been engaging in a stealth critique of liberalism, particularly its relationship to forms of religious discrimination.

It is not a coincidence that many forms of religious appropriation are motivated by liberal goals. Liberalism helps to justify appropriating the religious practices of others by framing these actions as the pursuit of universal goods, such as solidarity, knowledge, and wellness. Liberalism also makes appropriation possible by emphasizing individual autonomy and freedom over the rights of social groups, including religious communities. Finally, liberalism obscures various harms caused by religious appropriation by presenting religious tolerance as the primary goal. But tolerance has limitations. It relies on a distinction between "us" and "them" that reinforces a hierarchy and does very little to fight the problem of hatred or create space for new freedoms.[3]

One of the takeaways of this book is that liberal motivated forms of religious appropriation are not as progressive as they are intended to be. In fact, they are quite the opposite. The liberal impulse to offer respite yoga to inner-city schools is a form of racial conditioning of Black youth. The politics of solidary hijab alleviates the guilt of non-Muslims so that they feel less urgency to address systemic anti-Muslim hate. It thus contributes to, instead of combating, gendered Islamophobia. The goal of religious literacy in my Camino program depends on constructing an experience of authentic pilgrimage in ways that are comfortable to non-Catholic students. This means students learn more about themselves than about a religious tradition.

And yet, since I think religious borrowing is widespread and impossible to eradicate, I want to spend some time thinking constructively about the best way forward. Is there a way to borrow our religion in more responsible ways?

One way forward would be to develop a set of principles to follow when engaging with religious practices as an outsider. Such principles could include recognizing any power differentials between ourselves and the religious community in question. Another could be pursuing forms of religious engagement beyond tolerance that take religious difference as a source of new values and ways of life. And finally, we might have to be explicit that the expression of our individual autonomy needs to be curtailed so as to recognize, respect, and allow the freedom and flourishing of others.

In some cases, applying these principles would lead us to decide the harm outweighs the benefit of religious borrowing. As someone familiar with debates within the Muslim community about the obligatory nature of hijab, I wouldn't adopt it as symbol of solidarity. When I realized my Camino program was reinforcing the idea that we have a right to consume religion when we are invested in remaining outsiders, I stopped offering it. The more I learn about respite yoga, the more I seek out a way to practice that does not rely on unpaid labor or centering whiteness. The ability to say "No, I shouldn't do this thing, even though I know I can" is a powerful acknowledgment of personal privilege and a commitment to not allowing inherited entitlement to continue unchecked.

However, avoiding religious borrowing entirely isn't always feasible or even desirable, since it could prevent meaningful forms of engagement. The question becomes, How do we mitigate risk when borrowing religion? In other words, how do we borrow without appropriating? My answer might surprise you. I don't think the solution is stealing less religion, but stealing more.

Let me explain. Engaging the religion of others is not the problem. The exploitation of religious appropriation lies in the partialness of the borrowing, the delinking of practices from communities and complex webs of meaning, based not only on the assumption that we can consume a religious practice without embracing the "religion" per se, but also that we are entitled to do so. For "nones," who think that "organized religion" is problematic, religious practices are safe only if untethered from larger systems of thought and practice. For folks who have their own sincerely held religious beliefs or values, the religion of other people is treated as a repository of cultural artifacts to be tried on for personal goals while simultaneously rejecting the religious ideas that give meaning to the practices. There is an implied superiority, either as a none who has no religion or as a religious believer who is sure only theirs is correct, which allows us to steal the religion of others.

One way to prevent the exploitations that result from the partialness of religious appropriation is to reconnect the practices to religious communities and traditions that claim them. Part of this is education. Once the borrower understands the religious meaning of the practice and its associated cosmologies, metaphysics, and systems of value, it is more difficult to consume the practice as a mere political, pedagogical, or therapeutic commodity. What I learned from the research for this book means I do not feel comfortable wearing hijab as a symbol of protest, requiring participation in a religious ritual for course credit, or chanting "namaste" in a yoga class.

And yet religious literacy is not enough. I think equally important is giving up the hierarchical framing of "us" versus "them" that animates the appropriation in the first place. This can occur only when the borrower is willing to abandon the idea that we have the right to universalize and domesticate any religious practice deemed to have value. It would mean, in other words, giving up core tenets of American religious liberalism.

What I am suggesting is no less than a radical rethinking of freedom. Liberalism privileges individual freedom and autonomy and ignores that freedom justified as "self-optimization" often comes at the expense of others. Instead, the rights of social groups need to be part of our assessment of religious borrowing, including groups that are marginalized within religious communities such as female, Black, or brown believers. This more deferential stance is necessary for meaningful cultural exchange, one that looks less like theft and more like reciprocity. And yet we should be careful to not assume kinship with religious traditions and communities not our own. Much as fences make good neighbors, acknowledging and respecting boundaries of religious communities makes us better partners and collaborators within the context of religious pluralism.

But what if we wanted to go further? What if, rather than merely understanding and tolerating religious difference, we let difference change us and become a source of values?[4] It turns out that the devotional aspects of practices deemed too dangerous for the mainstream liberal consumer can help mitigate some of the risks of the appropriation. So, the remedy to the exploitations of religious appropriation could be borrowing more, not less.

On the most general level, religious worldviews can help challenge liberalism's overemphasis on personal sovereignty by shifting our attention from individuals to communities. They also deemphasize the importance of human agency in general, thus providing ways for us to get beyond self-reliance and self-actualization as the primary modes and goals of human activity.

On a more specific level, religious values can be recruited to help prevent some forms of exploitation that religious appropriation creates. Modesty gets a bad rap, especially when it is narrowly conceptualized as the submission of women to men. But taken seriously as a value that should inform political action, modesty could prevent non-Muslim women from adopting hijab for their feminist politics. Solidarity hijab not only attracts unnecessary attention to non-Muslim women by centering them in the conversation of Islamophobia—the opposite of what modesty would require—it also exacerbates the power of an already privileged group. Modesty can be a form of humility, which is precisely the virtue we need to cultivate as an antidote to the arrogance of liberalism's unchecked individualism.

There are lessons within the religious practice of pilgrimage that might help improve the Camino as an educational destination. One is the role of displacement. A medieval pilgrim temporarily left his life to engage in a time of reflection. This worked in part because he valued a period of liminality, or in-betweenness, when assumptions about what is true and good could be reassessed. The Camino can likewise be framed for educational purposes as an experience not of authenticity, but one in which everything we assume about what makes something authentic is up for reevaluation.

The Camino is also a place where travelers can observe multiple roles of religious institutions ranging from village albergues to monastic communities to the bureaucracy of the Pilgrim Office in Santiago. Religious institutions are part of what nones and SBNR object to in religion, but this is based on a very anemic view of religious institutions as hierarchical structures that set out only to control believers. Understanding how a variety of religious institutions support pilgrimage on the Camino is an opportunity to think about how such institutions bolster, not only curtail, human experience.

Finally, let's take the example of respite yoga. Remember that yoga was popularized in the United States by erasing, leaving behind, or softening devotional elements to make yoga accessible to the US consumer who was on a quest for self-realization. But these devotional aspects, deemed too Eastern, foreign, or disruptive to American life, are also potential resources for critiquing the systems of structural injustice that can make yoga exploitative. At a very general level, yoga philosophy challenges assumptions that self-care should be our goal or that self-optimization can come without justice for the broader community.

For instance, Patañjali's *Yoga Sutras* contains ethical guidance—the yama (restraints) and niyama (observances). Most American yoga practitioners don't consider the yama or niyama obligations. Outside Kripalu, I have rarely heard them discussed by a yoga teacher in a class. But if adopted with as much enthusiasm as asana, they would change the impact of respite yoga. As codes that help us in our relationship to others, the yama offers ethical guidance that might mitigate exploitations of respite yoga, such as sexual abuse and unpaid labor. For instance, the yama of brahmacharya originally referred to sexual celibacy and honoring the boundaries of others. It provides a potential resource to critique widespread sexual abuse in the US yoga industry.

When the US yoga industry chooses to invoke seva to justify unpaid labor, this reinforces dominant capitalism norms. An economic system based instead on *ahisma*, the first yama, which can be translated as "nonharm," would look very different. It would certainly require the fair compensation of labor. But ahisma operationalized could also encourage reparations, suggests Susanna Barkataki in her activist handbook *Embrace Yoga's Roots*.[5] One specific recommendation she makes is to "spend your money on those from whom this practice came," which can take the form of hiring more South Asian yoga teachers, buying books written by South Asian authors, or donating money to organizations doing humanitarian work in India.[6] This is all to say that yoga has a resource not only for preventing economic exploitation but also for addressing it once it has occurred. But this resource is part of what is left behind when yoga is reinvented as a personal wellness practice.

Careful engagement with the religion of others has the potential to help us understand communities different from our own. But it can also fundamentally change the way we see the world and provide ways for dismantling structures of privilege, inequity, and alienation. This would involve more, not less, religion. Let me leave you with one last personal story that illustrates this point.

A ten-day meditation training at Kripalu in March 2020 was the last stint of fieldwork I conducted for this book. According to the welcome letter in the front of my training binder, the goal of the program was to "learn about the ancient traditions of yoga meditation from a historical perspective: the stages it went through, the understanding that inspired it, the desired goal, and the techniques that emerged to lead to that goal." In other words, the training was focused on the ideas specific meditation practices were originally tethered to. The program was, at least in part, about devotional yoga.

The meditation training was led by Yoganand Michael Carroll, the former dean of Kripalu school. A masterful teacher, Yoganand taught us about ancient forms of South Asian philosophy, such as Vedanta, Sankhya, and Tantra, by telling stories. Each tradition we learned about had developed slightly different cosmologies, which depended on different beliefs about the relationship between an individual and an ultimate reality, sometimes called Brahman. But what they had in common was that all arose in periods of immense human suffering. Life was unpredictable and hard, Yoganand told us. People physically toiled, had no guarantee of food or shelter, and died early. The spiritual techniques that arose from these traditions were ways to cope with that harsh reality.

After story-based lectures, Yoganand led us through techniques of meditation based on these ancient South Asian philosophies. We tried to embody the idea, for instance, that we are all part of a greater, unchanging reality, through mantra, visualization, and breath retention. The practices were meant to give us a taste of the power of devotional yoga so that we could use them in our own spiritual work, or as inspiration for creating respite practices for our students.

"Scholar Liz" was uneasy when Yoganand insisted, "I am not a preacher, I'm a teacher," and that we could engage in these practices without religious implications. To me, it seemed clear the techniques were grounded in, as Paul Tillich would say, an ultimate concern. And the most accurate way I knew to describe the supernatural metaphysics and cosmologies we were learning was that they were religious. By engaging in the techniques, and feeling their benefits, we were implicitly externalizing the religious ideas behind them as well.

Yoganand and I had several conversations about my discomfort with "trying on" these powerful practices. I wanted him to acknowledge we were in an ethical gray area when we offered these techniques to students without mentioning these religious connections. But from his point of view, most people don't want their yoga, whether asana or meditation practice, to be devotional work. They just want to feel better. "If a technique works," he told me, "we should offer it."

And then, three days into the training, the world changed. On Monday, March 9, word of infection rates in China and Italy dominated the news. On Wednesday, March 11, COVID-19 was declared a pandemic by the World Health Organization. There was a confirmed case of COVID-19 in my daughter's school, which was traced back to a parent who had attended a local Biogen conference that turned out to be a superspreader event. Her school closed for a deep cleaning. On Friday, March 13, my father-in-law was exposed to COVID-19 in Canada and put into quarantine.

Despite my intellectual reservations about whether the meditation techniques we were learning could be secularized, my embodied experience became less fraught. As someone who usually dislikes sitting meditation of all forms, I was surprised to find participating in meditation for six hours a day calming. As the reality of COVID-19 became more and more upsetting, I began engaging in these devotional practices with more and more focus.

Kripalu shut down on March 14, and as I drove home, I formed a plan to continue my own meditation practice at home as well as teach some techniques to my family to help deal with COVID-19 uncertainty. That didn't happen, at least not in the way I intended.

I had no time to fit meditation into my day while trying to figure out to how to pivot courses online and homeschool a sixth grader. My daughter was resistant to my suggestions to meditate. When my partner had time for self-care, he just wanted to go for a run.

And yet, multiple times a day I found myself returning to the devotional ideas behind the respite techniques, the philosophical, cultural, and religious systems and worldviews that gave rise to the practices. Vedanta helped me remember that this too shall pass; Sankhya, that I can't control what is going on, but I can control my reaction to it; and Tantra reminded me to appreciate family, a sunny day, and a pantry-based home-cooked meal. I had, quite unintentionally, walked away from that meditation training with new ways to understand the world. Religious ideas I had internalized through engaging in religious practices were shaping my reaction to a reality that was suddenly more uncertain, scary, and dangerous. Religious appropriation was functioning as a resource for resilience, but only because I was borrowing more, not less, of the associated religion.

And I was not alone. As COVID-19 spread that spring, nonessential businesses temporarily closed, schools shut down, stock market and retirement funds plummeted, unemployment and food insecurity soared, and communities began to enforce different levels of lockdown—and something else happened: downloads of mindfulness apps increased. During the week of March 29, 2020, mindfulness apps were downloaded 750,000 times, a 25 percent increase from their weekly average in February. The popular Los Angeles–based meditation app Headspace reported its downloads doubled from mid-March to mid-April 2020, the time when most Americans began sheltering in place for the first time.[7] During that period, Headspace curated a "Weathering the Storm" collection of meditations and movement exercises and made it free to everyone. It also offered its premium membership "Headspace Plus" for free to health-care professionals. There is evidence that people were spending more time using yoga and meditation apps. The *Washington Post* reported that the use of such apps on Androids was up 85 percent by the end of March.[8]

The ethicist who started this project would have been critical of this uptick. When I began the research for this book, my intention was to highlight cases of religious borrowing that I found problematic, cases often ignored by the same liberals who denounced other forms of cultural appropriation. I began wanting to scold.

And yet as I engaged in various forms of religious appropriation, and read, interviewed, and wrote about them, I realized different types of borrowing have different ethical implications. Yes, some are ill-conceived, perpetuating stereotypes of religious minorities and expressing entitlement in many forms. But I find myself defending religious borrowings in some cases, particularly when it seems that the borrowers are taking the time to learn about and from religious practitioners and welcome uncomfortable conversations about privilege and power. In these cases, the agents of appropriation are transformed.

I want to continue to insist that religious practices are connected to religious ideas, institutions, and communities, and if you are doing the practices, you are doing religion. You might even begin "to believe." But in some cases that might be okay. During COVID-19, my own religious appropriation—which was motivated by research, not personal spiritual growth—had a significant role in how I responded to the pandemic. In this case, I wasn't only stealing my religion, I was also finding it. And yet admitting that makes me incredibly uncomfortable.

If you, too, are ending this book uncomfortable, I have achieved my goal. There are no quick fixes to the ethical dilemmas of religious appropriation. We avoid conversations about appropriation for a reason. They are hard. They are sticky. They are contentious. They strike at the core of who we think we are. While writing this book, I was often uncomfortable—especially when I discovered how my own actions made me part of the problem. But being able to confront, sit with, and then try to resolve discomfort is a hallmark of ethical learning. It is how we make visible what seems natural. It is how we change what we assume is right and good. Discomfort is the first step to realizing we have work to do so that religious borrowing can contribute to the inclusion of religious difference instead of merely participate in its oppression.

Notes
Acknowledgments
Index

Notes

Preface

1. Gregory Smith, "About Three-in-Ten U.S. Adults Are Now Religiously Unaffiliated," Pew Research Center, December 14, 2021, https://www.pewforum.org/2021/12/14/about-three-in-ten-u-s-adults-are-now-religiously-unaffiliated/.

Introduction

1. See Lynn Neal's recent account of this history in Lynn S. Neal, *Religion in Vogue: Christianity and Fashion in America* (New York: New York University Press, 2019).

2. R. Davies, "Beating Off the Backward Bigots," *Sunday Mail (QLD)*, July 8, 1990.

3. Indigenous religion: see, for example, James O. Young, *Cultural Appropriation and the Arts* (Oxford: Wiley-Blackwell, 2010); Loretta Todd, "Notes of Appropriation," *Parallelogramme* 16, no. 1 (1990): 24–32; Lenore Keeshig-Tobia, "Stop Stealing Native Stories," *Globe and Mail*, January 26, 1990; and Rosemary J. Coombe, "The Properties of Culture and Politics of Possessing Identity: Native Claims in the Cultural Appropriation Controversy," *Canadian Journal of Law and Jurisprudence* 6, no. 2 (1993): 249–285. Eastern spiritual practices: see, for example, Véronique Altglas, *From Yoga to Kabbalah: Religious Exoticism and the*

Logics of Bricolage (Oxford: Oxford University Press, 2014); and Amanda Lucia, *White Utopias: The Religious Exoticism of Transformational Festival* (Oakland: University of California Press, 2020).

4. See, for example, Susan Scafidi's definition of cultural appropriation as "taking intellectual property, traditional knowledge, cultural expressions, or artifacts from someone else's culture without permission," in Susan Scafidi, *Who Owns Culture? Appropriation and Authenticity in American Law* (New Brunswick, NJ: Rutgers University Press, 2005), 9.

5. See, for example, Allison Fish, "The Commodification and Exchange of Knowledge in the Case of Transnational Commercial Yoga," *International Journal of Cultural Property* 13, no. 2 (2006): 189–206, and Allison Fish, "Authorizing Yoga: The Pragmatics of Cultural Stewardship in the Digital Era," *East Asian Science, Technology and Society: An International Journal* 8 (2014): 439–460.

6. James O. Young, for instance, a philosopher who has published widely on the artistic appropriation of Native cultures, argues that cultural appropriation can result in the production of aesthetically successful works of art and therefore is not always morally objectionable; see Young, *Cultural Appropriation*.

7. Anonymous, "Hoop Earrings Are My Culture, Not Your Trend," *Vice*, October 10, 2017, https://www.vice.com/en/article/j5ga5x/hoop -earrings-are-my-culture-not-your-trend.

8. As quoted in Catherine Rampell, "Political Correctness Devours Yet Another College, Fighting over Mini-Sombreros," *Washington Post*, March 3, 2016.

9. Full transcript of keynote address published as Lionel Shriver, "Lionel Shriver's Full Speech: 'I Hope the Concept of Cultural Appropriation Is a Passing Fad,'" *Guardian*, September 13, 2016.

10. Yassmin Abdel-Magied, "As Lionel Shriver Made Light of Identity, I Had No Choice but to Walk Out on Her," *Guardian*, September 10, 2016.

11. Abdel-Magied, "As Lionel Shriver Made Light of Identity."

12. Fish, "The Commodification and Exchange of Knowledge," 192. For an analysis of the possibility and limits of using intellectual property rights to protect the market value of cultural knowledge and practice, such as yoga, see Fish, "Authorizing Yoga."

13. C. Thi Nguyen and Matthew Strohl, "Cultural Appropriation and the Intimacy of Groups," *Philosophical Studies* 176 (2019): 989.

14. Nguyen and Strohl, "Cultural Appropriation and the Intimacy of Groups."

15. Erich Hatala Matthes, "Cultural Appropriation without Cultural Essentialism?," *Social Theory and Practice* 42, no. 2 (2016): 346; also see Suzy Killmister, "Group-Differentiated Rights and the Problem of Membership," *Social Theory and Practice* 37 (2011): 233.

16. Jessica Andrews, "No, This Year's Met Gala Was Not Cultural Appropriation," *Teen Vogue*, May 11, 2018.

17. For a philosophical summary of the oppression account of cultural appropriation, see Erick Hatala Matthes, "Cultural Appropriation and Oppression," *Philosophical Studies* 176 (2019): 1003–1013.

18. Iris Marion Young, "Responsibility and Global Justice: A Social Connection Model," *Social Philosophy & Policy* 23, no. 1 (2006): 116.

19. James Martin, "The Last Acceptable Prejudice?," *America Magazine*, July 1, 2015.

20. Iris Young identifies five faces of oppression caused by structural injustice, of which exploitation is only one. The other four are powerless, marginalization, cultural imperialism, and violence. I use exploitation throughout this book because I found that attempts to classify harms within Young's five faces of oppression required drawing boundaries between these types, when my observation was that harms often entailed multiple "faces." Iris Marion Young, "Five Faces of Oppression," in *Justice and the Politics of Difference* (Princeton: Princeton University Press, 1990), 39–65.

21. Joel Feinberg, *The Moral Limits of the Criminal Law*, vol. 2, *Offense to Others* (Oxford: Oxford University Press, 1985), ch. 9. James Young made this connection between the harm of cultural appropriation and a profound offense in his 2005 article "Profound Offense and Cultural Appropriation," *Journal of Aesthetics and Art Criticism* 6, no. 2 (2005): 135–146.

22. See Véronique Altglas, "'Bricolage': Reclaiming a Conceptual Tool," *Culture and Religion* 15, no. 4 (2014): 490. See also Paul Heelas and Linda Woodhead, *The Spiritual Revolution: Why Religion Is Giving Way to Spirituality* (Oxford: Blackwell, 2008), 2.

23. Tara Isabella Burton, *Strange Rites: New Religions for a Godless World* (New York: Public Affairs, 2020), 2.

24. A much-cited Pew Forum on "nones" concludes that the religious unaffiliated are less religious than other Americans, but measures religion in ways that assume the validity of religion versus spirituality that is based on a Protestant idea of religion, such as belief in God, heaven, and daily prayer. For an excellent critique of the Pew Forum methodology, see Andrea R. Jain, *Peace, Love, Yoga: The Politics of Global Spirituality* (New York: Oxford University Press, 2020), 48–49.

25. There are cases of religious appropriation where the appropriator might identify as a religious insider. The Canadian anthropologist Rosemary Coombe, for instance, discusses this phenomenon in the context of New Age appropriation of Native American practices. Rosemary J. Coombe, "The Properties of Culture and Politics of Possessing Identity: Native Claims in the Cultural Appropriation Controversy," *Canadian Journal of Law and Jurisprudence* 6, no. 2 (1993): 276, 278. See also Richard Rogers, "From Cultural Exchange to Transculturation: A Review and Reconceptualization of Cultural Appropriation," *Communication Theory* 16 (2006): 487. I also think it is possible to appropriate your own religion because the asymmetrical power dynamics within religious communities can make internal debates about orthopraxy feel exploitative to some marginalized members. I'll have more to say about this in the chapters that follow.

26. Hillel Steiner, "Exploitation, Intentionality, and Injustice," *Economics and Philosophy* 34, no. 3 (2018): 376.

27. Hanna Flanagan, "Cardi B Apologizes after Being Accused of Appropriating Hindu Culture on Footwear News Cover," *People*, November 11, 2020, https://people.com/style/cardi-b-apologizes-after-being-accused-of-cultural-appropriation/.

28. @My_DesiGirl, Twitter, November 16, 2020, https://twitter.com/My_DesiGirl/status/1328250897034604549.

29. @GeetaChelseaFC, Twitter, November 10, 2020, https://twitter.com/GeetaChelseaFC/status/1326340455886430211.

30. Richard Delgado and Jean Stefancic, *Critical Race Theory: An Introduction*, 3rd ed. (New York: New York University Press, 2017), 79.

31. Jason Chester, "'Maybe I Should've Done My Research!' Cardi B Apologises after Being Accused of Cultural Appropriation for 'Sick, Disgusting and Disrespectful' Hindu Inspired Footwear Shoot," *Mail Online,* November 11, 2020, https://www.dailymail.co.uk/tvshowbiz/article -8937985/Cardi-B-apologises-accused-cultural-appropriation.html.

32. Chester, "'Maybe I Should've Done My Research!'"

33. The formation of religion as an object of study doesn't occur until the sixteenth and seventeenth centuries, even if human activity that we might today call religion predates this. See Brent Nongbri, *Before Religion: A History of a Modern Concept* (New Haven: Yale University Press, 2013), 152.

34. Malory Nye has a useful overview about what is at stake in this enterprise, in Malory Nye, "Decolonizing the Study of Religion," *Open Library of Humanities* 5, no. 1 (2019): 43, https://www.doi.org/10.16995/olh.421.

35. This ultimate concern is manifested, according to Tillich, ethically "as the unconditional seriousness of moral demand," intellectually as "the passionate longing for ultimate reality," and aesthetically as the "desire to experience ultimate meaning." Paul Tillich, *Theology of Culture,* ed. Robert Kimball (New York: Oxford University Press, 1959), 7–8, as quoted by Jonathan Z. Smith, "Religion, Religions, Religious," *Critical Terms for Religious Studies,* ed. Mark Taylor (Chicago: University of Chicago Press, 1998), 280–281.

36. Clifford Geertz's anthropological definition of religion is a classic example: "1) A system of symbols which act to 2) establish powerful, pervasive, and long-lasting moods and motivations in men [*sic*] by 3) formulating conceptions of a general order of existence and 4) clothing these conceptions with such an aura of factuality that 5) the moods and motivations seem uniquely realistic." Clifford Geertz, "Religion as a Cultural System," in *The Interpretation of Cultures* (New York: Basic Books, 1973), 90. The limitation of Geertz's definition, according to such scholars as Talal Asad, is that Geertz neglects that religious symbols and truth claims shift over time, and that this change is because of specific histories of power dynamics and discourse. See Talal Asad, *Genealogies of Religion: Discipline and Reasons of Power in Christianity and Islam* (Baltimore: Johns Hopkins University Press, 1993), 32–33.

37. Malory Nye, *Religion: The Basics*, 2nd ed. (New York: Routledge, 2004), 55.

38. My thanks to my colleague Fadeke Castor for suggesting to me that decentering human agency is central to religion.

39. Ralph Waldo Emerson, *Ralph Waldo Emerson* (Oxford Authors), ed. Richard Poirier (New York: Oxford University Press, 1990), 3.

40. Leigh Eric Schmidt, *Restless Souls: The Making of American Spirituality* (Berkeley: University of California Press, 2012), xiii.

41. Robert Fuller, *Spiritual, but Not Religious: Understanding the Unchurched in America* (New York: Oxford University Press, 2001), 112–113.

42. Catherine Albanese, "The Culture of Religious Combining: Reflections for the New American Millennium," *CrossCurrents* 50, no. 1/2 (2000): 17–19.

43. George Gallup Jr., *The Gallup Poll Public Opinion 1999* (Wilmington, DE: Scholarly Resources, 2000), 281.

44. Robert A. Orsi, *Between Heaven and Earth: The Religious Worlds People Make and the Scholars Who Study Them* (Princeton: Princeton University Press, 2007).

45. Malory Nye, "Religion Is Religioning? Anthropology and the Cultural Study of Religion," *Scottish Journal of Religious Studies* 20, no. 2 (1999): 224.

46. J. Kameron Carter, *Race: A Theological Account* (New York: Oxford University Press, 2008), 4.

47. Numerous scholars working at the intersection of religion and critical race theory have shown that the theological problem of whiteness is institutionalized in the United States in ways that adversely affect religious diversity. See, for example, Winnifred Fallers Sullivan, *The Impossibility of Religious Freedom* (Princeton: Princeton University Press, 2005); Tracy Fessenden, *Culture and Redemption: Religion, the Secular, and American Literature* (Princeton: Princeton University Press, 2007); Orsi, *Between Heaven and Earth*; and Tisa Wenger, *Religious Freedom: The Contested History of an American Ideal* (Chapel Hill: University of North Carolina Press, 2017).

48. A textual basis for this includes Quran 16:125: "Invite (all) to the Way Of thy Lord with wisdom And beautiful preaching; And argue with them In ways that are best And most gracious: For thy Lord knoweth best,

Who have strayed from His Path, And who receive guidance." Translated by Abdullah Yusuf Ali, 1946, https://quranyusufali.com/16/.

49. Scholars have shown that Pilates has its own ethical implications. For example, Sarah Woolverton Holmes argues that the teaching practices of the hips, spine, and core commonly found in Pilates educational manuals are orientalist insofar as they reinforce behaviors of racial whiteness and European aesthetics. See Sarah Woolverton Holmes, "A Critical Dance Studies Examination of the Teaching Methodologies, Exercises, and Principles of Pilates" (PhD diss., University of California, Riverside, 2013), https://escholarship.org/uc/item/7sj2k7f7.

50. Abdel-Magied, "As Lionel Shriver Made Light of Identity."

Chapter One: Solidarity Hijab

1. Interview with Sabirah Mahmud by Aqsa Ahmad, "Joe Biden Used a Teenage Bernie-Supporting Climate Activist's Photo for 'Hijabi Clout' in an Ad. We Talked to Her about It," *Jacobin Magazine*, February 7, 2020, https://www.jacobinmag.com/2020/02/us-youth-climate-strike-joe-biden-hijab-campaign-ad.

2. Ahmad, "Joe Biden Used a Teenage Bernie-Supporting Climate Activist's Photo."

3. Erum Salam, "'Hijabi Clout': The Women of Color Unknowingly Used by 2020 Campaigns," *Guardian*, February 8, 2020.

4. Salam, "Hijabi Clout."

5. Sikh Coalition, "Identity," https://www.sikhcoalition.org/about-sikhs/identity/.

6. This was how the headpiece was described on Nordstrom's website at the time (no longer accessible) and quoted in Allyson Chiu, "'Not a Cute Fashion Accessory': Gucci's $800 'Indy Full Turban' Draws Backlash," *Washington Post*, May 16, 2019.

7. Elizabeth Bucar, *The Islamic Veil: A Beginners Guide* (Oxford: Oneworld Publications, 2012), 45–48.

8. "U.S. Muslims Concerned about Their Place in Society, but Continue to Believe in the American Dream," Pew Research Center, July 26, 2017, https://www.pewforum.org/2017/07/26/religious-beliefs-and-practices/.

9. Bozena C. Welborne, Aubrey L. Westfall, Özge Çelik Russell, and Sarah A. Tobin, *The Politics of the Headscarf in the United States* (Ithaca, NY: Cornell University Press, 2018), 32.

10. See Elizabeth Bucar, "Islamic Virtue Ethics," in *The Oxford Handbook of Virtue*, ed. Nancy E. Snow (Oxford: Oxford University Press, 2017); Elizabeth M. Bucar, "Cultivating Virtues through Sartorial Practices: The Case of the Islamic Veil in Indonesia," in *Character: New Directions from Theology*, ed. Christian B. Miller et al. (Oxford: Oxford University Press, 2015), 590–602; and Elizabeth M. Bucar, "Islam and the Cultivation of Character: Ibn Miskawayh's Synthesis and the Case of the Veil," in *Cultivating Virtue: Perspectives from Philosophy, Theology, and Psychology*, ed. Nancy E. Snow (Oxford: Oxford University Press, 2014), 197–226.

11. Barbara Metcalf, "Remaking Ourselves: Islamic Self-Fashioning in a Global Movement of Spiritual Renewal," in *Accounting for Fundamentalisms: The Dynamic Character of Movements*, ed. Martin E. Marty and R. Scott Appleby (Chicago: University of Chicago Press, 1994), 710.

12. As the anthropologist Saba Mahmood concludes from her study of the Islamic piety movement in Egypt, pious acts "inhabit" norms. In Saba Mahmood, *Politics of Piety: The Islamic Revival and the Feminist Subject* (Princeton: Princeton University Press, 2005), 15.

13. Leila Ahmed, "The Discourse of the Veil," in *Women and Gender in Islam: Historical Roots of a Modern Debate* (New Haven: Yale University Press, 1992).

14. Besheer Mohamed, "New Estimates Show U.S. Muslim Population Continues to Grow," Pew Research Center, January 3, 2018, https://www.pewresearch.org/fact-tank/2018/01/03/new-estimates-show-u-s-muslim-population-continues-to-grow/.

15. See Lila Abu-Lughod, *Do Muslim Women Need Saving?* (Cambridge, MA: Harvard University Press, 2013); Charles Hirschkind and Saba Mahmood, "Feminism, the Taliban, and Politics of Counter-Insurgency," *Anthropological Quarterly* 75 (2002): 339–354; and Yvonne Haddad, "The Post-9/11 *Hijab* as Icon," *Sociology of Religion* 68, no. 3 (2007): 254–255.

16. Human Rights Watch, as quoted in Ashraf Zahedi, "Muslim American Women in the Post-11 September Era," *International Feminist Journal of Politics* 13, no. 2 (2011): 188.

17. FBI, "2016 Hate Crime Statistics: Victims," https://ucr.fbi.gov/hate-crime/2016/topic-pages/victims.

18. ACLU, "Discrimination against Muslim Women-Fact Sheet," https://www.aclu.org/other/discrimination-against-muslim-women-fact-sheet#17.

19. G.E. v. City of New York et al., No. 2012 Civ. 05967 (E.D.N.Y. 2017) ($60,000 per person); Soliman v. City of New York et al., No. 2015 Civ. 05310 (E.D.N.Y. 2018) ($60,000 per person); Kirsty Powell v. City of Long Beach et al., No. 2016 Civ. 02966 (C.D. Cal. 2017) ($85,000); Al-Kadi v. Ramsey County et al., No. 2016 Civ. 02642 (Minn. Dist. Ct. 2019) ($120,000); Musa v. City of New York, Index. No. 151601/2017 (N.Y. Supreme) ($85,000); Jennifer Hyatt v. County of Ventura et al., No. 2018 Civ. 03788 (C.D. Cal. 2018) ($75,000).

20. Gayatri Chakravorty Spivak, "Can the Subaltern Speak?," in *Marxism and the Interpretation of Culture*, ed. Cary Nelson and Lawrence Grossberg (Urbana: University of Illinois Press, 1988), 271–313.

21. Spivak, "Can the Subaltern Speak?"

22. Haddad, "The Post-9/11 *Hijab* as Icon," 254.

23. Asra Q. Nomani and Hala Arafa, "As Muslim Women, We Actually Ask You Not to Wear the Hijab in the Name of Interfaith Solidarity," *Washington Post*, December 21, 2015.

24. Ruth Graham, "The Professor Wore a Hijab in Solidarity—Then She Lost Her Job," *New York Times*, October 13, 2016.

25. Tim Wallace and Alicia Parlapiano, "Crowd Scientists Say Women's March in Washington Had 3 Times as Many People as Trump's Inauguration," *New York Times*, January 22, 2017.

26. Matt Broomfield, "Women's March against Donald Trump Is the Largest Day of Protests in US History, Say Political Scientists," *Independent*, January 25, 2017; Erica Chenoweth and Jeremy Pressman, "This Is What We Learned by Counting the Women's Marches," *Washington Post*, February 7, 2017.

27. Holly Derr, "Pink Flag: What Message Do 'Pussy Hats' Really Send?," *Bitch Media*, January 17, 2017, https://www.bitchmedia.org/article/pink-flag-what-message-do-pussy-hats-really-send.

28. Kirsten Jordan Shamus, "Pussyhat Project Is Sweeping Nation Ahead of the Women's March on Washington," *Detroit Free Press/USA Today*, January 14, 2017.

29. Amiya Nagpal, "I Didn't Go to the Women's March—It Was Inaccessible, White Tokenism," *Cambridge Student*, January 26, 2017, as quoted in Banu Gökarıksel and Sara Smith, "Intersectional Feminism beyond U.S. Flag Hijab and Pussy Hats in Trump's America," *Gender, Place & Culture* 24, no. 5 (2017): 635.

30. Stephy Chung, "'Hope' Artist Shepard Fairey Reveals New Posters to Protest Trump," CNN, January 19, 2017, https://www.cnn.com/style/article/shepard-fairey-trump-inauguration-posters-trnd/index.html.

31. Gökarıksel and Smith, "Intersectional Feminism," 633.

32. Gökarıksel and Smith, "Intersectional Feminism," 629.

33. Azad Essa, "Why Many Muslim Women in the US Are Skipping the Women's March This Year," *Middle East Eye*, January 17, 2020, https://www.middleeasteye.net/news/why-many-muslim-women-are-skipping-womens-march-year.

34. Hoda Katebi, "Please Keep Your American Flags Off My Hijab," *Mondoweiss*, January 25, 2017, https://mondoweiss.net/2017/01/please-american-flags/.

35. Janelle Zara, "Shepard Fairey: I'm Not Going to Be Intimidated by Identity Politics," *Guardian*, November 14, 2017.

36. "U.S. Muslims Concerned about Their Place in Society, but Continue to Believe in the American Dream," Pew Research Center, July 26, 2017, https://www.pewforum.org/2017/07/26/religious-beliefs-and-practices/.

37. Katebi, "Please Keep Your American Flags Off My Hijab."

38. Katebi, "Please Keep Your American Flags Off My Hijab"; Gökarıksel and Smith, "Intersectional Feminism."

39. Katebi, "Please Keep Your American Flags Off My Hijab."

40. Ali Shakir, "Don't Let Jacinda Ardern's Headscarf Send the Wrong Message," *Stuff*, October 2, 2019, https://www.stuff.co.nz/national/christchurch-shooting/116195738/dont-let-jacinda-arderns-headscarf-send-the-wrong-message.

41. Mehrbano Malik, "My Issue with Kiwis Being Encouraged to Wear Headscarves in Solidarity," *Stuff*, March 21, 2019, https://www.stuff.co.nz/national/christchurch-shooting/111462185/my-issue-with-kiwis-being-encouraged-to-wear-headscarves-in-solidarity.

42. Anonymous, "Headscarves Movement Means Well but It Is 'Cheap Tokenism,'" *Stuff*, March 22, 2019, https://www.stuff.co.nz/national /christchurch-shooting/111473440/headscarves-movement-means-well-but -it-is-cheap-tokenism.

43. Sarah J. Jackson, Moya Bailey, and Brooke Foucault Welles, *#Hashtag Activism: Networks of Race and Gender Justice* (Cambridge, MA: MIT Press, 2020), xxv.

44. @krw18, Twitter, March 22, 2019, https://twitter.com/krw18/status /1109244337848750080.

45. @krw18, Twitter, March 23, 2019, https://twitter.com/krw18/status /1109592824549441536.

46. @LaylaAPoulos, Twitter, March 22, 2019, https://twitter.com/Layla APoulos/status/1109083117061632000.

47. @BaconTribe, Twitter, March 22, 2019, https://twitter.com/Bacon Tribe/status/1109196580324823040.

48. @TinyMuslimah, Twitter, March 23, 2019, https://twitter.com/Tiny Muslimah/status/1109532138871885824.

49. @fizzydizzy, Twitter, March 24, 2019, https://twitter.com/fizzydizzy /status/1109821644099465217.

50. @SanaSaeed, Twitter, March 23, 2019, tweet deleted.

51. @KameelahRashad, Twitter, March 24, 2019, https://twitter.com /KameelahRashad/status/1109826366671867904.

52. @LaylaAPoulos, Twitter, March 25, 2019, https://twitter.com/Layla APoulos/status/1110281548786479104.

53. @TinyMuslimah, Twitter, March 24, 2019, https://twitter.com/Tiny Muslimah/status/1109868293094076417.

54. Jackson, Bailey, and Welles, *#Hashtag Activism*, 181, 183.

55. "Demographic Portrait of Muslim Americans," Pew Research Center, July 26, 2017, https://www.pewforum.org/2017/07/26/demographic -portrait-of-muslim-americans/.

56. Katebi, "Please Keep Your American Flags Off My Hijab."

57. Katebi, "Please Keep Your American Flags Off My Hijab."

58. Amaney A. Jamal, "Trump(ing) on Muslim Women: The Gendered Side of Islamophobia," *Journal of Middle East Women's Studies* 13, no. 3 (2017): 474.

59. Koa Beck, *White Feminism: From the Suffragettes to Influencers and Who They Leave Behind* (New York: Atria Books, 2021), 176.

60. Minh-Ha Pham calls this romantic orientalism; see Minh-Ha T. Pham, "China: Through the Looking Glass. Race, Property, and the Possessive Investment in White Feelings," in *Fashion and Beauty in the Time of Asia*, ed. S. Heijin Lee, Christina H. Moon, and Thuy Linh Nguyen Tu (New York: New York University Press, 2019), 41–42.

61. "New Zealanders Wear Headscarves in Solidarity with Mourning Muslim Community," SBS News, March 22, 2019, https://www.sbs.com .au/news/new-zealanders-wear-headscarves-in-solidarity-with-mourning -muslim-community.

62. Shannon Sullivan, *Revealing Whiteness: The Unconscious Habits of Racial Privilege* (Bloomington: Indiana University Press, 2006), 10.

63. Helen Ngo, "Stimulating the Lived Experience of Racism and Islamophobia: On 'Embodied Empathy' and Political Tourism," *Australian Feminist Law Journal* 43, no. 1 (2017): 123.

64. The Hijabinist, "Here's What's Wrong with Hijab Tourism and Your Cutesy 'Modesty Experiments,'" *Ms. Muslamic* (blog), July 21, 2013, https://msmuslamic.wordpress.com/2013/07/21/heres-whats-wrong-with -hijab-tourism-and-your-cutesy-modesty-experiments/.

65. The Hijabinist, "Hijab Tourism Redux: World Hijab Day Edition," *Ms. Muslamic* (blog), February 1, 2014, https://msmuslamic.wordpress .com/category/islam-and-muslims/.

66. Phil Pasquini, "Women's March: Muslim Women's Contingent Calls for End to Muslim Ban," *Washington Report on Middle East Affairs*, January 21, 2019, https://www.wrmea.org/human-rights/women-s -march-muslim-womens-contingent-calls-for-end-to-muslim-ban.html.

67. "Meet the Hijab-Wearing Police Constable Who Stood in Solidarity with the Muslim Community," MiNDFOOD, March 23, 2019, https://www.mindfood.com/article/meet-the-hijab-wearing-police -constable-who-stood-in-solidarity-with-the-muslim-community/; "Hijab Wearing Police Officer's Photo Makes Powerful Statement in Wake of Christchurch Mosque Shootings," *Stuff*, March 22, 2019, https://www .stuff.co.nz/national/christchurch-shooting/111491996/hijab-wearing -police-officers-photo-makes-powerful-statement-in-wake-of-christchurch -mosque-shootings.

68. *Stuff*, "Hijab Wearing Police Officer's Photo."

69. The Hijabinist, "Hijab Tourism Redux: World Hijab Day Edition."

70. Hannah Parry, "Women Don Stars and Stripes Headscarves in New York Rally on World Hijab Day Just Days after President Trump's 'Muslim Ban,'" *Daily Mail*, February 1, 2017, https://www.dailymail.co.uk/news/article-4182600/Women-don-stars-stripes-headscarves-New-York-rally.html.

71. The Hijabinist, "Hijab Tourism Redux: World Hijab Day Edition."

72. Edward W. Said, *Orientalism* (New York: Vintage Books, 2003), 2–3.

73. Pham, "China: Through the Looking Glass," 41–42.

74. The Hijabinist, "Here's What's Wrong with Hijab Tourism and Your Cutesy 'Modesty Experiments.'"

75. Rafia Zakaria, *Against White Feminism: Notes on Disruption* (New York: W. W. Norton, 2021), ix.

76. Zakaria, *Against White Feminism*, ix.

77. Beck, *White Feminism*, xvii.

78. Zakaria, *Against White Feminism*, 179.

79. Namira Islam, "Soft Islamophobia," *Religions* 9, no. 280 (2018): 3.

80. Margari Hill et al., *Study of Intra-Muslim Ethnic Relations: Muslim American Views on Race Relations* (Alta Loma, CA: Muslim Anti-Racism Collaborative, June 4, 2015), 19–20.

81. Jamillah Karim, *American Muslim Women: Negotiating Race, Class, and Gender within the Ummah* (New York: New York University Press, 2008); Sharmila Sen, *Not Quite Not White: Losing and Finding Race in America* (New York: Penguin Books, 2018).

82. Kayla Renée Wheeler, "On Centering Black Muslim Women in Critical Race Theory," *Maydan*, February 5, 2020, https://themaydan.com/2020/02/on-centering-black-muslim-women-in-critical-race-theory/#_ftnref10.

83. See Sylvia Chan-Malik, *Being Muslim: A Cultural History of Women of Color* (New York: New York University Press, 2018); and Megan Goodwin, "Gender, Race, and American Islamophobia," in *The Routledge Handbook of Islam and Gender*, ed. Justine Howe (New York: Routledge, 2020).

84. As quoted in Tara Golshan, "Clinton's Defense of 'Peace-Loving Muslims' Is a Bad Response to Trump's Offensive Comments," Vox.com,

June 13, 2016, https://www.vox.com/2016/7/31/11963134/anti-muslim
-clinton-trump.

85. Mychal Denzel Smith, "The Seductive Danger of Symbolic Politics," *Nation*, January 21, 2016.

86. I am drawing here on a similar argument Jakobsen and Pellegrini make in reference to sexual difference in Janet R. Jakobsen and Ann Pellegrini, *Love the Sin: Sexual Regulation and the Limits of Religious Tolerance* (New York: New York University Press, 2003), 50.

Chapter Two: Playing Pilgrim

1. As quoted in Isabel Burton, *The Life of Captain Sir Richard F. Burton* (London: Chapman and Hall, 1893), 1:178.

2. Richard Burton, *Personal Narrative of a Pilgrimage to Mecca and Medina*, 3rd ed. (Leipzig: Bernhard Tauchnitz, 1874), 1:2–3.

3. Hillary Kaell, *Walking Where Jesus Walked: American Christians and Holy Land Pilgrimage* (New York: New York University Press, 2014), 99.

4. In the introduction to their edited volume on pilgrimage, *Contesting the Sacred*, British anthropologists John Eade and Michael Sallnow described this contestation as follows: "Pilgrimage is above all an arena for competing religious and secular discourses, for both the official co-optation and the nonofficial recovery of religious meanings, for conflict between orthodoxies, sects, and confessional groups, for drives towards consensus and communitas, *and* for counter-movements towards separateness and division." John Eade and Michael J. Sallnow. eds., *Contesting the Sacred: The Anthropology of Christian Pilgrimage* (Chicago: University of Illinois Press, 1991), 2; emphasis in the original.

5. Victor Turner, "Liminal to Liminoid in Play, Flow, and Ritual: An Essay in Comparative Symbology" *Rice University Studies* (1974): 232.

6. The Turners call this human interrelatedness "communitas." For them it is spontaneous, normative, or ideological. See Victor Turner and Edith Turner, *Image and Pilgrimage in Christian Culture* (New York: Columbia University Press, 1978), 32, 252.

7. Martin Luther, *Luther's Work*, vol. 44, *The Christian in Society I*, ed. Hartmut Lehmann and James Atkinson (Philadelphia: Fortress Press, 1966), 171.

8. Pilgrimage as a duty: "Those who make pilgrimages do so for many reasons, very seldom for legitimate ones," Luther wrote. "The first reason for making pilgrimages is the most common of all, namely, the curiosity to see and hear strange and unknown things. This levity process from a loathing for and boredom with the worship services, which have been neglected in the pilgrims' own church. Otherwise one would find comparably better indulgences at home than in all the other places put together." Martin Luther, *Luther's Works*, vol. 31, ed. Jaroslav Pelikan, Helmut T. Lehmann, and Christopher Boyd Brown (St. Louis: Concordia Publishing House, 1955), 198. Pilgrimage and extramarital sex: "Every false religion is contaminated by libidinous desires. Just keep an eye on sex. What were pilgrimages [under the papacy] but opportunities to get together? What does the pope do now but besmirch himself unceasingly with lust? In order that they might satisfy lust the more well-situated places, beautiful fountains, trees, hills, and rivers were sought out for pilgrimages." Martin Luther, *Luther's Works*, 54:1542.

9. Yaniv Belhassen, Kellee Caton, and William P. Stewart, "The Search for Authenticity in the Pilgrim Experience," *Annuals of Tourism Research* 35, no. 3 (2008): 676.

10. Kaell, *Walking Where Jesus Walked*, 9, 12.

11. Brian Graham and Michal Murray, "The Spiritual and the Profane: The Pilgrimage to Santiago de Compostela," *Ecumene* 4, no. 4 (October 1997): 397.

12. Sasha Pack, "Revival of the Pilgrimage to Santiago de Compostela: The Politics of Religious, National, and European Patrimony," *Journal of Modern History* 82 (June 2010): 366.

13. Pack, "Revival of the Pilgrimage to Santiago de Compostela," 337.

14. Oficina del Peregrino, "Informe estadístico: Año Santo 2010," http://oficinadelperegrino.com/wp-content/uploads/2016/02 /peregrinaciones2010.pdf; Oficina del Peregrino, "Informe estadístico: Año Santo 2015," http://oficinadelperegrino.com/wp-content/uploads /2016/02/peregrinaciones2015.pdf; Oficina del Peregrino, "Informe estadístico: Año Santo 2019," http://oficinadelperegrino.com/wp-content /uploads/2016/02/peregrinaciones2019.pdf.

15. Oficina del Peregrino, "Informe estadístico: Año Santo 2019."

16. Darla K. Deardorff, "Identification and Assessment of Intercultural Competence as a Student Outcome of Internationalization," *Journal of Studies in International Education* 10, no. 3 (2006): 247–248.

17. Northeastern University, "Experiential Learning: In the Classroom," https://www.northeastern.edu/experiential-learning/in-the-classroom/index.html.

18. Northeastern University, "Experiential Learning: Global Experience," https://www.northeastern.edu/experiential-learning/global-experience/.

19. Elijah Siegler, "Working Through the Problems of Study Abroad Using the Methodologies of Religious Studies," *Teaching Theology and Religion* 18, no. 1 (January 2015): 38.

20. All student names are pseudonyms.

21. Nancy Louise Frey, *Pilgrim Stories: On and off the Road to Santiago* (Berkeley: University of California Press, 1998).

22. Alexander Moore, "Walt Disney World: Bounded Ritual Space and the Playful Pilgrimage Center," *Anthropological Quarterly* 53, no. 4 (1980): 207–218.

23. Moore, "Walt Disney World," 216.

24. Charles Lindholm, "The Rise of Expressive Authenticity," *Anthropological Quarterly* 86, no. 2 (2013): 364.

25. Lindholm, "The Rise of Expressive Authenticity," 364.

26. Ning Wang, "Rethinking Authenticity in Tourism Experience," *Annals of Tourism Research* 26, no. 2 (1999): 358.

27. Keith Egan, "Days of Wine and Walking: Leisure, Excess, and Authenticity on the Camino," in *Leisure and Death: An Anthropological Tour of Risk, Death, and Dying,* ed. Adam Kaul and Jonathan Skinner (Boulder: University Press of Colorado, 2018), 51–52.

28. Egan, "Days of Wine and Walking," 52.

29. Marlien Lourens, "Route Tourism: A Roadmap for Successful Destinations and Local Economic Development," *Development Southern Africa* 24, no. 3 (2007): 475.

30. Reinaldo Fraile, "Are 'Smelly' Hipsters Ruining Spain's Camino de Santiago Pilgrim Route?," *El País,* July 31, 2017, https://english.elpais.com/elpais/2017/07/28/inenglish/1501234923_239922.html.

31. Sara Scott, "Spent: An Examination into the Economic Impact of Pilgrims & Tourists on the Camino de Santiago" (unpublished undergraduate paper, Boston: Northeastern University, 2017).

32. See Maria Rosa Menocal, *The Ornament of the World: How Muslims, Jews, and Christians Created a Culture of Tolerance in Medieval Spain* (Boston: Back Bay Books, 2003); and Richard Fletcher, *Moorish Spain* (New York: Henry Holt, 1992).

33. John D. Barbour, "'Oh Events' for the Professor: Studies and Stories of Religious Studies Abroad," *Teaching Theology and Religion* 18, no. 1 (2015): 88–96.

34. Ninety percent: Elizabeth Redden, "Study Abroad Numbers Grow," *Insider Higher Education*, November 13, 2018. Cost: Karin Fischer, "A Global Education Opens Doors but Leave Many Shut Out," *Chronicle of Higher Education*, May 29, 2015.

35. Andrea R. Jain, *Peace Love Yoga: The Politics of Global Spirituality* (New York: Oxford University Press, 2020), 26. See also Kathryn Lofton, *Consuming Religion* (Chicago: University of Chicago Press, 2017), 6.

36. Oficina del Peregrino, "Consulta rápida de estadísticas mensuales: Junio 2019" and "Consulta rápida de estadísticas mensuales: Junio 2020," https://catedral.df-server.info/est/index.html.

37. Daniela Flesler, *The Return of the Moor: Spanish Responses to Contemporary Moroccan Immigration* (West Lafayette, IN: Purdue University Press, 2008), 57.

38. See, for instance, Winnifred Fallers Sullivan, *The Impossibility of Religious Freedom* (Princeton: Princeton University Press, 2005); Tracy Fessenden, *Culture and Redemption: Religion, the Secular, and American Literature* (Princeton: Princeton University Press, 2007); Robert A. Orsi, *Between Heaven and Earth: The Religious Worlds People Make and the Scholars Who Study Them* (Princeton: Princeton University Press, 2007); Janet R. Jakobsen and Ann Pellegrini, *Love the Sin: Sexual Regulation and the Limits of Religious Tolerance* (New York: New York University Press, 2003); and Mark Silk, *Unsecular Media: Making News of Religion in America* (Champaign: University of Illinois Press, 1997).

39. Andrew Greeley, "Protestant and Catholic: Is the Analogical Imagination Extinct?," *American Sociological Review* 54, no. 4 (August 1989): 485.

40. Sullivan, *Revealing Whiteness*, 10.

41. Anthony Ogden, "The View from the Veranda: Understanding Today's Colonial Student," *Frontiers* 15 (2007).

42. Siegler, "Working Through the Problems of Study Abroad," 57.

43. Michael Fielding, "Target-Setting, Policy, Pathology and Student Perspectives: Learning to Labour in New Times," *Cambridge Journal of Education* 29 (1999): 277–287.

44. Wendy Wiseman, "The Politics of Teaching of Indigenous Traditions in Aotearoa / New Zealand," *Teaching Theology and Religion* 18, no. 1 (2015): 79.

45. Kerry Mitchell, "The Immersion Experience: Lessons from Study Abroad in Religion," *Teaching Theology and Religion* 18, no. 1 (2015): 56.

46. Alison Cook-Sather and Zanny Alter, "What Is and What Can Be: How a Liminal Position Can Change Learning and Teaching in Higher Education," *Anthropology and Education Quarterly* 42 (2011): 38.

47. Cook-Sather and Alter, "What Is and What Can Be," 51.

48. Siegler, "Working Through the Problems of Study Abroad," 42–43.

49. My thinking on this point was helped by Theodossopoulos's 2013 discussion of authenticity. See Dimitrios Theodossopoulos, "Laying Claim to Authenticity: Five Anthropological Dilemmas," *Anthropological Quarterly* 86, no. 2 (2013): 347.

Chapter Three: Respite Yoga

1. Kumari Devarajan, "How 'Namaste' Flew Away from Us," *Code Switch: Word Watch*, January 17, 2020, https://www.npr.org/sections/codeswitch/2020/01/17/406246770/how-namaste-flew-away-from-us.

2. Devarajan, "How 'Namaste' Flew Away from Us."

3. See Candy Gunther Brown, "Sedlock v Baird," in *Debating Yoga and Mindfulness in Public Schools: Reforming Secular Education or Re-establishing Religion?* (Chapel Hill: University of North Carolina Press, 2019), 113–139.

4. The first time I heard this distinction was from Michael Carroll, the former dean of Kripalu school and known as Yoganand, during the

Kripalu meditation training in March 2020 that I discuss in the Conclusion that follows.

5. Tejal Patel and Jesal Parikh, two desi yoga instructors who host the popular podcast *Yoga Is Dead*, describe monsters that live under our yoga mats as the things that are killing yoga. See yogaisdeadpodcast.com.

6. K. Pattabhi Jois, interview by Alexander Medin, "3 Gurus, 48 Questions: Matching Interviews with Sri T. K. V. Desikachar, Sri B. K. S. Iyengar & Sri K. Pattabhi Jois," ed. Deirdre Summerbell, *Namarupa* (Fall 2004): 18.

7. Andrea R. Jain, *Peace Love Yoga: The Politics of Global Spirituality* (New York: Oxford University Press, 2020), 61.

8. See, for example, Mark Singleton, *Yoga Body: The Origins of Modern Posture Practice* (New York: Oxford University Press, 2010); and James Mallinson and Mark Singleton, *Roots of Yoga* (New York: Penguin Books, 2017).

9. Tantra also grounds Hatha yoga's a system of subtle physiology: the idea that the human body is made up of *nadis* (channels), and that such practices as asanas purify and balance. In the Hatha yoga tradition, which much of modern postural yoga draws from, the purpose of the physical practices was to transform the body so that it is immune from decay, immortal even.

10. Hugh Urban, "The Cult of Ecstasy: Tantrism, the New Age and the Spiritual Logic of Late Capitalism," *History of Religions* 39 (2000): 270. See also Jeffrey Kripal's work on what he calls "the Tantric transmission," the preference for the erotic and heterodox Tantric traditions in American counterculture. Jeffrey J. Kripal, *Esalen: America and the Religion of No Religion* (Chicago: University of Chicago Press, 2007).

11. Kripalu School of Yoga, "200-Hour Teacher Training Manual," Yoga Philosophy section, Stockbridge, MA, 2018, 2.28.

12. Singleton, *Yoga Body*, 82–84.

13. Most generally, we can see that this, considered one of the classic yoga texts, named eight parts or "limbs" of yoga, including the ethical duties of the yamas (restraints) and niyamas (observances), breath control (*pranayama*), and forms of concentration and meditation (such as Pratyahara, Dharana, Dhyana, and Samadhi).

14. Kate Imy, "Fascist Yogis: Marial Bodies and Imperial Impotence," *Journal of British Studies* 55 (2016): 320–343.

15. Andrea R. Jain, *Selling Yoga: From Counterculture to Pop Culture* (Oxford: Oxford University Press, 2015), 27.

16. Jain, *Selling Yoga*, 49.

17. Sanjoy Chakravorty, Devesh Kapur, and Nirvikar Singh, *The Other One Percent: Indians in America* (Oxford: Oxford University Press, 2016).

18. Jain, *Selling Yoga*, 183n14.

19. Hugh B. Urban, *New Age, Neopagan, and New Religious Movements: Alternative Spirituality in Contemporary America* (Berkeley: University of California Press, 2015), 5.

20. Urban, *New Age, Neopagan, and New Religious Movements*, 202.

21. Urban, *New Age, Neopagan, and New Religious Movements*, 202.

22. Urban, *New Age, Neopagan, and New Religious Movements*, 213.

23. Urban, *New Age, Neopagan, and New Religious Movements*, 213.

24. Jain, *Selling Yoga*, 66–67.

25. Ilyse Morgenstein Fuerst, "Locating Religion in South Asia: Islamicate Definitions and Categories," *Comparative Islamic Studies* 10, no. 2 (2014): 223–224.

26. Morgenstein Fuerst, "Locating Religion in South Asia," and Sheldon Pollock "The Death of Sanskrit," *Society for Comparative Study of Society and History* (2001): 392–393.

27. Véronique Altglas, *From Yoga to Kabbalah: Religious Exoticism and the Logics of Bricolage* (Oxford: Oxford University Press, 2014), 79.

28. The Christian theologian Paul Tillich is often credited with introducing the idea of religion as being an issue of ultimate concern, and that faith arises out of an individual's awareness that she is part of the infinite and yet does not own and cannot master this infinity. See Paul Tillich, *Dynamics of Faith* (New York: HarperCollins, 1957).

29. Kripalu School of Yoga, "200-Hour Teacher Training Manual," Yoga Philosophy section, 2.2.

30. Marilyn Robinson Waldman, "Tradition as a Modality of Change: Islamic Examples," *History of Religions* 25, no. 4 (1986): 326.

31. Kripalu School of Yoga, "What Is Yoga?," https://kripalu.org/content/what-yoga.

32. See Danna Faulds, *Into the Heart of Yoga: One Woman's Journey* (Greenville, VA: Peaceable Kingdom Books, 2011), 198–207.

33. Faulds, *Into the Heart of Yoga*, 159–161.

34. Stephen Cope, *Yoga and the Quest for the True Self* (New York: Bantam Books, 1999); Faulds, *Into the Heart of Yoga*; Aruni Nan Futuronsky, *Already Home: Stories of a Seeker* (Nashville, TN: Cold River Studio, 2010); Aruni Nan Futuronsky, *Recovering My Voice: A Memoir of Chaos, Spirituality, and Hope* (Bloomington: iUniverse, 2008).

35. Max Weber, *Theory of Social and Economic Organization*, trans. Talcott Parsons and A. M. Henderson (Oxford: Oxford University Press, 1947).

36. Cope, *Yoga and the Quest for the True Self*, 149.

37. Kripalu School of Yoga, "Our History," https://kripalu.org/content /our-history.

38. T. A. Swain and G. McGwin, "Yoga-Related Injuries in the United States from 2001 to 2014," *Orthopaedic Journal of Sports Medicine* 4, no. 11 (2016).

39. J. Mikkonen, P. Pedersen, and P. W. McCarthy, "A Survey of Musculoskeletal Injury among Ashtanga Vinyasa Yoga Practitioners," *International Journal of Yoga Therapy* 18 (2008): 59, 62–64.

40. David Keil, "Negative Experiences in Yoga Practice: What Do Practitioners Report," *Yoga Anatomy*, March 21, 2017.

41. Cope, *Yoga and the Quest for the True Self*, xii.

42. Cope, *Yoga and the Quest for the True Self*, xiii.

43. John Welwood, *Toward a Psychology of Awakening: Buddhism, Psychotherapy, and the Path of Personal and Spiritual Transformation* (Boulder: Shambhala, 2002).

44. Ingrid Clayton, "Beware of Spiritual Bypass," *Psychology Today*, October 2, 2011.

45. Tracey Anne Duncan, "'Spiritual Bypassing' Is the 'All Lives Matter' of the Yoga World. Don't Buy It," Mic.com, June 29, 2020, https://www .mic.com/p/spiritual-bypassing-is-the-all-lives-matter-of-the-yoga-world -dont-buy-it-27631880.

46. Duncan, "'Spiritual Bypassing.'"

47. Duncan, "'Spiritual Bypassing.'"

48. Amanda Lucia, *White Utopias: The Religious Exoticism of Transformational Festival* (Oakland: University of California Press, 2020), 212–213.

49. I take this to be one of Goodwin's findings in *Abusing Religion*. In her epilogue, she argues that the abuse in American religious communities is not (just) a religious problem, it is an American one. "We protect the shape of America by closing ranks, insisting that abusers are not us—and thus that the problem isn't ours to address" and this in turn makes it harder for us to punish offenders and prevent abuse in the first place. See Megan Goodwin, *Abusing Religion: Literary Persecution, Sex Scandals, and American Minority Religions* (New Brunswick, NJ: Rutgers University Press, 2020), 12.

50. Goodwin, *Abusing Religion*, 147.

51. Statista Research Department, "Revenue of Yoga Industry in the United States from 2012 to 2020," https://www.statista.com/statistics/605335/us-yoga-industry-revenue/.

52. Alice Hines, "Inside CorePower Yoga Teacher Training," *New York Times*, April 6, 2019.

53. Hines, "Inside CorePower Yoga Teacher Training."

54. Traci Childress and Jennifer Cohen Harper, eds., *Best Practices for Yoga in Schools* (Atlanta: YSC-Omega Publications, 2015), 21.

55. Childress and Harper, *Best Practices for Yoga in Schools*, 22.

56. Lucia, *White Utopias*, 93.

57. Lucia quoting Rivers, *White Utopias*, 92.

58. Lucia, *White Utopias*, 93.

59. *Yoga Journal* editors, "Yoga and Hinduism," *Yoga Journal*, November 27, 2007, https://www.yogajournal.com/teach/yoga-and-hinduism/.

60. Suhag Shukla, "Letter to *Yoga Journal*," Hindu American Foundation, 2010, https://www.hinduamerican.org/wp-content/uploads/2020/03/YogaJournalLetter.pdf.

61. Aseem Shukla, "The Theft of Yoga," *Newsweek*, April 18, 2010. Article has since been removed from *Newsweek*'s and *Washington Post*'s (where debate originated) websites.

62. Jain, *Selling Yoga*, 142.

63. Philip Goldberg, *American Veda: From Emerson and the Beatles to Yoga and Meditation How Indian Spirituality Changed the West* (New York: Three Rivers Press, 2010), 3.

64. See, for example, Wilhelm Halbfass, *India and Europe: An Essay in Understanding* (Albany: State University of New York Press, 1988); Richard King, *Orientalism and Religion: Postcolonial Theory, India and "the Mystic East"* (New York: Routledge, 1999); and Brian K. Pennington, *Was Hinduism Invented? Britons, Indians, and the Colonial Construction of Religion* (New York: Oxford University Press, 2005).

65. Pew Research Center, "Most Indians, Including Hindus, Do Not Practice Yoga," July 6, 2021, https://www.pewresearch.org/fact-tank/2021/07/06/most-indians-including-most-hindus-do-not-practice-yoga/.

66. United Nations, "International Day of Yoga 21 June," https://www.un.org/en/observances/yoga-day.

67. Jain, *Peace Love Yoga*, 136.

68. Jason Burke, "Modi's Plan to Change India and the World through Yoga Angers Religious Minorities," *Guardian*, June 6, 2015.

69. See, for example, Expedia, "Taj Ganj," https://www.expedia.com/Agra-Taj-Ganj.dx553248633981695063.

70. Charlotte Ward and David Voas, "The Emergence of Conspirituality," *Journal of Contemporary Religion* 26, no. 1 (2011): 103–121.

71. Sonia Vadlamani, "What Is a Lightworker and What Do They Do Exactly?," Happiness.com, https://www.happiness.com/magazine/inspiration-spirituality/what-is-a-lightworker-and-what-do-they-do-exactly/; *Plandemic:* Martin Enserink and Jon Cohen, "Fact-Checking Judy Mikovitz, the Controversial Virologist Attaching Anthony Fauci in a Viral Conspiracy Video," *Science*, May 8, 2020, https://www.sciencemag.org/news/2020/05/fact-checking-judy-mikovits-controversial-virologist-attacking-anthony-fauci-viral.

72. "Redpilled," Conspirituality.net, accessed February 5, 2022, https://conspirituality.net/redpilled/.

73. Dheepa Sundaram, "Namaste Nationalism: Yoga, Whiteness and Extremism on Jan. 6," Religion News Service, August 20, 2021, https://religionnews.com/2021/08/20/namaste-nationalism-yoga-whiteness-and-extremism-on-january-6/.

74. Brittany Martin, "Wellness and Yoga Influencers Are Taking a Stand against QAnon," *Los Angeles Magazine*, September 15, 2020, https://www.lamag.com/citythinkblog/wellness-influencers-q-anon/.

75. Martin, "Wellness and Yoga Influencers Are Taking a Stand against QAnon."

76. Sarah Wilson, "The Wellness Realm Has Fallen into Conspiritualism—I Have a Sense Why," *Guardian*, September 14, 2020.

77. Susanna Barkataki, "How to Decolonize Your Yoga Practice," Open Democracy, July 13, 2015, https://www.opendemocracy.net/en/transformation/how-to-decolonize-your-yoga-practice/.

78. Rumya Putcha, "On Yoga and White Public Spaces," *Namaste Nation* (research blog), March 28, 2018, http://rumyaputcha.com/on-yoga-and-white-public-spaces/.

79. Creative Wellness, "Yoga Industry Growth, Market Trends & Analysis 2020," April 29, 2020, https://www.wellnesscreatives.com/yoga-industry-trends/.

80. Ibis World, "Pilates & Yoga Studios Industry in the US," December 31, 2018, https://www.ibisworld.com/united-states/market-research-reports/pilates-yoga-studios-industry/Sell.

81. Commodification of religion: For a book-length treatment of this argument, see Jeremy Carrette and Richard King, *Selling Spirituality: The Silent Takeover of Religion* (New York: Routledge, 2005).

82. Kathryn Lofton, *Consuming Religion* (Chicago: University of Chicago Press, 2017), 6.

83. Jain, *Peace Love Yoga*, 26

84. Sophia Rose Arjana, *Buying Buddha, Selling Rumi: Orientalism and the Mystical Marketplace* (London: Oneworld Publications, 2020), 5.

85. White supremacy: Shreena Gandhi and Lillie Wolff, "Yoga and the Roots of Cultural Appropriation," Praxis Center, December 19, 2017, http://www.kzoo.edu/praxis/yoga/.

86. "Yoga: An Instrument of White Supremacy?," *Tucker Carlson Tonight*, Fox News, January 29, 2018.

87. Email correspondence with author, January 23, 2020.

88. Email correspondence with author, January 23, 2020.

89. Centers for Disease Control and Prevention, "Risk for COVID-19 Infection, Hospitalization, and Death by Race / Ethnicity," July 16, 2021, https://www.cdc.gov/coronavirus/2019-ncov/covid-data/investigations-discovery/hospitalization-death-by-race-ethnicity.html.

90. Comparison of Brookline and Chelsea census data: United States Census, "Quick Facts: Chelsea City, Massachusetts; Brookline CDP, Massachusetts," accessed August 26, 2021, https://www.census.gov/quickfacts/fact/table/chelseacitymassachusetts,brooklinecdpmassachusetts/PST 045219. Chelsea's essential workers: Lauren Chambers, "Data Show COVID-19 Is Hitting Essential Workers and People of Color Hardest," ACLU Massachusetts, July 4, 2020, https://data.aclum.org/2020/04/07/COVID-19-disproportionately-affects-vulnerable-populations-in-boston/.

91. bell hooks, "Eating the Other: Desire and Resistance," in *Black Looks: Race and Representation* (Boston: South End Press, 1992), 39.

92. Down Under School of Yoga, "Dialogues of Social Justice with Stephen Gresham," https://www.downunderyoga.com/special-events-listing/free-accomplice-circle-dialogues-on-justice-with-stephen-gresham.

Conclusion

1. James O. Young, "Profound Offense and Cultural Appropriation," *Journal of Aesthetics and Art Criticism* 6, no. 2 (Spring 2005): 135–146.

2. Leigh Eric Schmidt, *Restless Souls: The Making of American Spirituality* (Berkeley: University of California Press, 2012), xv.

3. Janet R. Jakobsen and Ann Pellegrini, *Love the Sin: Sexual Regulation and the Limits of Religious Tolerance* (New York: New York University Press, 2003), 50.

4. Jakobsen and Pellegrini, *Love the Sin*, 50.

5. Susanna Barkataki, "Yogis and Reparations," in *Embrace Yoga's Roots: Courageous Ways to Deepen Your Yoga Practice* (Orlando: Ignite Yoga and Wellness Institute, 2020), 167–170.

6. Barkataki, "Yogis and Reparations," 169.

7. Rachel Lerman, "Feeling Stressed? Meditation Apps See Surge in Group Relaxation," *Washington Post*, April 21, 2020.

8. Lerman, "Feeling Stressed?"

Acknowledgments

Books happen because of a community of support, and it is time to give thanks to mine.

I formed my understanding of religious appropriation in conversation with others who were willing to give me the gift of their insight and experience. Some of these were thought leaders who offered commentary on social media platforms. Some were my students, including the seventy-five who followed me through northern Spain. And some were the members of my Kripalu *sangha*. They all pushed me to sit in discomfort, which is where I learned. This book is entirely dependent on them.

It is generous to read a manuscript in draft form and offer feedback in the best of times, but it is an extraordinary act of friendship to do so during a global pandemic. I am thankful to Megan Goodwin, Bill Hart, Brian Henderson, Grace Kao, Jung Lee, Michael McGregor, Ilyse Morgenstein Fuerst, Irene Oh, and Rumya Putcha for sharing feedback at key points of this project. My student Dayna Archer read the entire manuscript, and her enthusiasm for the subject matter was the extra boost I needed to get this book over the finish line. Two anonymous readers for Harvard University Press offered feedback on the first draft of the manuscript that guided my revisions and made for a much better book.

My Northeastern colleague and writing partner, Liza Weinstein, deserves credit for hundreds of 5:30 a.m. writing sessions over the last three years. While our families slept, we coordinated timers and sent encouraging texts, which made the process of writing alone so much less lonely. I am fortunate to have had a department chair, Ron Sandler, and dean, Uta Poiger, who helped make sure I had time and funding for research even as my institutional responsibilities increased. Leadership like theirs is rare and allows faculty to do our best work.

My partner, Alexis, allowed me to steal the family dog and sneak away to our cabin whenever I needed a writing retreat. And although our daughter, Zoe, wishes I would write a dystopian novel instead of "all this boring ethics stuff," she has put up with my regimen of weekend writing units.

Finally, I want to thank Sharmila Sen, whom I affectionately call my editrix. She convinced me to write this book. She was patient as I struggled to stay on schedule during COVID-19 work disruptions. She was tough when I needed it, and a cheerleader when I was ready for that. And though I could have written a book on religious appropriation without her, I could not have written a better book.

Index